FOCUS

Globalization

WRITING TEAM

William Bosshardt

Bonnie T. Meszaros

Sandra J. Odorzynski

Phillip J. VanFossen

Michael Watts, Chair

WITH AN INTRODUCTORY ESSAY BY

David Hummels

AUTHORS

William Bosshardt
Associate Professor of Economics
Director, Center for Economic Education
Florida Atlantic University

David Hummels
Associate Professor of Economics
Purdue University

Bonnie T. Meszaros
Associate Director,
Center for Economic Education and Entrepreneurship
University of Delaware

Sandra J. Odorzynski
Professor of Economics
St. Norbert College

Phillip J. VanFossen
Associate Professor of Social Studies Education
Director, James F. Ackerman Center for Democratic Citizenship
Associate Director, Center for Economic Education
Purdue University

Michael Watts
Professor of Economics
Director, Center for Economic Education
Purdue University

FUNDING

The National Council on Economic Education gratefully acknowledges the funding of this publication by the U.S. Department of Education, Office of Safe and Drug-Free Schools, under PR Grant # Q304B050002. Any opinions, findings, conclusions, or recommendations expressed in the publication are those of the authors and do not necessarily reflect the view of the U.S. Department of Education.

ISBN 1-56183-635-4

CONTENTS

CONTENTS

FOREWORD

Focus: Globalization is the latest volume in a series of National Council on Economic Education (NCEE) publications dedicated to increasing the economic literacy of all students. The *Focus* publications, a centerpiece of NCEE's comprehensive EconomicsAmerica program, build on over five decades of success in delivering effective economic education to America's students.

The *Focus* series is innovative, using economics to enhance learning in subjects such as history, geography, civics, and personal finance, as well as economics. Activities are interactive, reflecting the belief that students learn best through active, highly personalized experiences with economics. Applications of economic understanding to real-world situations and contexts dominate the lessons. In addition, the lessons are correlated with NCEE's *Voluntary National Content Standards in Economics*.

Globalization has become highly controversial in recent years and is therefore a timely topic for the NCEE *Focus* series. As the subject of increasing interest in the mass media, ranging from prominent publications to radio talk shows, many ideas related to globalization evoke strong emotion even as they reveal economic misconceptions. This growing public attention makes it difficult for teachers to ignore or dismiss the issues. *Focus: Globalization* addresses this challenge through a comprehensive overview of globalization that equips teachers to grasp the concepts underlying the debates, and it provides 12 classroom-ready lessons featuring a student-centered, active-learning approach.

The development of this publication was undertaken as part of the Cooperative Civic Education and Economic Education Exchange Program (CCEEEEP) funded through the U.S. Department of Education, Office of Safe and Drug-Free Schools (PR Grant # Q304B050002), and carried out in coordination with the U.S. Department of State. NCEE extends its deep appreciation to Ms. Rita Foy Moss for her support as CCEEEEP program officer. We are grateful that the U.S. Congress had the foresight to recognize the need for economic education in developing market economies and the vision to see how an international education exchange program such as this could benefit U.S. teachers and students.

NCEE thanks the authors, Michael Watts, Director of the Center for Economic Education at Purdue University, who took the lead on this project; William Bosshardt, Director of the Center for Economic Education at Florida Atlantic University; Bonnie T. Meszaros, Associate Director of the Center for Economic Education and Entrepreneurship at the University of Delaware; Sandra J. Odorzynski, Department of Economics, St. Norbert College; and Phillip J. VanFossen, Associate Director of the Center for Economic Education at Purdue University. NCEE also thanks David Hummels of Purdue University for his introductory essay.

Robert F. Duvall, Ph.D.
President and CEO
National Council on Economic Education

ACKNOWLEDGMENTS

The members of the writing team are grateful for the support from Patty Elder, Barbara DeVita, and other staff members at the National Council on Economic Education (NCEE) who commissioned this publication, and supported its development in many other ways.

Generous financial support to the NCEE from the U.S. Department of Education, Office of Safe and Drug-Free Schools, for this publication and a wide range of other activities involving economic educators from the United States and over 20 transition and developing economies, is also greatly appreciated.

David Hummels' essay was immensely helpful for us as we planned and wrote the lessons. We believe it will be an even more valuable resource for social studies teachers, and it was especially gratifying to see how well the essay was received by 13 teacher/reviewers, listed below.

Our special thanks to Suzanne Becker for her careful, considerate, and comprehensive copy editing, and to April Fidler for her work in preparing camera-ready masters for the volume as well as handling uncounted administrative tasks on the project, great and small.

Finally, this publication was substantially improved by the following reviewers, classroom teachers who field-tested rough drafts of the new lessons on short notice and for little financial reward.

Robert Becker, Fox Valley Lutheran High School, Appleton, WI
Brett Burkey, Spanish River High School, Boca Raton, FL
Dean Duehring, Oshkosh West High School, Oshkosh, WI
Edwina Eichner, South Broward High School, Hollywood, FL
Michelle Foutz, Carmel High School, Carmel, IN
Jill Hahn, Evansville Central High School, Evansville, IN
Davis Kiger, Nova High School, Davie, FL
Patrick Lombardozzi, A.I. DuPont High School, Wilmington, DE
John Netzer, Lourdes High School, Oshkosh, WI
Julie Patterson, Indiana University - Bloomington, Center for the Study of Global Change, Bloomington, IN
Michael Renn, William Penn High School, New Castle, DE
Michael Singer, Coral Springs Charter School, Coral Springs, FL
Andrew Wiggins, North Central High School, Indianapolis, IN

PREFACE
TEACHING ABOUT GLOBALIZATON: WHAT, WHERE, AND HOW?

Globalization has become an extremely controversial topic over the past decade, with well-organized demonstrations now commonplace and even expected whenever and wherever the international organizations that are seen as promoting it have their meetings. Although the term globalization clearly means different things to different people, it usually encompasses many other economic and public policy issues, including: rising levels of international trade; debates over the benefits and costs of free trade, or policies that limit trade to promote "fair trade"; the changing distribution of income and wealth across nations, and across workers with different education and skill levels within particular nations; environmental effects of economic growth and international trade; the appropriate role and historical effectiveness (or not) of the leading international institutions that promote international trade and development; and government's role in assisting workers and/or firms that are adversely affected by international trade.

The scope and complexity of these issues is both an opportunity and a daunting challenge for economics instructors at any academic level, and especially in courses that introduce or incorporate basic economic concepts and principles but are not entirely devoted to economics. To address that problem we have prepared 12 lessons featuring student-centered instructional methods and providing teachers with the conceptual framework and basic data and information sources they need to cover these topics in an academically responsible and engaging way. All of the lessons can be used in a secondary economics course, but many of them will also be used in history, geography, government/civics, or contemporary issues courses.

An introductory essay by David Hummels provides a comprehensive overview of basic facts and ideas that lie behind the many debates related to the umbrella topic of globalization. The essay is intended as a teacher reference, but in class testing some teachers in AP-level economics courses had students read the essay, too, with positive responses.

Lesson 1 features an engaging "readers theatre" skit that involves all the students in a class in (fictional) protests held during meetings of international agencies, introducing the wide range of issues involved and the positions various groups hold on these issues.

Lesson 2 is a simple demonstration of the powerful forces that lead people to specialize and trade, and establishes the idea that international trade is both inevitable and, generally, a source of increased production and consumption for people in all nations.

Lesson 3 personalizes the idea of trade by showing how individuals regularly gain from specialization and trade, and having students consider which of their own talents and interests represent a source of their own comparative advantage in making future career choices.

Lesson 4 illustrates how deeply our daily lives are affected by globalization and trade with other nations, and compares that to life experiences of a real person who lived and died in the United States about 200 years ago.

Lesson 5 reviews trade data to show how the mix of products traded internationally has changed over the past century although–to most people's surprise–the level of international trade as a percentage of GDP has not really changed dramatically. (In recent decades, however, it has rebounded rapidly from the low levels that were experienced during the Great Depression and World War II.) Lessons 4 and 5 are especially appropriate for use in world and U.S. history classes.

Lesson 6 looks at the effects of globalization on national and local cultures, and reviews the debate over whether this is a good or bad thing, or perhaps some of both.

Lesson 7 deals with environmental issues, including treaties dealing with global warming and waste products, nations that become pollution havens, and the link between levels of national income and public demand for stronger environmental policies.

Lesson 8 deals with the effects of international migration in both source and host countries. Migration by skilled and unskilled workers is considered separately, to deal with issues of wage effects on low-income workers on the one hand, and "brain drain" in developing nations on the other. Key similarities between the effects of international trade of goods and services and letting people migrate are established.

Lesson 9 reviews the two key reasons that lead the vast majority of mainstream economists to endorse free trade, productivity gains achieved through trade and from economic growth. Students then compare some statistical measures of different nations' globalization and standards of living to investigate whether those claims are supported. Finally, they compare the measures of globalization to poverty indexes computed for a group of developing nations, to see whether the same kinds of effects hold for those nations.

Lesson 10 deals with issues of outsourcing and protecting domestic firms and workers from foreign competition, using the U.S. sugar industry as an example. Policies that provide special assistance to U.S. workers who lose their jobs due to international trade are reviewed.

Lesson 11 is a review of barriers to international trade–especially tariffs, quotas, and subsidies–with a review of which groups gain or lose from these policies, or from free trade if the restrictions are repealed.

Lesson 12 deals with a topic that has become increasingly important in the United States in recent decades: What are the long term causes and effects of a country running large and sustained trade deficits, particularly in terms of foreign ownership of financial assets in the country? The accounting measures related to these issues are surprisingly straightforward, though rarely covered in the media or most social studies textbooks.

Few teachers are likely to have enough class time to cover all of these lessons, of course, and so all of the lessons are designed to stand alone, although a few are closely related or even linked, as suggested in the brief review above and noted in the lessons themselves.

For teachers who want to do more on some of these topics, many additional resources–both print and electronic–have been noted in the lessons. As this volume went to press, most official statistics featured in these lessons were available only through 2004, but most can be updated using the websites listed in the lessons.

Other NCEE sources for lessons, data, or information related to globalization include:

Focus: High School Economics, second edition, 2001 (21 lessons on general economic concepts and issues, including the topics of economic growth and development, productivity, human capital, saving and investing, and public choice issues for national policies, which are featured in this volume, too)

Focus: Economic Systems, 2001 (12 lessons on topics related to a comparison of different types of economic systems, including special interest groups and differences in national standards of living)

Focus: Institutions and Markets, 2003 (12 lessons on the key role of economic institutions and international differences in those institutions, with lessons on the WTO and other international institutions, investments in human capital, and social capital and norms)

Focus: International Economics, 1998 (20 lessons, most on topics that are at least somewhat related to globalization, including why people and nations specialize and trade, trade barriers, the balance of payments, international investments, and international comparisons of national income and economic growth)

Virtual Economics v.3, 2005 (a CD with a searchable database of 1200 lessons for all grade levels and basic economic concepts, keyed to the NCEE and state standards and benchmarks in economics, with a glossary of over 500 terms)

EconEdLink, http://www.econedlink.org/ (an Internet-based source of classroom-tested, K-12 economic lesson materials, with over 470 lessons posted)

Thinking Globally: Effective Lessons for Teaching about the Interdependent World Economy, 2005 (a CD-ROM with eight lessons covering international topics such as globalization, international economic institutions, comparative advantage, economic growth, and exchange rates)

INTRODUCTORY ESSAY
THE DEBATE OVER GLOBALIZATION

David Hummels
Purdue University

CONTENTS

I. What is Globalization?

The word *globalization* has been used to mean many different things. It may conjure up visions of fleets of container ships moving goods worth trillions of dollars across all the worlds' oceans, giant multinational firms with operations in every time zone, brand names and advertisements known by consumers on six continents, and telephone call centers in India providing customer service to American consumers who bought Japanese electronics while vacationing in the south of France. To some, globalization also conveys broader concerns and even fears, such as the erosion of labor and environmental standards or the loss of national sovereignty to international institutions that are not accountable to citizens of any nation.

In more general terms, however, **globalization** refers to increases in the degree of integration between national economies. **Integration** encompasses all of the ways national economies are connected in international markets, including trade in goods, services, and ideas; international movements of the factors of production; and coordination of public policies. After a brief look at historical trends in some measures of integration, the reasons why this growing integration has occurred and the effects it has had on national economies and different groups of people–including consumers and workers–will be discussed.

Trade in Goods and Services

One of the most important forms of international integration is merchandise trade. When U.S. firms sell goods and services abroad, these are U.S. **exports**. When people or firms in the United States buy goods and services from other countries, these are U.S. **imports**. Both U.S. exports and imports have risen rapidly since World War II.

From 1960 to 2003, after adjusting for inflation, U.S. exports increased by almost 800 percent. Over that same period U.S. imports increased even more, by 1300 percent. Part of this growth in both imports and exports simply reflects the growth in the size of the U.S. economy in these years, which expanded by a factor of about 400 percent. But international trade grew much faster than the national economy. Specifically, as shown in Figure 1, since 1960 imports grew from 4.2 to 13.8 percent of U.S. national income, or gross domestic product (GDP), while exports increased from 4.9 to 9.3 percent.

Despite this dramatic growth in international trade over the past five decades, the United States is far less reliant on trade than most other countries. For example, in 2003, exports of goods and services were about 25 percent of national output in France, 40 percent in Canada, and 80 percent in Belgium. And although U.S. exports as a percentage of GDP have grown sharply since 1960, they are comparable today to what they were in 1880, and actually less than they were at the end of World War I.

Another important trend in international trade, seen in the United States and in most other countries over the past 30 years, is that a growing share of trade takes place with countries that are nearby neighbors. Despite the relatively small size of their national economies, Canada and Mexico are the largest U.S. trading partners, purchasing over a third of U.S. exports and supplying a quarter of U.S. imports in 2003.

International Mobility of Labor and Capital

Another way national economies are integrated in the international marketplace is by movements of **factors of production**, or inputs, and in particular by labor (workers) and capital. Both labor and capital can cross national borders if the expected returns are high enough.

The United States is, of course, a nation of immigrants. Most current citizens can trace their ancestry back to migrants who arrived on these shores within the last three or four centuries. And migration is still important: in 2001 there were 31.8 million migrants in the United States, including 20 million in the U.S. labor force. That represents 11 percent of the nation's population and 13.9 percent of the labor force, both percentages about twice as high as they were in the 1960s and 1970s. Although the absolute number of migrant workers in the United States is much higher than in other countries, foreign-born workers are a comparable fraction of the workforce in many other countries.

Capital is the other mobile factor of production, and there are many ways to invest capital in a foreign country. Private investors can buy government or corporate bonds to earn the interest that is paid on the bonds. Or they can buy shares of stock in foreign companies on foreign stock markets. Private firms also engage in foreign direct investment (FDI) by building or purchasing affiliate operations in other countries. That is different from buying shares of stock in foreign companies, because with FDI a company controls the affiliate operation.

In 2003, U.S. agents (meaning individual citizens, banks, other corporations, and government agencies) owned $7.8 trillion dollars of foreign financial assets. Meanwhile, foreign agents owned $10.5 trillion dollars of U.S. financial assets, including $3.4 trillion of U.S. corporate bonds and stocks, $2.4 trillion in foreign direct investment, and $1.7 trillion in U.S. government bonds. To put those numbers in perspective, the total capitalization (value) of U.S. equities in 2003 was $14.3 trillion, and the total value of U.S. government bonds was $3.9 trillion. A sizable fraction of the total U.S. capital stock is owned by foreign citizens.

Integration: Old and New

Migration and merchandise trade is old news, in the sense that countries have experienced that for thousands of years. The level of U.S. trade today is roughly comparable in size to trade a century ago, and migrants are a considerably smaller portion of the labor force than they were for the nation's first 150 years. So why do many observers claim that we are experiencing an unprecedented era of globalization? Put differently, what's new about the current forms of globalization? Two things stand out. First, the kinds of things being traded are very different from what was traded in earlier eras. Second, the ways countries are integrated now go far beyond the simple trading of goods.

Suppose we were to go back to the first era of globalization in the late 1800s and look at the cargoes carried by the great steamships that made the first era possible. For the most part we would see bulk commodities–such as coal, wheat, cotton, and iron ore–and some very simple manufactured products. Trade today is quite different. Figure 2 (on page 4) shows the growth in world trade relative to output for manufacturing, agriculture, and mining products. While agriculture and mining trade/output has been steady since World War II, manufacturing trade has grown very rapidly. Bulk commodities have become far less important than trade in manufactures and services. That is important because trade in manufactures and services requires a much higher degree of sophistication and coordination in production, consumption, and regulation than trade in basic commodities.

To understand why this is true, think about what is involved in producing and exporting coal. First, of course, you have to have coal. If there are no coal deposits in a country you cannot just dig a mine and expect to produce coal. If there is coal you can dig it up, put it on railroad cars or ships, and sell it abroad. The product itself is not sophisticated, and it doesn't take extensive research and development to create it or to tailor it to

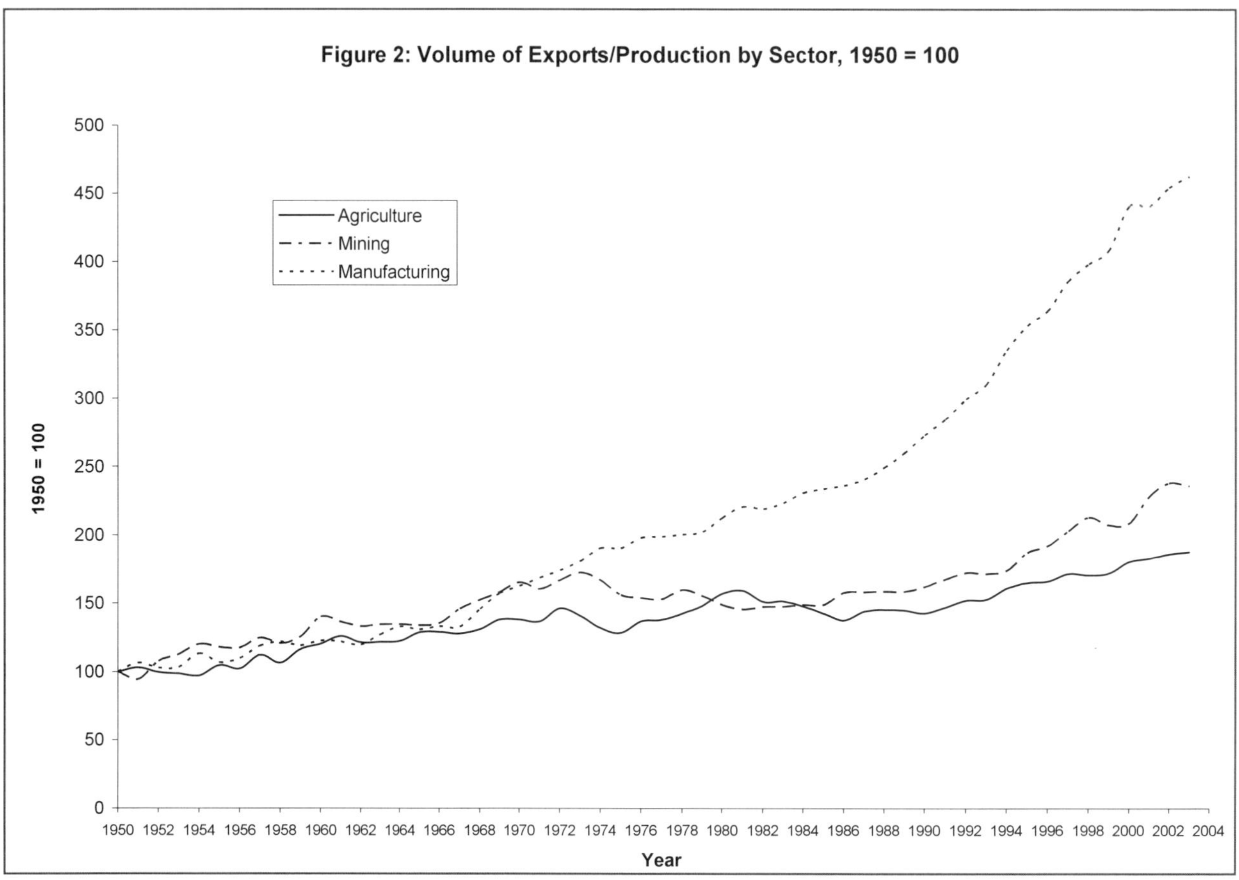

consumer uses. Nor are major marketing or education campaigns required to encourage consumers to buy the product. They buy the coal, throw it in a stove or furnace, and the transaction is done. The usefulness of the coal is a function of its natural physical properties: when you burn it, it produces heat.

In stark contrast, consider what is involved in producing and exporting a laptop computer. The first thing to note is that there are no natural deposits of computers to mine, so the location of natural resources does not determine where the computer can be produced. Instead, factories to produce computers can be built virtually anyplace in the world. That makes computer manufacturing much more "footloose," or mobile, which means inefficient firms quickly face tremendous competitive pressure from firms that can produce and sell laptops at a lower cost.

The second key characteristic of laptops and many other products that are internationally traded today is that the value of the physical materials in the final product is often trivial. With the computers nearly all the value comes from the ideas–the technology–incorporated into the central processing unit, the disk drives, the flat panel screen, the long-life battery, and so on. New technologies have to be researched and developed, and the intellectual property created through this research has to be protected from those who try to copy and steal it. Because production can be moved to any country in the world that protection must be international in scope, too. Protecting a patent at home doesn't save a company from foreign competitors.

The third characteristic of today's international trade is that technologies can be repeatedly reused once they are discovered. That gives firms that develop successful new technologies a major cost advantage over their competitors, allowing them to expand production, sales, and profits. Especially good innovations can lead to enormous profits and even monopoly power for the firms that create them. Although international trade in goods increases competitive pressures in many markets, monopoly power from innovations that are protected by internationally recognized patents, copyrights, etc. does not end at national borders. Increasingly, therefore, firms that dominate a market in one nation are likely to dominate that market in other countries, also.

A fourth key difference between old and new forms of international trade is that it has become increasingly rare to find a purely "Japanese" or "American" computer (or any other complex manufactured product). Because the laptop embodies so many different technologies and so many different kinds of expertise, it is rare to find one company or even one country that excels in producing every part. Instead, the technologies embodied in final products usually come from dozens of labs and manufacturing plants located all around the world. Research laboratories themselves are increasingly multinational in scope, and leading laboratories in the United States rely to an increasing degree on hiring foreign-born scientists and engineers who were trained at U.S. universities.

Managing trade in goods that require many different technologies and hundreds of component parts is more difficult and entails far more coordination problems than producing the basic commodities that were the staples of international trade in earlier centuries. The coordination problems can be especially difficult when transactions are conducted between independent firms. As a result, large firms often "internalize" these transactions (that is, bring them under the direct control of one corporation). When this involves goods and ideas that are produced in many different countries, the result is a **multinational corporation** (MNC).

As noted earlier, when an MNC makes investments in other countries that is called **foreign direct investment** (FDI). In recent decades the number of MNCs and the amount of FDI have skyrocketed. Currently there are over 60,000 multinational corporations that direct nearly a million affiliates. Their total investments in 2003 totaled $8.2 trillion, 10 times more than in 1982. MNCs have invested heavily in the United States, with the real (inflation-adjusted) value of their investments about 35 times higher in 2000 than in 1960.

Worldwide, the spectacular growth in FDI was partly a result of relaxing laws and regulations that limited foreign ownership of domestic companies. But the main cause for these trends, all around the world, was the shift in world trade away from simple products such as wheat and coal to more complex, technology-based products such as computers, airplanes, and pharmaceuticals.

Because production and trade have become more complex, international treaties governing trade have also become more complex. International agreements must now be negotiated and ratified dealing with protection of intellectual property, regulation of foreign investment and monopoly power, and the mobility of highly skilled scientists and other workers. These issues are highly controversial and difficult to negotiate.

II. Why Countries Trade

With all of these complications and controversies, it is easy to lose sight of the fundamental question: Why do countries trade with one another in the first place? The short, simple answer is because nations **specialize.** In other words, they produce more of some goods than they consume, but produce less than they consume of many other goods.

Specialization by countries is really very much like specialization practiced by individuals. For example, farmers grow more food than they eat themselves, doctors provide more medical care than they use themselves, and tailors sew more clothing than they can ever wear themselves. That way more and better food, medical care, and clothing can be produced than if each person had to grow their own food, be their own doctor, and sew their own clothes. But specialization is only possible with trade, so that the doctor can buy clothes from the tailor and food from the farmer, the farmer can buy clothes from the tailor and medical services from the doctor, etc.

That leads to a second key question: *why* do countries (or individuals) specialize in producing some goods or services, but not others? Three basic ideas from economics are used to answer this question: arbitrage, absolute advantage, and comparative advantage.

Arbitrage

Arbitrage is nothing more than "buying low and selling high." In the context of international trade, suppose an identical shirt can be bought for $15 in the United States or $10 in Mexico. A smart entrepreneur sees this and realizes she can make money by arbitrage, so she buys the low-priced shirts in Mexico and sells them at a higher price in the United States. Because the shirts have moved across an international border we say that they have been exported from Mexico and imported into the United States. If the same thing happened with shirts moving from Florida to Ohio it would still be arbitrage, but there would be no exports or imports.

Trading a few shirts will not have much effect on either the U.S. or Mexican economy. However, this entrepreneur (and others) can make money through arbitrage as long as the shirt sells for different prices in the two countries. Eventually, enough shirts may be exported to the United States to have important effects on output and price levels in both countries. Before the trade began, shirt factories in Mexico produced only for Mexican consumers, but after trading they are now producing for Mexican and American consumers. Shirt production in Mexico must increase to meet the higher demand, while shirt production in the United States will fall. This is precisely how specialization occurs: the low-price country produces more of the products it exports, while output of that product in the high-price country falls.

These changes in output also affect the prices of shirts on both sides of the border. Increasing output to meet both Mexican and U.S. demand raises costs for Mexican shirt producers and their prices begin to rise.[1] Meanwhile, the availability of more and lower-priced shirts in the United States pushes prices down. Arbitrage causes the price of goods to converge and eventually equalize on both sides of the border.[2]

How specialized will these two countries become? Once there is no price difference there is no further incentive for the entrepreneur to move goods between the two countries. If production costs are similar in the two locations, a small amount of arbitrage will equalize prices and only a small degree of specialization will occur. If production costs are very different, however, trade will cause Mexico and the United States to dramatically change their pattern of specialization.

This simple story captures important ideas about why countries trade and the effects of arbitrage, but it leaves several important questions unanswered:

1) How does the United States pay for the imported shirts (or put differently, is there anything it can export to Mexico)?
2) Are Mexico and the United States better or worse off as a result of the trade?

---

[1] Put differently, the supply curve for Mexican shirt slopes upwards and producing more shirts increases the marginal cost of production.

[2] Note that nowhere in this story did the governments of the United States and Mexico become involved in this process, or make decisions about how each country would specialize and trade. Instead, trade happened because an entrepreneur saw an opportunity to make money by moving goods from a low to a high-priced location. When we say that Mexico exports shirts to the U.S. we really mean that private individuals or firms produced goods in Mexico and sold them to consumers in the U.S. Entrepreneurs must also bear the cost of transporting goods internationally and paying international trade taxes, or tariffs, on their shipments. If these transactions costs are large, less arbitrage (trade) will take place and countries will be less specialized.

3) Why are the costs of production different in the United States and Mexico?

To answer these questions economists have developed the ideas of absolute and comparative advantage.

Absolute Advantage

Absolute advantage is defined as the ability to make a good or service with fewer inputs than another individual, company, or country would use to produce it. Some countries, such as the United States, have extremely high levels of productivity, which means they have an absolute advantage in producing many goods and services. It might seem that being more productive would also make the United States a low-cost producer and allow it to export almost any good or service, and that countries with very low productivity levels could never compete on international markets. This turns out to be wrong, however, because high-productivity countries also enjoy high wage rates, and higher wages can offset the productivity advantages.

To see this, consider a simple example. Suppose there is only a single good produced in the economy, rice, and only one input has to be paid to produce the rice, labor. Initially it takes four French workers or four German workers to grow a pound of rice. If this market is competitive, with many buyers and sellers who do not have any control over wages and prices, and given the assumption of only one output and one paid input, the price (*p*) of a unit of output will equal the number of inputs used to produce it multiplied by the cost of each input:

$$p(\text{rice}) = (\text{wage per worker}) \times (\text{number of workers /lb rice})$$

The price of rice in Germany will be (wage per German worker × four workers), and the price of rice in France will be (wage per French worker × four workers). As described in the earlier shirt example, arbitrage (trade) will tend to equalize prices of goods across locations. That means we can set the price of rice in France and Germany equal,

$$p(\text{rice})_{\text{Germany}} = p(\text{rice})_{\text{France}}$$

which means that the wage per German worker times the number of German workers per pound of rice equals the wage per French worker times the number of French workers per pound of rice. Rearranging terms shows that:

$$\frac{\text{wage per German worker}}{\text{wage per French worker}} = \frac{\text{4 French workers/ lb rice}}{\text{4 German workers/ lb rice}} = \frac{4}{4}$$

In other words, with labor productivity in producing rice equal in the two countries (four workers to produce a pound of rice in both countries), the price of rice in both countries will be equal to four, and there are no opportunities to arbitrage by trading rice. But now suppose workers in Germany become more productive, so that it only takes two German workers to grow a pound of rice. German firms now have an absolute advantage because they can produce rice with fewer inputs (fewer labor hours), and the right-hand term in the last equation will now be four divided by two. With the productivity increase, however, wages will no longer be equal in the two countries, either. Instead,

$$\frac{\text{wage per German worker}}{\text{wage per French worker}} = 2$$

In short, because German workers are now twice as productive as French workers, they will earn twice the wage. How does this come about, in practice? Starting from the point where wages are still equal, let's turn a clever entrepreneur loose on the problem.

As long as wages are equal, Germany's productivity advantage will allow it to produce rice at a lower cost, so the entrepreneur will start shipping rice from Germany to France. But as Germany's production of rice increases, the entrepreneur must hire more workers. That increases the demand for labor and bids up the wage, which means that Germany will eventually lose its cost advantage in exporting rice to France.

Although this is a very simplified example, it makes two key points. First, when we look at wage levels around the world they are primarily determined by productivity levels, with high productivity countries enjoying high wages. Second, having an absolute advantage in productivity does not mean that a country will be a low cost producer of a good (and thus an exporter), because the country will also have high wage rates that push up prices. In the rice example wages and productivity were eventually exactly offsetting.

Comparative Advantage

If absolute advantage doesn't mean that a country will be the low-cost exporter of a product, what does? It turns out that people and countries specialize and then trade based on what economists call comparative advantage. To understand comparative advantage, it is useful to start with the example of individuals choosing to specialize. Each person has only 24 hours in each day, and that means spending time and effort on one activity requires us to give up doing other activities. Economists call this an **opportunity cost**. A person or firm has a **comparative advantage** when they can produce a good or service at a lower opportunity cost than someone else.

People use their time most efficiently when they focus on activities in which they have a comparative advantage. For example, suppose a lawyer must decide between taking two hours to type a 50-page document and using those same two hours to do legal research for a client for which she will earn \$500. A secretary could type the document for the lawyer, but suppose the secretary doesn't type as well as the attorney, and will take four hours to complete the work. Given the local wage rate for a typist of \$12.50/hr, that will cost the attorney \$50. The lawyer could type the document herself twice as fast as her secretary, and save paying the secretary \$50. But in doing so the lawyer gives up \$500 she could have earned doing legal work. Hiring a secretary frees up time for work that has a higher value, such as doing case research, representing clients in court, etc.

The same idea explains why countries specialize. Countries are also endowed with limited resources–including labor, capital, human capital, and natural resources. When countries use these factors of production to produce one good, they cannot use them to produce another good. Countries trade because their opportunity costs for producing different goods are different. That is, just like the lawyer and the typist, they have different comparative advantages.

To illustrate this idea by extending the earlier example of Germany and France producing rice, now suppose that in addition to growing rice France and Germany can also produce bicycles. In Germany it takes one worker to produce a bicycle, but two workers to grow a pound of rice. In France it requires four workers to make a bicycle and four workers to grow a pound of rice. That means Germany has an absolute advantage in producing both goods, because it can produce both bicycles and rice with less labor than France. But that does not mean Germany has a comparative advantage in producing both goods, and in fact it does not.

To determine comparative advantage look at prices for both goods in both countries. Imagine for a moment that France and Germany cannot trade, and so must produce for themselves any goods they consume. In Germany bikes will be half as expensive as rice because they require half as much labor. Put differently, Germany's opportunity cost of producing one pound of rice is giving up production of two bicycles. Opportunity costs and prices are different in France, because making a bicycle requires the same number of workers as growing rice. Therefore, the opportunity cost of producing one pound of rice is only one bicycle.

Although France has a lower opportunity cost for producing rice, Germany has a lower opportunity cost for producing bikes. Producing one more bike in Germany requires giving up a half-pound of rice; producing one more bike in France requires giving up a full pound of rice. This is not a tricky or atypical example, but it illustrates a very general proposition: Being relatively good (that is, low-cost) at producing rice necessarily means being relatively bad (high-cost) at producing bicycles. Similarly, the person with a comparative advantage as an attorney must have a comparative disadvantage as a typist.

Returning to the Germany and France example, what happens if these countries can trade? Entrepreneurs buy goods where prices are low and sell where prices are high. The real price of rice is lower in France because it has a lower opportunity cost than in Germany, so entrepreneurs should export French rice to Germany. The relative price of bicycles is lower in Germany, so entrepreneurs will export German bicycles to France.

The Gains from Trade

How will these countries gain from international trade? An easy way to see that is to ask what each country can consume with and without international trade. Suppose Germany has 100 workers, and initially uses them to produce 50 bicycles (50 bikes × 1 worker per bike = 50 workers) and 25 pounds of rice (25 lbs rice × 2 workers per lb rice = 50 workers). To export bicycles from Germany to France, the entrepreneur must increase bicycle output in Germany. If she opens up a second bicycle factory and hires all 50 workers away from the rice farms, that increases bicycle output in Germany by 50 and reduces rice output by 25 lbs.

What will she get when she sells the 50 bikes in France? If she uses the money she earns to buy 50 pounds of rice and ships all 50 pounds back to Germany, Germany can still consume 50 bicycles, but now its rice consumption has increased from 25 to 50.

How does this work? Germany is relatively inefficient at producing rice and relatively efficient at making bikes. Trade with France allows Germany to shut down its rice farms and use its scarce resources (workers) more efficiently. It is as if Germany discovered a new technology for producing rice that allows it to make 50 pounds of rice with 50 workers, instead of the 25 pounds it could make before. And in fact it *has* discovered a new technology: France's technology. The only catch is that to utilize this technology it has to export bikes and import rice.

As it turns out, both countries can gain from the trade. To convince yourself of this, simply go back and repeat the exercise above for France, shipping rice to Germany in exchange for cheaper bicycles, and you will find that it works in both directions. That really shouldn't be too surprising, because like all voluntary exchanges, international trade only occurs when both parties expect to gain.

Note too that arbitrage and trade opportunities do not depend on absolute advantage, but only on comparative advantage. That would be true even if absolute advantages in producing rice and bicycles became larger for Germany, or if they suddenly shifted to France instead of Germany. For example, suppose France experienced a huge increase in labor productivity and could reduce labor inputs for both bicycles and rice by half without reducing the amount of each product produced. France now has the absolute advantage in producing both goods, but the opportunity costs of producing either product in France would be unaffected. The pattern of trade would continue just as it did before, and the gains from trade would be the same. The only difference would be that French wages would be higher than before.

Finally, note that achieving the gains from trade requires that inefficient firms be shut down. (In this example, German rice farms and French bicycle factories were relatively inefficient, high-cost producers.) Doing this frees up resources that can be used more efficiently and does not create long-term unemployment. Instead, workers who are laid off in Germany's rice farms are re-employed in Germany's bike factory, and French workers in bicycle factories are re-employed producing rice. More of both products are produced and consumed, so the standard of living rises in both countries.

Sources of Comparative Advantage

As shown in the example above, nations have different comparative advantages and can gain from trading because they have different productivities in producing different goods. In the real world there are large differences in relative productivity across countries. There are many reasons for this. A few of the most important reasons are discussed below.

First, differences in endowments of natural resources are important in some industries. For example, agricultural productivity differs across countries because of climate and soil quality. Comparative advantage in energy production depends on differences in natural endowments of crude oil, rivers suitable for hydroelectric production, and windy coastlines or plains for wind turbines.

Second, government services and regulations also play a role in shaping productivity. Worker productivity may vary because of differences in school quality, because laws require students to complete more years of schooling, or because schools in a particular country emphasize some subjects over others. Government regulation of factory emissions can leave a nation with a comparative disadvantage in polluting industries and a comparative advantage in clean industries.

The third and probably most important source of comparative advantage and productivity differences across countries results from decisions by firms to invest in technology. For example, the United States has strong comparative advantages in airplane manufacturing and pharmaceuticals because U.S. firms in these industries have spent billions of dollars researching and developing state-of-the-art technologies.

Economies of scale arising from investments in technology are an important source of productivity differences and comparative advantage. In producing large commercial jet airplanes, for example, a company must spend large sums for research and development (R&D) before a single airplane is produced. The more jets a firm can produce and sell, thc more the fixed costs of that investment can be spread out and thus represent a smaller part of the price for each unit sold. For example, the new super-widebody A380 plane produced by the European Airbus consortium required $13 billion in R&D costs. If Airbus sells only 100 of these planes, the R&D cost per plane will be $130 million. If Airbus can sell 250 planes, the R&D cost per plane falls to $52 million. Airbus executives have said they will "break even," covering their R&D costs, if they can sell 250 planes. If Airbus meets its goal of selling 1000 planes, the R&D cost per plane becomes very small, and Airbus will make a great deal of money.

Suppose Boeing (the U.S. rival to Airbus) has precisely the same schedule of average costs for its new superjet. Which company will end up enjoying the greatest profits? That depends on which company sells more planes. It becomes a kind of virtuous circle: selling more planes lowers average costs, which allows the company to lower prices, sell more planes, and make more money. Put another way, in industries with strong increasing returns to scale, achieving a greater level of sales and output can become a source of comparative advantage. These tend to be industries in which very few firms can successfully operate at one time, but where the few successful firms earn high profits.

A fourth source of comparative advantage is differences in the supply of key inputs. In the earlier examples with France and Germany, for simplicity labor was treated as the only input. But usually firms require multiple inputs: land and other natural resources, different kinds of skilled labor, capital, energy, and material supplies. Industries differ in the intensity with which they use these different kinds of inputs. For example, agriculture uses land intensively, so if land is very expensive (in Japan, for example), the cost of agricultural production will be high and the nation is likely to import, but not export, agricultural products. Other countries, including the United States, Canada, Australia, and Brazil, are endowed with much more land. Land prices in these countries are relatively low, which lowers the cost of producing agricultural products.

A few more examples may be instructive: Producing aluminum uses electricity intensively, which is why Canada, with relatively abundant supplies of low-cost hydroelectric energy, has a comparative advantage in aluminum production. Textiles and apparel use unskilled labor intensively, so China, with an abundant supply of unskilled labor, has a comparative advantage in textile and apparel production. Automobiles use capital intensively, and so Japan, with relatively abundant supplies of capital (reflecting its high national savings rate), has a comparative advantage in automobile production.

International Migration and Capital Flows

Differences across countries in the relative supply of inputs are not only an important source of comparative advantage, they are also an important reason for international migration and capital flows.

To understand this, consider a simple example involving agricultural trade between the United States and Mexico. Some crops, such as wheat, are most efficiently produced on very large farms where harvesting can be done with advanced machinery. Other crops, such as tomatoes and many fruits, cannot be effectively harvested by machinery. Instead they are labor intensive, requiring field workers to hand pick produce and avoid the damage machines would cause. The United States has relatively abundant supplies of land and capital, but labor is relatively scarce. In other words, labor productivity and wage rates are high. For large-scale agriculture that means the cost of machinery is low and the cost of hiring field workers is high. The reverse is true in Mexico: machinery costs are high but the cost of hiring field workers is low.

Those differences in factor supplies and factor prices will lead the United States to export wheat while Mexico will export tomatoes and fruit. This occurs for the same reasons Germany exported bicycles and France exported rice in the earlier example of comparative advantage. There is another way for the United States and Mexico to gain from trade, however. Rather than importing tomatoes and fruit from Mexico, U.S. produce and fruit farmers can import Mexican laborers. This lowers the price (wages) of field workers and allows U.S. tomato and fruit farms to be competitive. Similarly, instead of exporting wheat to Mexico, the United States could export (loan) financial capital to Mexico to be used in the purchase of machinery. That would make Mexican wheat farms more competitive.

This suggests an interesting parallel between trade in goods and trade in the factors of production, including labor migration and international capital flows for investment. If countries differ in their relative supplies of factor inputs, the relative price of those inputs will also be different. That difference creates the potential to gain from trade, which can be realized either by trading final goods and services or by trading the factors of production.

Most international immigration today is motivated by the economic forces just described. Latin American migrants move to the United States, while North African and Eastern European migrants move to Western Europe. The migrants are able to command higher wages in the United States and Western Europe than in their home nations because they have more capital to work with (and therefore higher productivity). In earlier centuries, a similar situation motivated migration from Western Europe and Asia to the United States. In those periods migrants left densely populated regions in which land was scarce and expensive for the United

States, where land was abundant and inexpensive.

Other Reasons for Trade

Not all world trade is easily explained by cost differences and comparative advantage. As noted above, the gains from trade resulting from comparative advantage are greatest when countries are very different from one another; but a great deal of world trade occurs between very similar countries. This is sometimes called "North-North" trade, because it takes place between the rich, industrialized countries in the Northern Hemisphere (mainly between the nations of Western Europe, Asia, and the United States and Canada). Furthermore, these economies often engage in "intra-industry" trade, meaning that these countries simultaneously import and export similar products from the same industry.

Much of this trade is explained by what economists call "differentiated products." For example, although cars have the basic function of providing transportation, there are important differences in car makes and models in terms of size, fuel efficiency, horsepower, styling, etc. Different consumers prefer different features, and these tastes often overlap with the kinds of products produced in particular nations. As a result, there are many Americans buying Honda sedans from Japan, Germans buying American sports utility vehicles, and Japanese buying German luxury vehicles.[3]

The same pattern holds true for many other kinds of goods, too: American consumers wear Italian leather shoes, play Japanese video games, listen to British music, and eat French cheese. McDonalds restaurants can be found in over 100 other countries, and the latest Hollywood hits dominate box offices worldwide. Brands such as Coca-Cola, Mercedes, Xerox, and Sony are known globally. Recent estimates suggest that the gains from trading "differentiated" products and expanding the set of consumer choices may yield even larger gains from trade than those resulting from simple comparative advantage.[4]

Trade increases product diversity in styling and other characteristics, but another result of trade is a greater degree of worldwide convergence in consumer culture. Some critics of globalization decry the loss of unique national cultures, and worry about large multinational firms driving small, local firms out of business.[5] Proponents of globalization point out that no one forces consumers to eat at McDonalds, drink French wine, or play Nintendo. They argue that because consumers are free to choose or ignore these products, having them available cannot make consumers worse off, whereas "protecting" consumers by excluding the international products often makes them pay higher prices for products they do not like as much.

Increasingly, firms that produce differentiated goods are moving production facilities to be closer to their final consumers in different countries. When firms begin to operate facilities in many countries, by making foreign direct investments, they become **multinational firms**. The automobile industry provides an excellent example of this. The first cars Honda and Toyota sold to U.S. consumers were produced in Japan and exported. During the 1980s these companies built car factories in the United States to accomplish several goals: First, this

[3] Producing distinct, or differentiated, cars requires firms to invest substantial research and development resources. These fixed costs prevent any one company, or country, from producing every conceivable type of car. Being able to export to many markets allows auto firms to spread their fixed costs over more units and lower unit costs.

[4] Paul Romer, "New Goods, Old Theory and the Welfare Costs of Trade Restrictions," *Journal of Development Economics, 43*(1): 5-38, 1994.

[5] Perhaps the best known is Jose Bove, a French farmer who spent three weeks in jail in 1999 for ransacking a McDonalds in Millau, France. Of course the same concerns arise within countries, too, including complaints about national chains of groceries, fast-food restaurants, and retail superstores driving out small, local "mom and pop" businesses.

eliminated the cost of shipping cars from Japan. Second, the surge of Japanese auto exports to the United States in the 1980s displaced sales by U.S. automobile firms (General Motors, Ford, and Chrysler). That created a political backlash that eventually led to **quotas**, or limits, on the number of Japanese cars that could be sold in the United States. Moving the production of these cars to the United States allowed these firms to avoid the trade restrictions. Third, by locating in the United States they were able to better customize the products to meet the specific demands of U.S. consumers.

In the simple examples of trade based on comparative advantage, trade is driven entirely by cost differences. If a country is the low-cost supplier, it will be an exporter. When we think about trade in differentiated products cost is still an issue, but it is not the only factor, because consumers may be willing to pay more for a higher priced product if it has the particular characteristics they prefer. As a result, the ability of firms to identify consumer tastes and shape their products to meet them becomes a critical factor in shaping trade.

III. Trade Policy

Most economists view free trade as a desirable policy. Because of the mutual gains from trade–whether that trade is between individuals and firms in the same country or in different countries–they believe people in all countries will generally be better off if competition in the international marketplace determines which firms succeed and which fail. Despite this consensus among economists, however, governments routinely interfere with international trade by imposing a variety of policy restrictions. What these restrictions are, how they affect markets, why governments choose to use these restrictions, and how certain international rules and institutions have been developed to limit the use of national policies that restrict international trade are the focus of this section.

Tariffs and Trade Barriers

One of the earliest and most common restrictions on international trade is the **tariff**, a sales tax on imported goods. Most tariffs are ad-valorem, meaning that they are set as a percentage of a good's price. In the United States, the average tariff on imported goods today is only about 5 percent, but for some goods (such as textiles and steel) they are much higher.

To understand the effect of tariffs, suppose the U.S. steel industry finds that Korean steel firms can now produce and sell steel at a lower price than they can. As shown earlier, free trade allows steel consumers to purchase more steel and pay lower prices, making consumers (including companies that use steel to produce their products) better off. However, U.S. firms that produce steel, and their employees, are worse off. Inefficient U.S. firms will be driven out of the market, but even the U.S. firms that are able to continue producing steel will see the prices they can charge driven down by competitive pressure from the Korean firms.

Not surprisingly, U.S. steel firms and workers have a strong incentive to encourage the government to "protect" the market from foreign steel producers. The U.S. government may do this by levying a tariff on Korean steel, and in 2002 that is exactly what happened, with tariffs rising by up to 30 percent.

The tariff effectively reverses the changes in the market caused by free trade. Steel prices rise by the amount of the tariff, which makes consumers worse off because they must pay a higher price for steel and other products made with steel. On the other side of the market, U.S. steel suppliers are "protected" from foreign competition and can sell their output at higher prices. The output of steel produced in the United States expands and inefficient firms that would otherwise have gone out of business can still produce.

The tariff hurts consumers and helps producers, but what is the effect on the economy as a whole? Tariffs almost always result in net economic losses because consumer losses far outweigh producer gains. Although there are some interesting theoretical arguments for special cases in which tariffs could make a country better off, in practice this is rarely the case.

Political Explanations for Protection

If tariffs, quotas, and other kinds of trade barriers generally make the country as a whole worse off, why do governments adopt these policies to restrict international trade? There are at least three possible explanations. One, politicians may not realize that these policies reduce or eliminate the gains from trade and usually do more harm than good. Perhaps they were not fortunate enough to have taken a course in international economics in high school or college, or maybe they sat in the back row and napped.

Two, politicians may have objectives other than maximizing economic welfare. For example, national security is often cited as a reason for protecting domestic firms from international competition.[6] The argument goes something like this: without steel we cannot build tanks and planes, and we cannot trust that foreign steel supplies will be available in times of national crisis. Therefore, for security reasons, it is important to keep domestic steel firms in business even if they are not economically efficient. Although this argument does make sense on some level, there are two key problems with it. First, the United States is not likely to face armed conflict with any of the countries that are its major trading partners, and even if such a conflict did break out with one or two countries, most of these goods are supplied by dozens of exporting nations and would still be available. The second problem with the national defense argument for trade barriers is that, in practice, it is soon extended in literally silly ways to justify, for example, protective policies for domestic shoe and scissors manufacturers. These are not products that immediately come to mind in listing products that are essential to national defense, but after all, barefoot soldiers cannot fight effectively. So where do policy makers draw the line, short of protecting every product that is purchased by the Armed Forces, which means erecting trade barriers on almost everything?[7]

The third possible reason why politicians may impose trade barriers it that they may be more concerned about who wins and who loses from trade, rather than focusing on the overall net gains from trade. They may do that because, even though gains are greater than losses, the gains are often spread out across large numbers of consumers, whereas losses are concentrated among a few firms and a relatively small number of workers. For example, the U.S. International Trade Commission (USITC) estimates that if import restrictions on textiles and apparel were lifted, U.S. consumers would gain between $9 and $14 billion each year.[8] That is a lot of money, but divided among 300 million consumers it amounts to no more than $30-$50 per person. Moreover, most consumers have no idea that trade restrictions cause them to pay a few extra dollars for each shirt and pair of pants they buy, so individually they have very little incentive to demand that import restrictions be lifted.

On the other hand, the USITC also estimates that removing the trade restrictions on textiles would reduce output and employment in the U.S. textile apparel industry by 10 to 14 percent. These losses would be concentrated among a small number

[6] Another possible objective is to increase government revenues. In many small and poor countries, governments are incapable of monitoring or taxing economic transactions that take place inside their borders. They may, however, be able to control entry points at their borders, which makes tariffs one of their few feasible sources of tax revenues.

[7] One famous leader, Lycurgus, did just that by intentionally putting an end to all international trade in ancient Sparta. Today, not many consumers in any country–including Greece–want to be that Spartan.

[8] "The Economic Effects of Significant U.S. Import Restraints," June 2004, U.S. International Trade Commission.

of firms and workers, which creates a strong incentive for those people to lobby to keep the status quo of high import restrictions. Once trade restrictions are in place they are politically very difficult to remove, even when the overall benefits of removing the restrictions are substantially greater than the costs.

IV. Losses from Trade in Factor Markets

When countries specialize and trade, efficient sectors expand production to export goods, and inefficient sectors decline and are replaced by foreign competitors. There is no question that specialization and trade causes some redirection of resources in the economy. Indeed, there can be no gains from trade without eliminating inefficient firms. But what are the consequences of this dislocation for workers at inefficient firms, in the short run and the long run?

Unemployment

As briefly discussed in the example of France and Germany trading rice and bicycles, there are strong theoretical arguments suggesting that international trade does not create long-run unemployment. Those arguments are strongly supported by empirical evidence, too, because countries that are more open to trade have unemployment rates no different from countries that are more closed to trade. Even countries that have experienced especially rapid trade growth have not faced increases in their unemployment rates. In short, international trade may cause short-run dislocations as workers change jobs. In time, however, displaced workers find new jobs working in firms that are more efficient, which increases national output and consumption levels.

Specific Factors and Mobile Factors

Telling displaced workers everything will work out for the best in the long run still leaves them facing serious problems, and as it turns out some workers face more serious problems than others. In the (overly) simple France-Germany example, no workers were hurt by switching jobs and they all shared equally in the gains from trade by enjoying lower prices for the products they consumed. One key to this kind of smooth transition was that workers could do either job equally well. In other words, they had no skills that were specific to growing rice or building bikes, so they did not have to retrain to take the new jobs and they did not have to pay to relocate their families. The real world is, of course, more complicated than that, so the idea that everyone shares equally in the gains from trade has to be modified.

The difference between mobile and specific factors is easy to see by comparing **financial capital** (or investment funds)–which is very liquid, and easy to move from one use to another–to a piece of physical capital that is designed to do one highly specialized task. Suppose you have $100 in savings that you want to invest. The $100 could easily be invested in any sector of the economy, but you decide to invest it in the textile sector to buy a machine for cutting cloth. Once that machinery is purchased the investment has become specific. It can be used to produce apparel, but not to grow rice or build a bicycle.

People also make specific investments. They take courses that prepare them to be doctors *or* engineers *or* shop foremen. Learning cell biology is very important for a person who wants to be a doctor, but will not help that person design airplanes or run a production line. Workers also learn from on-the-job training and work experience that is not taught in the classroom at all, but is still essential knowledge for the work being done at a particular business.

So, in the real world, what would happen to the inputs used to produce textiles and apparel if the United States removed import restrictions and output and employment levels in the industry fell, as the USITC has estimated they would? First, if textile mills close down some of their specific capital investments–plants and machinery–becomes much less valuable. The owners of that capital would incur a large loss on the investment, which is another reason why textile mill owners oppose reducing or eliminating the trade restrictions.

How much would workers suffer, and which workers would suffer most? That depends on whether the work in textile mills required specific training that cannot be used elsewhere. Generally, studies by economists find that workers suffer greater earnings losses from displacement when they have been employed at the same firm for a long time, and when they are unable to find re-employment in the same sector of the economy.[9]

Workers displaced because of import competition experience more difficulty in becoming re-employed than workers displaced for other reasons, but this seems to be mainly explained by the characteristics of the workers themselves. For example, women displaced from jobs for any reason are more likely to leave the labor force than men, and so are re-employed at lower rates.[10] Because women are overrepresented in import-competing industries, especially textiles and apparel, displaced workers from these industries are less likely to be re-employed.

Although job displacements from international trade clearly impose costs on some workers, and more on some workers than others, do the costs of job displacement represent a significant argument against globalization? Not necessarily. First, although some layoffs occur because of import competition, it is much more common for layoffs to be caused by competition from domestic firms, or because of changes in consumers' tastes and technology. Job turnover from globalization is a very small component of overall job turnover in the United States, reflecting the fact that trade (exports and imports) accounts for less than 25 percent of U.S. GDP.

Second, the federal government uses Trade Adjustment Assistance programs to ease the transition between jobs when import competition leads to displacement. Workers are eligible for up to 18 months of unemployment insurance, and for additional retraining and re-employment assistance. These benefits are considerably more generous than those provided to workers who are displaced for any other reason.

Trade and the Returns to Education

The costs of dislocation and unemployment from trade are primarily a short-run phenomenon that diminishes over time as workers move out of declining industries. Over a longer time span globalization does not cause unemployment, but it can still affect workers by changing wages and the returns to education.

Over the past three decades one of the most pronounced changes in U.S. labor markets has been the increase in what economists call the skill premium, which refers to how much more skilled workers earn than unskilled workers. Skill is typically associated with education levels, so we can think of the skill premium as the ratio of wages for college-educated workers to wages for workers who have only a high school education. Specifically, in 1973 college-educated workers earned 32 percent more a year than workers with high school educations, but by 1993 college-educated workers earned 56 percent more each year.[11]

---

[9] One study (Alfred J. Field and Edward M. Graham, "Is There a Special Case for Import Protection for the Textile and Apparel Sectors?" *The World Economy,* 1997) examined labor market outcomes in 1992 for workers displaced between 1986 and 1991. For manufacturing as a whole 94 percent of displaced workers were re-employed, after an average of six months of unemployment. Workers re-employed in the same industry saw a small drop in earnings (2.8 percent), while those re-employed in a different industry experienced a 24 percent drop in earnings, suggesting that less of their training transferred to their new jobs.

[10] Lori G. Kletzer, *Job Loss from Imports: Measuring the Costs*. IIE Press, 2001.

[11] Figure 1.7 in William Cline, *Trade and Income Distribution,* IIE Press, 1997.

Many people have connected the rise in the skill premium to globalization. To see why, recall that one source of comparative advantage is the relative supply of factor inputs. The United States has a relatively abundant supply of college-educated workers, whereas countries like Mexico and China are relatively abundant in workers with less than a college education. We therefore expect to see the United States exporting goods and services that use college-educated (skilled) workers intensively, and importing goods that intensively use unskilled workers.

It was also noted above that the effect of importing goods produced using unskilled workers is identical to allowing the migration of unskilled workers from Mexico and China into the United States. If migration leads to an increase in the supply of unskilled workers in the United States, wages for unskilled workers will fall. This fits the data on the skill premium.

Given that, should those concerned with growing income inequality in the United States oppose globalization? There are two important counterarguments to that position.

First, globalization is not the only explanation for the rising skill premium in recent decades. This period also corresponds to the introduction and rapid spread of computer technology throughout the U.S. economy. Information technology complements educated workers by making them more productive, and substitutes for less educated workers by replacing them. That leads to a rise in the skill premium. Although there is still considerable debate about the causes of the rising skill premium, a consensus among economists is emerging around the view that technological changes are the main factors, with globalization playing a smaller but still important role. If that is true, even if all international trade had been banned, there still would have been a sharp rise in the skill premium.

Second, restricting trade is a very inefficient way to equalize the distribution of income. Trade barriers help some firms and workers, but only by hurting consumers and other firms and workers.[12] If policymakers are only concerned with helping low-income workers to make the distribution of income more equal, they can directly subsidize the hiring of workers or supplement their incomes using policies like the Earned Income Tax Credit. These policies help low-income workers more directly, with smaller negative effects than trade restrictions.

V. Trade and International Institutions

All governments face a tug-of-war between competing economic interests in many different arenas, including the winners and losers from free trade policies. Today it is widely acknowledged by most economists and governments that free trade is the best economic policy for a country as a whole, but despite that it is difficult to prevent or eliminate trade barriers in the face of withering pressure to "protect" domestic producers and workers. Recognizing this trap, most nations in the world have now joined international institutions or signed international agreements that limit how and how much they can impede trade. The most important examples are the World Trade Organization (WTO), formerly known as the General Agreement on Tariffs and Trade (GATT), and regional free trade agreements such as the North American Free Trade Agreement (NAFTA).

How did these institutions and agreements come to exist? In the decades before World War I international trade grew very rapidly, driven by improvements in transportation technology and a web of bilateral (two-nation) trade agreements that lowered tariff rates among major trading countries. This system worked reasonably well until the 1920s and 1930s, when the United States and the leading European powers engaged in a series of "trade wars." The infamous Smoot-Hawley tariff was passed in 1930, steeply raising U.S. tariff

[12] See Lesson 11 in this volume for a review of the effects of tariffs, quotas, subsidies, and other trade barriers.

rates, and Europe quickly retaliated. World trade quickly ground to a halt, which made the Great Depression even more severe.

After World War II, the allied nations founded GATT, with the goal of trying to convert all national trade barriers into tariffs and then negotiate sharp tariff reductions.[13] The GATT was designed to be a dynamic treaty, and at roughly 10-year intervals the member nations completed new "rounds" of negotiations that lowered tariffs and addressed other trade issues. When it proved difficult to agree on tariff cuts in sensitive sectors, such as agriculture and textiles, these special issues were handled in side agreements, in essence sidelining the most contentious issues so that agreements could be achieved on other issues. Over time the GATT was extremely successful in reducing tariff rates, with successive rounds lowering world-wide rates from an average of 40 percent to only 5 percent.

In 1990 the WTO was formed from the GATT. Unlike the GATT, the WTO is not a treaty but an international institution, like the United Nations or the World Bank. While the WTO continues to focus on tariff reductions, it also covers areas not dealt with by the GATT such as trade in services, intellectual property protection, product and production standards, and competition (also known as anti-trust) policy. The WTO has also instituted a settlement process through which trade disputes can be mediated and, if necessary, adjudicated. Not surprisingly, this expansion of the WTO's influence has been the source of considerable debate and conflict. Some of the most important current issues and areas of debate are described below. What becomes clear from even this brief discussion is that while many groups are displeased with WTO, they are sharply divided in terms of their preferred remedies for these problems. In fact, many of those who criticize the WTO want it to do much more, while others want it to do much less.

Agriculture and Textiles

For a variety of reasons, high income nations–especially the United States, Japan, and Western Europe–have historically chosen to protect their markets from imported agricultural and textile and apparel products. This is surprising in at least one sense, because all of these nations have strong comparative disadvantages in textiles and apparel, and Japan and Western Europe have strong comparative disadvantages in agriculture. Therefore, protecting these particular goods means throwing away some of the largest potential gains from trade. Moreover, many of the poorest countries in the world regard agriculture and textiles/apparel as their only comparative advantage industries. Denying their access to markets in the high income nations means denying them gains from trade as well.

In addition to unusually high tariffs, trade in textiles and apparel is further impeded by a system of quotas called the Multi-Fiber Accord (MFA). The MFA was put in place in 1974, but under strong political pressure from many developing countries a termination of the MFA was agreed to in 1994, with an expiration date set for January 2005. When it expired Chinese textiles and apparel were shipped into the United States and Europe at unprecedented rates, and by May 2005 the United States had re-imposed quotas, effectively reneging on the agreement to end the MFA.

In addition to tariff protection, agriculture in high income nations is also provided heavy subsidies. Exporters in developing countries complain that these subsidies prevent them from selling to consumers in the high income nations by artificially lowering prices, and also that by increasing supplies of agricultural products on world markets the subsidies lower prices they receive in other parts of the world. Low food prices are very beneficial for consumers (importers) of agriculture, of

[13] This was a very busy period of international institution building that also gave rise to the United Nations, the World Bank, and the International Monetary Fund, among others.

course, but they are very harmful for the developing countries trying to export agricultural products.

These agriculture, textile, and apparel policies leave two very different groups unhappy with the WTO. Farmers and textile/apparel producers in the United States, Japan, and Western Europe are outraged that future trade agreements might remove their tariff, quota, and subsidy protections. Farmers and textile/apparel producers in the developing nations are outraged that the WTO has not gone far enough in removing these protections.

Environmental Standards

Globalization can lead to convergence in public policies in different nations. To see why this happens, imagine two cities sitting on either side of a river. One city (call it Windsor, Ontario) charges high sales taxes on food and gasoline. The second city (call it Detroit, Michigan) charges low sales taxes on these products. At first most citizens in Windsor grumble about their sales tax, but there isn't much they can do about it. As long as they cannot easily cross the river, they must pay the high sales tax when they buy these goods and services. But then a bridge is built across the river, so Windsor citizens can now buy the same goods in Detroit without paying the high sales tax, and sales at retail stores in Windsor fall. The owners of those stores soon demand a repeal of the sales tax, or that the bridge be closed.

The same kind of thing can happen with other kinds of regulations and public policies when countries open their markets to international trade, because there are often important differences between countries in terms of their preferred tax and regulatory policies. Higher taxes and strict regulations may have only moderate effects on business when they apply equally to all firms in a nation. But as soon as some firms can avoid the taxes or regulations by producing abroad, competition becomes especially difficult for firms that are still subject to the taxes and regulations.

In effect, regulation can become an important source of comparative advantage and trade. To see how this happens, suppose both the United States and Mexico produce some output in "dirty" and "clean" industries. Without regulation the United States has an absolute advantage in both industries, but neither country has a comparative advantage because the opportunity cost of production is the same in both nations. That means there are initially no gains from trade, so both countries produce some output in both clean and dirty industries.

If the United States then decides to regulate air and water emissions, production costs in the U.S. dirty industries will rise. If Mexico does not regulate, its production costs are unchanged. The regulations therefore leave the United States with a comparative advantage producing in the clean industries and Mexico with a comparative advantage in the dirty industries. After specializing, dirty industry output rises in Mexico and falls in the United States. Output produced in the dirty industries will be imported from Mexico into the United States, and output from the clean industries will be exported from the United States to Mexico.

If the pollution in dirty industries is local in scope, meaning that it mainly affects communities close to where the production occurs, free trade is great news for U.S. citizens who want a clean local environment. Without trade the United States had to produce its own dirty-industry output, and reducing emissions in the United States required the use of resources that could then not be used to produce other goods or services. With trade the United States can shift its dirty-industry production to Mexico at no cost, and U.S. water and air will be cleaner, too. So what's not to like, or is there a catch?

Although this example conveys some simple truths, it also ignores some important issues that concern environmental critics of globalization. First, there are likely to be specific factors (labor and capital) invested in the dirty industries in the United States, so there will be financial losses to capital owners and short-term unemployment issues if trade is adopted. In fact, the combination of environmental regulations plus globalization will impose particularly high costs on these groups, so the capital owners and workers in these industries will lobby very hard to prevent either the environmental regulations or free trade, or both.

Many environmentalists fear the political pressure that business interests will bring to bear against the regulatory standards, and they also do not want to promote a "race to the bottom" in which some nations choose to give up environmental quality to get more jobs and income. To prevent such a race and/or to avoid losing jobs in these industries, some people have suggested that developing countries be required to adopt the same environmental regulations as the United States or, if they do not, that any international trade that is driven by differences in environmental regulations be prohibited. Of course another solution would simply be to resist the lobbying pressure to lower U.S. environmental standards and enjoy the gains from trade.

An even broader problem, however, is that some pollution problems are global rather than local in scope, with effects felt well beyond the immediate area where pollution is created and released into the environment. One current example of this involves carbon emissions, which scientists believe contribute to global warming. To address this problem, many nations have signed the Kyoto Protocols, calling for strict limits on carbon emissions. But not all countries have signed these agreements–including the United States –and one controversial part of the protocols is that they set very different emission standards for industrialized and developing nations. If, as a result, carbon-emitting industries leave a highly regulated Europe to begin producing in unregulated China, global carbon emissions will remain high and the effects on global warming will be minimal or nil.

Another example of environmental damage with global scope is at the heart of a recent trade dispute between the United States and Mexico over tuna fishing. A low-cost technique to catch tuna uses nets that also catch and kill dolphins. When the United States passed laws banning these nets, the tuna fishing fleet began operating from Mexico to avoid the U.S. regulations. Environmentalists argued that letting Mexico's fishing fleet export tuna to the United States undermined the global goal of reducing dolphin kills.

A third issue raised by environmental critics of globalization is that, even if pollution effects are local in scope, it is wrong to allow developing countries to suffer pollution on our behalf. This basically argues that developing countries are incapable of making proper decisions about the desired levels of regulation and pollution in their own nations, and that it is necessary to dictate their policies to them. The same kind of issue arises in the following discussion of labor standards, and will be discussed at greater length there.

Labor Standards

Labor standards are laws and regulations governing how firms must treat their workers. These can include prohibitions on forced labor or child labor, workers' rights to organize and bargain collectively, non-discrimination in employment, workplace safety requirements, and minimum wage laws. These standards–especially those dealing with minimum wages and workplace safety–vary widely across countries.

Critics of globalization have argued that trade with countries that have low labor standards is wrong for two reasons. First, it undermines U.S. labor standards; second, it harms workers in the developing world. The effect of trade on U.S. wages has already been discussed, so only the second argument will be considered here.

Stories of children working long hours in dangerous factories to earn a dollar a day or less are upsetting, and lead many people to the instinctive conclusion that U.S. firms should be prevented from hiring foreign workers under those conditions. But to see whether that kind of policy makes sense, it must also be asked whether the hiring by these firms is the cause of low labor standards and poverty, and whether developing nations would be better off without U.S. firms hiring these workers.

The short answer to both of these questions is almost certainly no. As shown earlier, wages are low in these countries because labor productivity is low, not because workers are exploited by firms to export goods back to markets in developed nations. Several facts support this view. First, there is a nearly one-to-one relationship between worker productivity and worker wages. Second, the incidence of troubling labor practices such as the use of child labor is strongly related to income levels in a country, but negatively correlated with how much a country trades.[14] Third, studies of multinational firms operating in the developing world have shown that they generally pay higher wages than other employers in these nations.[15]

What would happen if the United States restricted trade with developing countries unless those countries raised their labor standards? The most likely consequence would be to eliminate all trade with these countries. That sounds extreme, but recall the example of trade in bicycles and rice in which France had a lower productivity level than Germany in both sectors. France still had a comparative advantage in producing rice, and so could export rice to Germany. But that required French wages to be substantially lower than Germany wages, to compensate for the French workers' lower productivity. If Germany required French workers be paid the same wages as German workers, there would be no trade between these countries. The result would be lower production and consumption of both goods, and therefore lower living standards, in both countries.

Eliminating trade with the developed world would almost certainly reduce the living standards of workers in those countries, which is the group we supposedly wanted to help with the tighter labor standards. There is considerable disagreement among economists about why some countries are rich and others are poor, but one thing seems clear: Countries that are more open to trade enjoy higher income levels. For that reason, most economists' response to the problem of low labor standards in poor nations is that these countries should pursue policies, including free trade, that allow them to increase productivity and incomes. When incomes rise, higher labor standards follow.

The same argument also seems to explain differences in environmental standards. Low-income, low-productivity countries can ill-afford to use many of their resources to reduce pollution. Instead, these countries may initially choose to accept and benefit from their comparative advantage in dirty, polluting, industries. At first trade causes pollution to increase, but as productivity and incomes rise, consumers in these nations demand more of most goods and services, including a cleaner environment. As that happens stricter environmental laws and regulations are adopted, and pollution levels begin to drop.

Product Standards

One of the more difficult issues facing the WTO is how to handle differences across countries in the way they regulate health and safety standards, especially what are called sanitary and phytosanitary standards for food. Some of these standards cover the content of the product by dictating which chemical additives and preservatives it may contain,

[14] Eric Edmonds and Nina Pavcnik, "International Trade and Child Labor: Cross-Country Evidence," NBER Working Paper 10317. Cambridge MA: National Bureau of Economic Research, 2004.

[15] Drusilla K Brown, Alan V. Deardorff, and Robert M. Stern, "The Effects of Multinational Production on Wages and Working Conditions in Developing Countries," NBER Working Paper 9669. Cambridge MA: National Bureau of Economic Research, 2002.

setting acceptable contamination levels, and so on. In general, for most goods that are traded internationally nations are free to set whatever content standards they deem appropriate, as long as they apply equally to all firms, regardless of nationality. Rules about how the foods are grown or raised are much more complex and controversial.

That provides the background for an example at the heart of some recent trade disputes between the United States and Europe, concerning the use of hormones to stimulate growth in cattle. U.S. producers argue that these are production standards, rather than a standard related to the final content of the product itself. Europeans argue that because these production techniques may create health risks they can be regulated under WTO rules as long as the regulations are applied equally to all firms regardless of nationality. The European Union banned imports of U.S. beef produced using bovine growth hormones (BGH), which led to a U.S. action against Europe at the WTO.

Although the European standard was clearly applied equally to all firms, regardless of nationality, the WTO decided to examine and rule on the scientific validity of the standard. The panel agreed with U.S. producers and exporters, saying that the Europeans could not demonstrate health risks from using BGH, and ruled that the standard was an illegal trade restriction. That outraged many Europeans, who felt the WTO had no business determining what legitimate science was, or what constituted a reasonable level of precaution for food products.

Whatever the merits of the bovine growth hormone case and the WTO's ruling, it should be pointed out that the WTO cannot and has not forced the European Union to change its policies. At the end of the day all member countries in the WTO remain sovereign, and are free to ignore WTO rulings–at some cost. In this case, the cost of maintaining the ban may turn out to be retaliation by the United States in the form of higher tariffs on European goods, which would now be sanctioned by the WTO and therefore not subject to further reprisals from Europe. If Europe chooses to maintain its policies in this case, however, the policies cannot be directly overridden by the WTO.

Still, this shows once again how globalization creates incentives for countries to harmonize regulations and other public policies, informally as a result of competitive market forces in some cases, or in this case explicitly through organizations such as the WTO. Because of that, some critics of globalization argue that belonging to the WTO results in some loss in national sovereignty. At least in the general sense that any mutual agreement for nations to restrict their behavior gives up some sovereignty, that is true. After all, when nations agree to jointly lower tariffs and other barriers to trade under the auspices of the WTO, they are agreeing to limit the use of some policies.

VI. Conclusion

Globalization presents a kind of paradox: Countries gain from trade because of their differences, but trading makes them more similar. The gains from trade are greater the more different two countries are, but countries converge as trade equalizes the availability, price, and cost of products. This is all good news for consumers who enjoy lower prices, and for exporting firms that find new markets. It creates serious problems, however, for inefficient firms that are unable to compete with lower priced imports, and for the specific factors of production that are employed at those firms, including some capital and labor inputs.

Cultures also converge with globalization. As multinational firms extend their reach (and their brand names) all over the world, the places we shop, the cars we drive, and the things that we eat, drink, listen to, and wear become increasingly similar. For consumers who want and like global brands, or who enjoy sampling new varieties of products from other countries, this is good news. For those who dislike or fear the influence of foreign cultures, and want to maintain local traditions, products, and employment patterns, globalization can pose a great threat.

Globalization also creates pressures on national governments to make their policies more similar. Sometimes this pressure is implicit and driven only by competitive market forces, whereas in other cases it is a formal, even legal and multinational effort, to coordinate policies across dozens of countries. Because some national policies are harmful–such as trade barriers supporting the interests of relatively small, but powerful, special-interest groups–pressure to conform to better international standards can be greatly beneficial in some cases. When there are more legitimate disagreements about the direction in which international policy standards are headed, these pressures to conform can breed tremendous resentment against globalization.

Appendix A: Critics of Globalization and the International Monetary Fund

Shortly after World War II, the International Monetary Fund (IMF) was founded as part of a new focus on international cooperation and international development, with a specific focus on macroeconomic stabilization policies and financial crises.[16] From its headquarters in Washington DC, just a few blocks from the White House (reflecting the leading role of the United States in funding and influencing IMF programs), the IMF provides economic policy advice to national governments and aid to countries facing financial crises.

To see why IMF aid and policies have become so controversial requires a bit of basic background in macroeconomic stabilization policies. **Fiscal policy** (adjusting the overall level of a national government's spending and taxes) and **monetary policy** (controlling the supply of money and interest rates) are often used to try to reduce unemployment or inflation, and to promote higher and steadier rates of economic growth.

National governments often spend more money providing goods and services than they take in through taxation. The resulting budget deficit must be financed by private lenders, who receive a promise from the government to pay the loan back with interest. There is nothing inherently wrong with this practice, and there are some very good reasons for governments to engage in deficit spending. For example, war efforts are often financed through borrowing, as are major investments in public infrastructure. In addition, many macroeconomists believe that deficit spending is an effective way to bring a national economy out of recession. The idea is that government spending provides a stimulus to aggregate demand that kick-starts an economy facing temporarily high unemployment and/or slow rates of economic growth.

If governments run large and perpetually growing deficits, however, the result is rising levels of public debt. Because interest must be paid on this debt, debt service becomes a growing portion of public expenditures, which can lead to more debt, which raises debt service, and so on, until the nation faces a financial crisis. This is similar to consumers who charge too much on their credit cards and can only afford to make minimum payments. Interest charges plus new purchases can cause the account balance to rise and debt begins to accumulate beyond the ability of the consumer making minimum payments to ever pay it off.

Unlike private citizens, however, national governments have a sneaky way out of this trap. Because they control the money supply they also control what money is worth. By deliberately increasing the money supply governments can lower the value of their currency, which reduces the real value of the debt and the interest they owe and pay. In other words, while governments promise to pay a certain dollar amount of debt and interest, they don't promise what those payments will be worth, in terms of the value of the nation's money.[17]

Many countries with severe debt trouble have tried printing money, known as "monetizing debt," as a short-term solution. But of course the major lenders to these countries know that governments can print money and do not want be left holding government IOUs that are made worthless by inflation. When danger signs appear they demand higher interest rates to compensate for

[16] The IMF was originally created as part of a system of "fixed" exchange rates that tied the value of national currencies to the U.S. dollar. This system sometimes led to crises in which countries were unable to balance their imports and exports, requiring an international lender to assist with payments. After the fixed exchange rate system broke down in the 1970s, the IMF broadened its focus from balance of payments crises to financial crises more broadly defined.

[17] A classic case was Germany's reparations to its victorious opponents after World War I, which could only be repaid by inflating the currency. During the German hyperinflation workers were eventually paid several times a day so that their spouses could spend their wages before the next round of price increases, and stacks of currency became more valuable as fuel than as money.

the risk they are taking, or they quit holding debt. That moves a country closer to financial crisis and collapse, and may make governments more likely to try to bail themselves out by printing money.

This vicious circle lies behind many of the financial crises experienced by developing countries in the last few decades. To stem these crises, the IMF has used a two-pronged approach. First, it loans money to troubled governments at better rates than they could get from private lenders worried about inflation risks. Second, as a condition of these loans the IMF negotiates fiscal austerity measures with loan recipients, typically in the form of dramatically reduced government spending. Because of concerns about an out-of-control debt spiral being the primary cause of many crises, the IMF makes controlling deficit spending an important piece of the solution.

This is where critics of the IMF, including Nobel-prize winning economist Joseph Stiglitz, find several key faults with the IMF's policies. First, by asking governments to give up the ability to run fiscal deficits, the IMF takes away an important tool for stimulating economies that are facing recessions. This may allow unemployment to become or remain a more severe social problem. Second, because budget cuts often reduce or eliminate assistance programs, such as food subsidies, the cost of the IMF policies is often borne by the most vulnerable members in these poor nations. In stark contrast, the international lenders who benefit by eliminating the risk of loan defaults or higher inflation are often multinational banks from the world's wealthiest nations. Third, the IMF's approach has not always or obviously been successful, with many countries that take the IMF's medicine proving very slow to recover and prosper.

Proponents of the IMF's policies offer three key responses to these charges. First, the IMF does not force any government to take loans from the IMF, so no nation is forced to accept these austerity measures. A government is free to try to solve its own problems if it prefers to do so, and some have. Second, blaming the IMF for the failure of countries facing financial crises is like seeing sick people in the hospital and concluding that the hospital made them ill. Typically, by the time the IMF is asked to provide loans to a country, the situation is already dire. Third, IMF proponents concede that austerity measures reduce the ability of national governments to use deficit spending to boost the economy, but point out that it is precisely the misuse of those policies that is often the root cause of these crises.

The controversy continues.

Appendix B: What Is a Trade Deficit?

The U.S. balance of trade figures are widely reported every month by the financial press, daily newspapers, and even television news broadcasts. But exactly what is the trade deficit, and what–if anything–makes it so important?

The **trade balance** is calculated by subtracting a country's imports of goods and services from its exports. When this number is positive (exports exceed imports), a country is running a **trade surplus**. When it is negative (exports are less than imports), a country is running a **trade deficit**. To most people (apparently including most of the reporters who write stories about the trade balance), a deficit sounds bad while a surplus sounds good. In terms of current consumption of real goods and services, however, there are clearly advantages in getting more goods and services from other countries than you send to them. So the question of why deficits or surpluses are good or bad is not always easy to answer, and depends partly on whether the deficits or surpluses last for just a year or two, or much longer.

The United States has had a negative trade balance, or a trade deficit, every year since 1981. That is a key reason why the issue is now seen by most economists as an important long-term issue facing the national economy. To explain how and why it is so important, the rest of this Appendix deals with three related topics: 1) the link between trading goods and services (exports and imports) and trading capital assets–which are not included in the balance of trade statistics, 2) the underlying causes of trade deficits or surpluses, and 3) under what circumstances a trade deficit is, or is not, a serious problem for a country.

Linking Trade and Investment

For centuries, U.S. citizens and companies have owned financial assets in foreign countries, and foreign citizens and companies have owned financial assets in the United States. The difference between these two values at any point in time is called net foreign wealth. Countries with positive net foreign wealth are net creditors, and countries with negative net foreign wealth are net debtors. (Similarly, a person can simultaneously own financial assets such as a banking account, and owe debts such as mortgages or student loans. If assets exceed debts, the person is a net creditor; if debts exceed assets, the person is a net debtor.)

Table B1 lists values for the international investment position of the United States over recent years. In 1985, U.S. citizens and companies held $1,288 billion dollars in financial assets abroad, while foreign citizens and companies held $1,160 billion dollars of U.S. financial assets. The difference, $128 billion, represented positive net foreign wealth for the United States. By 1990, however, foreign citizens and companies held $224 billion more in U.S. assets than U.S. citizens and companies held abroad. By 2003 the U.S. net foreign debt had grown to an astonishing $2.6 trillion.

Table B1: International Investment Position of the United States (in billions of dollars)

	Foreign assets owned by U.S. citizens and companies	U.S. assets owned by foreign citizens and companies	U.S. net foreign wealth position
1985	1,288	1,160	128
1990	2,166	2,390	-224
1995	3,874	4,292	-418
2000	7,190	9,377	-2,187
2003	7,864	10,515	-2,651

Source: *Statistical Abstract of the United States*, various years.

Why and how is this topic related to the trade balance for exports and imports? The trading of goods and capital are directly connected as shown in the following equation:

$$(\text{exports} - \text{imports}) = \text{change in net foreign wealth}$$

Typically a country pays for its imports by exporting goods. When trade is balanced (exports − imports = 0), export earnings

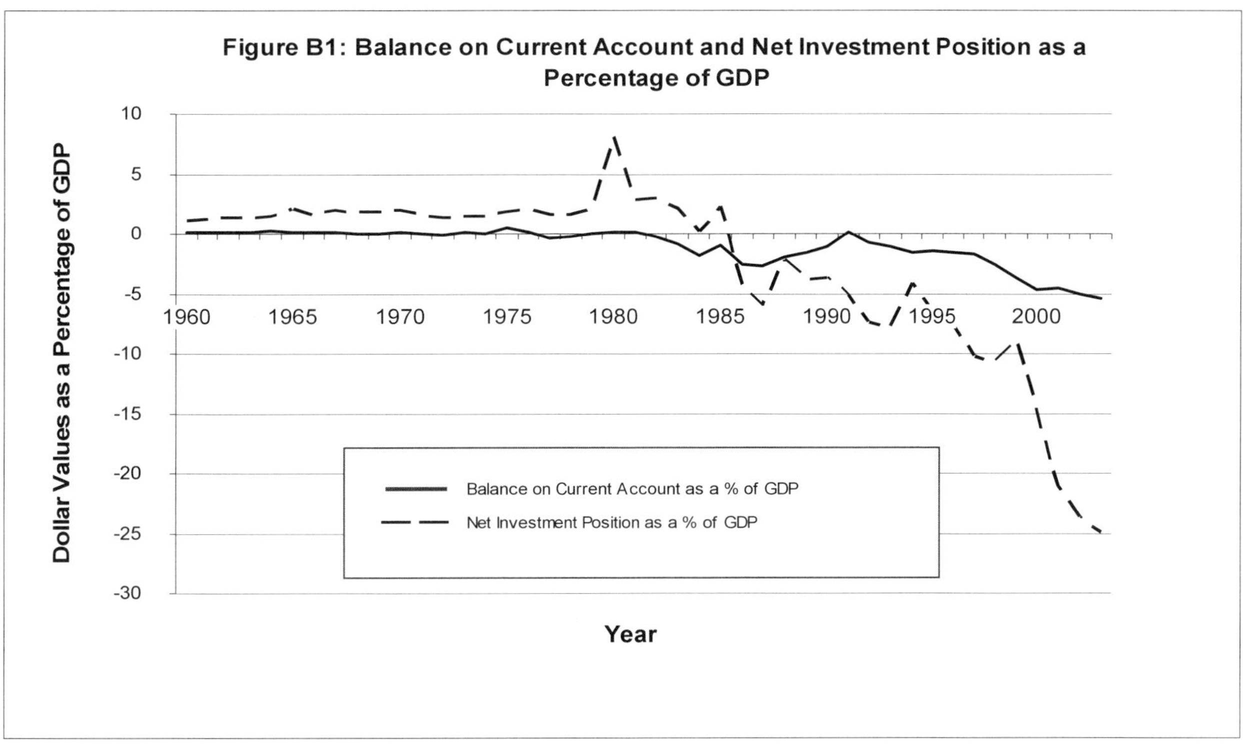

exactly offset import payments. When that is the case the trade in goods and services (imports and exports) results in no change in net foreign wealth. Similarly, when a family's after-tax income exactly equals their consumption expenditures, they are not adding to savings or to their debts.

The United States ran a trade deficit every year from 1981-2004, meaning that it spent more on imports than it earned from its export sales. To pay for those imports U.S. citizens and companies borrowed from abroad, leading to a decrease in U.S. net foreign wealth.[18] The cumulative effects of these deficits are shown in Figure B1 above.

Of course, there are two sides to any transaction. If the United States runs a trade deficit (importing more than it exports), some other country must be running a trade surplus (exporting more than it imports). For example, for the last several years China has run a large trade surplus with the United States. What do people and companies in China do with the export earnings from the United States that are not spent on imports from the United States? China lends this money back to the United States by buying financial assets, including bonds issued by the U.S. government, banks, or other firms and institutions. That provides funds that allow the United States to pay for the rest of its imports from China, but the catch is that eventually these loans must be paid back, and the earnings from China's investments in the United States will go back to China. To do that, the United States will someday have to reverse its trade balance so that its export earnings exceed its import payments. When that happens, U.S. households will have less to consume.

This situation is similar to one in which a consumer wants to buy a car but cannot pay the full price out of his or her current income. To make the purchase the consumer may first sell off some assets (for example, taking money out of savings accounts), but then borrows the rest of the purchase price from the

[18] The United States could also have sold off foreign assets rather than borrowing from abroad, but as shown in Table B1, the United States is both lending and borrowing internationally. Therefore, the decline in U.S. net foreign wealth occurred because the United States borrowed more money than it loaned.

car dealership.[19] The dealership gives the consumer a car, and a loan. The consumer gets the car to use now, and promises to pay the money back. The dealer is willing to do this because he makes a sale and earns interest on the money loaned to the consumer.

Another way to understand the link between international merchandise trade (exports and imports) and trade of capital assets is to ask where an economy can decide to place its savings, and where it gets funds to make investments. Domestic savings can go toward domestic investment, but can also be used to make foreign investments. As already seen, a country that is making net investments abroad experiences growth in its net foreign wealth. On the other hand, to finance domestic investments a country can either look toward domestic savers or to foreign savers. A country that receives net investments from other counties gets the current benefit of greater investment spending, with gains in future production capacity and (it hopes) profits and earnings, but it experiences a decline in its net foreign wealth. That means the equation that shows the link between net exports (exports – imports) and the change in net foreign wealth can be rewritten as:

domestic saving – domestic investment
= change in net foreign wealth

or

exports – imports = domestic saving – domestic investment

Why Countries Run Trade Deficits

What the last equation makes clear is that the trade balance is affected by savings and investment behavior.[20] Specifically, trade deficits can result from an increase in domestic investment or a decrease in domestic savings. But the effects of a trade deficit that results from increasing domestic investment are very different from those that result from decreasing savings.

An increase in investment means that a country's productive capacity is increasing, so in the future there will be greater ability to repay debts, perhaps even without reducing future consumption. A decrease in savings that increases current consumption of goods and services (including imports) does not increase future output or productivity.

To make this point clear for students, use the example of two kinds of personal borrowing. John takes out thousands of dollars in student loans, which he uses to pay for a college education. Jill takes out thousands of dollars in credit card loans to pay for a vacation and eating out at nice restaurants. Both face the same level of debt, but John's debt finances an investment in his future productivity, income, and ability to repay the loans. Without these loans John might not be able to afford college, and he could be much worse off in the long run. Jill, on the other hand, is only shifting future income and consumption to the present, paying a hefty premium (interest) on those loans to do so, and putting herself at considerable financial risk.

Countries engage in international borrowing for very similar reasons. They may lack domestic savings required to make investments in their future productivity. For example, many European countries borrowed heavily immediately after World War II to rebuild their economies. During this period the United States was the major creditor nation in world financial markets, but as

[19] To extend the analogy, the consumer did not have to borrow from the dealership, but could have borrowed from his or her bank. Similarly, while the United States does borrow heavily from the Chinese to pay for imports from China, it could just as easily borrow from Germany, France, or some other nation.

[20] The trade balance has very little to do with whether a country has strong or weak comparative advantages, or whether a country protects its markets from foreign trade. These factors will cause exports and imports to rise and fall together, with little or no effect on the trade balance.

already discussed that changed dramatically by the early 1980s.

Since 1981, capital inflows from other nations have contributed to high levels of capital investment in the United States, leading to increased productivity, output, and income levels. In recent years, however, an increasing fraction of foreign capital inflows were used to fund current consumption and spending, and in particular the federal budget deficit.

Domestic saving consists of private saving (the difference between income and consumption for private citizens) and public savings (the different between tax receipts and government expenditures). Between 1981 and 2004, the U.S. federal government ran budget deficits (expenditures exceeding tax receipts) in all but two years. From 2001 to 2004, the federal government spent $820 billion more than it collected in taxes. These deficits substantially reduced domestic savings and have contributed significantly to accumulated trade deficits of more than two decades experienced by the United States.

For any country that runs large government budget deficits, the ability to rely on foreign capital markets is, once again, a good news, bad news proposition. For the United States, the good news in recent years has been that the federal deficits have been financed in large part by inflows of foreign capital buying U.S. Treasury bonds. In 2003, $3.9 trillion of U.S. federal debt was held outside U.S. government accounts, with $1.7 trillion held by foreign lenders.[21] Without this foreign capital, the federal government would have had to pay higher interest rates to finance the debt, increasing the cost of borrowing and crowding out some private investment.

The bad news, once again, is that this loan of foreign capital must be repaid at some point. And to the extent that the government budget deficits are used to pay for current consumption expenditures rather than investments in capital projects, repaying these debts will be more difficult. Unlike repaying federal debt that is held by U.S. citizens and organizations, repaying foreign debt results in lower consumption for the United States as a whole.

[21] In 2003, the U.S. federal government had $6.76 trillion in total debt. $2.85 trillion was held by Federal government accounts, chiefly the Social Security system. Of the $3.9 trillion outside U.S. federal government accounts, $2.2 trillion was held by U.S. individuals and organizations, with the Federal Reserve System holding almost $700 billion.

LESSON ONE
WHY IS GLOBALIZATION SO CONTROVERSIAL?

LESSON DESCRIPTION

This lesson provides an overview of the major issues that have been raised in the debate over globalization. After a brief introductory reading, students are assigned to various roles in a much longer reader's theater activity depicting protests that take place at a (fictional) future meeting of the World Trade Organization in New York. Following a brief discussion of this skit students collect and organize arguments on both sides of the debate, and then work in small groups to design and produce signs that might be carried at the protests, by either supporters or opponents of globalization.

INTRODUCTION

Globalization is driven by an increasingly interdependent and international economic system, but entails many political, technological, and cultural changes that affect individuals, communities, businesses, and governments all around the world. Many people equate globalization with the growth of multinational or transnational corporations and with much more prominent roles for international institutions that oversee world trade and finance, such as the International Monetary Fund.

Few recent issues have generated more debate and public protest than globalization. For example, at 1999 meetings of the World Trade Organization (WTO) in Seattle, more than 50,000 protesters smashed windows of international corporations and confronted police for several days. One reason for protests at these and other WTO meetings (including meetings in Montreal and Brussels), is what many opponents of globalization see as unfair trade practices sanctioned by the WTO. They argue that the free trade policies supported by the WTO benefit large corporations and rich nations but lead to greater poverty, inequality, loss of local culture, and environmental damage, especially in poorer, less developed nations.

Supporters of free trade and globalization dismiss those claims, and instead argue that removing trade barriers such as tariffs and quotas allows production and capital to be allocated more efficiently. That increases production and competition, lowers prices, and gives consumers a greater range of choice in products. That in turn promotes economic growth and efficiency in general, and capital investments in developing nations in particular, raising income levels and the standard of living in all countries that are more open to trade. Supporters of the WTO argue that, far from being unfair, WTO policies reflect the desires and best interests of its nearly 150 member countries.

CONCEPTS

Economic institutions
Barriers to trade
Voluntary exchange
Specialization
Factor endowments
Gains from trade

CONTENT STANDARDS

Voluntary exchange occurs only when all participating parties expect to gain. This is true for trade among individuals or organizations within a nation, and among individuals or organizations in different nations.

When individuals, regions, and nations specialize in what they can produce at the lowest cost and then trade with others, both production and consumption increase.

BENCHMARKS

Voluntary exchange among people or organizations in different countries gives people a broader range of choices in buying goods and services.

Like trade among individuals within one country, international trade promotes specialization and division of labor and increases output and consumption.

As a result of growing international economic interdependence, economic conditions and policies in one nation increasingly affect economic conditions and policies in other nations.

Two factors that prompt international trade are international differences in the availability of productive resources and differences in relative prices.

OBJECTIVES

Students will:

- Identify who benefits and who loses when a trade barrier such as sugar or automobile import quotas is eliminated.
- Explain why the United States no longer has a comparative advantage in the production of some products it once exported.
- Identify and discuss major arguments for and against globalization, particularly policies that encourage free trade among nations.

TIME REQUIRED

Two class periods. In class periods of about one hour, the suggested coverage is: Period 1, Procedures 1–4; Period 2, Procedure 5, Closure, and Assessment

MATERIALS

- Visual 1: WTO Protests: Seattle, 1999
- Activity 1: The Debate over Globalization: A Brief Overview (one copy per student)
- Activity 2: "The Earth is Not For Sale: The Debate Over Globalization," A Reader's Theater (one copy per student)
- Activity 3: Summarizing the Arguments in the Globalization Debate (one copy per student)
- Activity 4: Representing the Debate: Making Protest Signs (one copy per student)
- Activity 5: Crossword: The Debate over Globalization (one copy per student)

PROCEDURES

1. Ask students if they remember the protests that occurred in Seattle, Washington in 1999, and what those protests were about. Display Visual 1; describe the protests and summarize the major issues involved.

2. Distribute Activity 1. Explain to students that this brief activity will give them an overview of the issues on both sides of the debate that sparked the protests in Seattle. Have students read the overview and answer the questions that follow. Briefly discuss student responses:

A. Which author(s) supports globalization? Why does he or she support it? *(Dr. Razeen Sally: "Globalization, then, is growth-promoting.")*

B. Which author(s) opposes globalization? Why does he or she oppose it? *(Duncan Green and Claire Melamed: "While globalization has led to benefits for some, it has not led to benefits for all.")*

C. What are two examples of the impact of increased globalization on your life?

(clothes and music from other countries, impact of terrorism, etc.)

3. Distribute copies of Activity 2: "The Earth is Not For Sale…" Assign students to take the 20 roles in the reader's theater script. Have students write in the names of those playing each role. Explain that the entire class will speak the lines for the "Group of Protesters," so all students will have at least a small speaking role.

4. Have students read Activity 2 in reader's theater format. Then distribute Activity 3, and give students 15-20 minutes to complete it. Allow students to review the reader's theater script as they answer the questions, if they wish. Review students' answers to the questions in Activity 3:

Character	For/against globalization?	Supporting evidence
Protester 1	*Against*	*Wearing "No More Sweatshops" T-shirt; "most people live on less than $1.00/day"*
Protester 2	*Against*	*"...dirty, dangerous. And the pay is awful..."*
Manager 1	*For*	*"...percent of people who are malnourished has dropped..."*
Manager 2	*For*	*"...making 2-3 times what she would make otherwise..."*
Protester 3	*Against*	*"...most making 11 cents to 17 cents per hour..."*
Union representative	*Against*	*"...now our jobs are going to China or Mexico."*
IT employee	*Against*	*"...2,500 U.S. companies have sent jobs overseas."*
Economics student 1	*For*	*"...between 1993 and 2002, the U.S. added more than 18 million jobs."*
Economics student 2	*For*	*"We still make plenty of things, just not the things we aren't competitive at."*
Mr. Singh, WTO delegate	*For*	*"...WTO agreements are designed to lower and eventually eliminate all trade barriers."*
Board Member, Ox-Fam International	*Against*	*"...the WTO continues to allow the U.S. to hold unfair advantages."*
Wall Street floor trader	*For*	*"...sounds like you are saying that you know what's better for them than they do."*
Art gallery owner	*Against*	*"...local cultures...get pushed out by the big, loud American culture."*
UN delegate 1	*For*	*"...best hope for developing nations."*
UN delegate 2	*Against*	*"...growth does not provide a solution to all problems."*

Arguments of those who support free trade and greater access to markets (globalists)	Arguments of those who oppose free trade and greater access to markets (anti-globalists)
1. Poverty, infant mortality, etc. all down as a result of increased trade.	**1.** Increases poverty and income inequality
2. Trade is the best hope for growth for developing nations, increasing income levels.	**2.** The U.S. is exporting jobs overseas to low - wage countries.
3. Multinational corporations often pay wage premiums above going wage rates in developing countries.	**3.** Multinational corporations exploit workers in sweatshops and pay less than $1.00/day.
4. Only 2% of U.S. manufacturing job loss is due to outsourcing, and the U.S. is a net service exporter.	**4.** The U.S. doesn't really play/trade fair–its agricultural subsidies are really trade barriers.
	5. Local cultures are crowded out by importing Western goods and ideas.

5. Ask students to recall the details of the 1999 Seattle protests. Remind students that demonstrators carried signs so their message could be captured by the media. (NOTE: HistoryLink.org has an excellent slideshow of images from Seattle: http://www.history link.org /essays/output.cfm?file_id=7117). Explain to students that they will be creating their own protest signs or posters that support one side or the other in the globalization debate. Distribute Activity 4, and assign groups of three students to represent either supporters or opponents. Have students review the directions and make certain they understand what is expected. Tell students that they will also be expected to make a brief (two or three minute) presentation describing their poster to the class. In these presentations, students should summarize how their poster represents some of the key arguments for their position on the debate.

CLOSURE

Ask students if they believe that consensus in the debate over globalization will be reached anytime in the near future. Why or why not? Ask students to briefly summarize one or two points (e.g., the impact of globalization on economic growth) for which each side differs substantially in their views. How could that disagreement be resolved, or can it never be resolved?

ASSESSMENT

Distribute Activity 5. Have students complete the crossword puzzle and review responses.

Key for Activity 5:

ACROSS

8 Companies that do business in more than one nation. **Multinational Corporations**

9 The globalization debate centers on free trade's impact on _**poverty**_; critics say free trade increases it, supporters claim free trade reduces it.

10 Critics of globalization argue that all workers deserve a _**living**_ wage.

DOWN

1 Supporters of globalization argue that the greater a nation's economic freedom, the greater its _**political**_ freedom will be as well.

2 Term used to describe U.S. businesses hiring workers in foreign countries because they have lower wage rates. **Outsourcing**

3 Critics of globalization claim the U.S. is hypocritical in arguing for free trade and keeping its own agricultural _**subsidies**_, which act as trade barriers.

4 In order to attract the best workers, corporations often pay their local workers in developing countries a wage _**premium**_, several times higher than the prevailing wage.

5 Supporters of globalization claim that free trade can result in greater _**economic**_ _**growth**_ for developing nations.

6 World merchandise trade has increased over the last 30 years, due in part to greatly reduced _**transportation**_ costs.

7 Organization responsible for negotiating and maintaining trade agreements among member states: **WTO.**

Visual 1
WTO Protests: Seattle, 1999

(www.bradandkathy.com/ photos/WTO/8/source/1.html)

Who: Union organizers, environmentalists, animal rights activists, and senior citizens protested during a World Trade Organization (WTO) meeting

What: Attempt by protesters to shut down the WTO meeting by blocking major roads, breaking windows of major downtown businesses, engaging police

When: November 30–December 2, 1999

Where: Downtown Seattle, Washington

Why: Protesters believed that WTO policies promoting greater free trade were bad for the environment, increased world poverty, and only made large corporations wealthy. WTO supporters believe that free trade improves living standards around the world, which in turn leads to increased human rights, literacy rates, and even life expectancies.

Activity 1
The Debate over Globalization: A Brief Overview

Reports about globalization, and the debate surrounding it, appear in the media almost every day. Even more important, globalization affects our everyday lives. For example, the clothes we wear are usually produced in other countries, while music by U.S. artists is heard by people in other countries, too. Some terrorist organizations have their own global networks. These are only a few examples of the how people in the United States are increasingly connected to people and countries around the world. Other examples can be seen when an American company hires workers in India to handle its technology support program, or in the proliferation and rising prominence of international organizations such as the United Nations, the World Bank, the World Trade Organization, and the International Monetary Fund, which were founded to deal with global problems including peace and security, economic growth and development, the environment, health, and international trade.

What is globalization, exactly? Nobel prize-winning economist Joseph Stiglitz defined globalization as "the closer integration of the countries and peoples of the world which has been brought about by the enormous reduction of costs of transportation and communication, and the breaking down of artificial barriers to the flows of goods, services, capital, knowledge, and (to a lesser extent) people across borders."[1] Over the past 50 years, the exponential growth of technology–primarily computer and communication technologies–has improved the ability of people and firms in all countries to access knowledge and to build links with people and firms in other parts of the world. Computers and other technologies have also reduced transportation costs, making it less expensive to import or export goods and services. This has led to dramatic increases in international trade and improved standards of living for millions of people.

Despite that, there are outspoken opponents of globalization. One key issue that divides supporters and opponents of globalization is the role it plays in causing or curing global poverty. Advocates of globalization want to continue to increase international trade and reduce trade barriers, such as tariffs and quotas, because they believe that offers a better chance for promoting economic growth in the developing nations of the world. Opponents claim that, instead, international trade and free markets have been a major cause of increased poverty and growing income inequality in developing nations. Here are two quotations that characterize this part of the debate:

> "Globalization, then, is growth-promoting. Growth, in turn, reduces poverty. ...(T)he liberalization of international transactions is good for freedom and prosperity. The anti-liberal critique is wrong: marginalization is in large part caused by not enough rather than too much globalization." (Dr. Razeen Sally, London School of Economics)[2]

> "While globalization has led to benefits for some, it has not led to benefits for all. The benefits appear to have gone to those who already have the most, while many of the poorest have failed to benefit fully and some have even been made poorer." (Duncan Green, Policy Analyst at the Catholic Aid Agency for England and Wales; and Claire Melamed, Head of Trade Policy, Christian Aid)[3]

---

[1] Joseph Stiglitz, *Globalization and Its Discontents.* W.W. Norton and Company, New York, NY: 2003.
[2] Razeen Sally, "Rival visions of globalisation - anything new after September 11th?" *Global Dimensions: London School of Economics,* accessed at (http://www.lse.ac.uk/collections/globalDimensions/research/rivalVisionsOfGlobalisation/) on September 26, 2005.
[3] "A Human Development Approach to Globalisation" (http://www.cafod.org.uk/archive/policy/polhumdevglobfull.shtml)

Activity 1 (continued)

Questions:

1. Which author(s) supports globalization, and why does he or she support it?

2. Which author(s) opposes globalization, and why does he or she oppose it?

3. List two ways that globalization has affected your life.

Activity 2
"The Earth is Not For Sale: The Debate Over Globalization"
A Reader's Theater

Characters	Played by
Narrator	
Sue Henry, news director	
David Richards, radio reporter	
Abbe Smith, radio reporter	
Protester 1	
Protester 2	
Manager 1	
Protester 3	
Manager 2	
Union representative	
IT employee	
Economics student 1	
Economics student 2	
Mr. Singh, WTO delegate	
Board member, Ox-Fam International	
Retiree	
Wall Street floor trader	
Art gallery owner	
UN delegate 1	
UN delegate 2	

Activity 2 (continued)

Setting (read by the Narrator):

New York City, near Wall Street. The World Trade Organization is meeting to discuss a new round of trade agreements, despite another round of protests from those who oppose globalism, and especially the expansion of free trade between the nations of the world. Protesters are lined up on either side of Wall Street, held back by barricades and police officers, including some on horseback. The police are there to keep Wall Street, the street that represents the heart of the U.S. and world financial network, open for business. Two reporters from a New York radio station are also walking the street, looking for a story and trying to understand what the debate is all about. Both reporters would admit, if asked, to knowing very little about the issues that so many of the protesters obviously feel strongly about. The reporters' job is to conduct live interviews with several protesters during the noon news show. The news show is hosted in the studio by the radio station's news director, who has decided to make this the top news story of the day. Because it is the lunch hour, many of the people who work in the financial district–traders, managers, and secretaries–will also be on the street, adding to an already chaotic situation. It's almost time for the live broadcast to begin.

Sue Henry, news director: ...(in a quiet voice) Ok, we are live in 3, 2, 1...(in regular voice) Welcome to WTRD, I am Sue Henry, your host for *Noon Magazine*, a show that focuses on one key story unfolding in our great city each day, with expanded live news coverage. Today's story is on the protests on Wall Street. The World Trade Organization is holding meetings in New York this week, and thousands of protesters have lined the street, chanting and singing. For more background we go to one of our reporters in the field, David Richards...David?

David Richards: Yes, Sue, I am here on a very crowded Wall Street with protesters chanting all around me...

Group of Protesters: People before profits! People before profits! People before profits!

David Richards: Many of these folks are against the growth of global free trade. They believe unfettered, so-called *laissez faire*, free trade, is to blame for increases in poverty, income inequality, and environmental damage in recent decades. They claim that the elimination of tariffs and other barriers to trade have simply allowed large, multinational corporations to move into and exploit developing nations, while hurting many U.S. workers and families, too.

Sue Henry: Thanks, David, stay close by...now we turn to Abbe Smith, also on Wall Street, but a bit closer to the New York Stock Exchange. Abbe, what can you add?

Abbe Smith: Sue, the other side of this global debate–you might call them free-trade advocates–argues that opening up markets and international borders to free trade has had all kinds of benefits for developing nations, as well as the United States and other industrialized nations. They cite data showing increased life expectancy, increased literacy, more political freedom, and a reduction in the proportion of people living on less than $1.00 per day in the developing nations.

Activity 2 (continued)

Sue Henry: David and Abbe, will you walk through the protesters there and see if you can get some interviews?

David Richards: I will, but it might be hard to hear over this shouting…

Group of Protesters: Capitalism? No thanks! We'll shut down your banks! Capitalism? No thanks! We'll shut down your banks!

David Richards: Ma'am, I'm from WTRD radio. Could I ask you why you are here?

Protester 1 (wearing a "No More Sweatshops" T-shirt): The unbridled expansion of capitalism and free trade has allowed large, multinational companies to exploit developing countries, and especially their poorest citizens who are often forced to work for less than $1.00 day.

Protester 2: That's right…once the borders of developing countries are open, big corporations can move in and set up factories. Many of the factories set up by these big companies are sweatshops–dirty, dangerous, and the pay is awful. We are here protesting for a 'living wage' for all foreign employees of U.S. corporations.

David Richards: These two people who don't look like protesters were walking by and shaking their heads at what you said. Let's see what they have to say.

Manager 1 (works for a large corporation; is on her way to lunch with a friend, Manager 2): I've been listening for the last few minutes and I want to correct some common misconceptions about globalization and large corporations. Evidence shows that the proportion of people living on $1.00 per day or less has decreased by 50% in the last 20 years, which was a period of rapid world economic growth, largely *because* of international trade. And the percentage of people who are malnourished has dropped from 56% in the 1960s to only 10% today. Again, during a period of global economic growth, fueled by trade.

Protester 1: I don't know about all these numbers, but I do know that the world's poor make our shirts and our shoes and get paid less than one-twentieth what U.S. workers make…

Manager 2: …but its not just about a simple comparison of wages. You have to ask about standards of living with and without investment by international firms. If a person making $ 0.50 an hour is making 2 to 3 times what she could make otherwise, isn't she better off?

Protester 3 (overhearing the conversation): Better off compared to whom, Bill Gates? To the Walton family? In Bangladesh, workers make shirts for large U.S. companies. Most are women who regularly work 14-hour days and sometimes even longer. Most make 11 cents to 17 cents an hour, hardly enough to support themselves, much less a family.

Manager 1: Look, our corporation has a factory in Vietnam. Last year our factory there paid 2 times the local wage. That was a big step up for those workers, and it made sense for us, too, because it meant we could get the most productive local workers.

Activity 2 (continued)

David Richards: Sue, this debate continues, but I am going to kick it back to you, because I know you want to get Abbe on the air…

Sue Henry: Thanks David. You know, in preparation for this show, I read a study by two economists that found that the more free and open to trade a country is, the lower its United Nations' Poverty Index. More trade, less poor…Interesting…we'll see if Abbe can shed some light on this question…Abbe?

Abbe Smith: Thanks Sue…

Group of Protesters: Teamsters and turtles…together at last! No, No, No, Don't Ship Our Jobs to Mexico! Teamsters and turtles…together at last! No, No, No, Don't Ship Our Jobs to Mexico!

Abbe Smith: As you can hear, the protesters on this side of Wall Street are opposed to 'outsourcing' American jobs. Sir, what brings you here today?

Union representative: I'm tired of these large, unfeeling corporations sending our good paying manufacturing jobs overseas to some factory where workers make $1.50 an hour…That's what's happening in the textile industry, the steel industry, and the auto industry, too. These are industries that built America and now our jobs are going to China or Mexico...

Information technology (IT) employee: That's right, in my company we just started outsourcing our tech support to India…Employees in India make only one-eighth of what we do here in the U.S.…I heard more than 2,500 U.S. companies have sent jobs overseas…

Union rep.: …that's right. And when all the manufacturing and technical jobs are gone to Mexico and India, we'll be a nation of short-order cooks, store clerks, and waitresses…not exactly a strong industrial base…

Economics student 1 (wandering by the conversation with Economics student 2): Wait a minute, you make it sound like the increase in global trade has led to these problems and that the U.S. is running out of jobs. I learned that people said the same thing in the 1960s and the 1980s–that we'd become a nation of burger flippers. That didn't happen. In fact, between 1993 and 2002, the U.S. added 18 million more jobs than it lost. High paying jobs in management and in specialized professions have grown by 20 million and now account for a third of all U.S. jobs…And only about 2% of the 15,000,000 American job losses each year are due to outsourcing.

IT employee:…My point exactly. We don't 'make' anything in this country any more, we 'manage' it…

Economics student 2: But industrial manufacturing climbed 93 percent between 1980 and 2003. We still make plenty of things, just not the things we aren't competitive at. For example, China now makes most of the worlds T-shirts, while the U.S. makes most of the world's large commercial aircraft. We could take over the T-shirt industry, but at what cost–we'd have to use resources and workers from our aircraft, and other, industries. Is this what we really want?

Activity 2 (continued)

Union rep.: But how can we compete with countries that don't have child labor laws, don't enforce pollution controls, and don't have worker safety laws…Of course they will have an advantage over us. We can bring back our manufacturing jobs by only buying "made in America!"

Economics student 1: That's a popular view, and an old one–that we should just buy American and our manufacturing jobs will return. But we just read a study of the American automobile industry, and only 21% of the employees in the industry are actually employed in making the cars. More than three-quarters are in *service* industries like mechanics and sales people. These folks don't really care where the car is made…so long as it's sold and used in the U.S.! Service industries employ more and more people, in highly trained, professional jobs in medicine, law, and financial services, too–not just flipping burgers at McDonalds or selling things at stores in the malls, although those are still good jobs for a lot of people, too.

Abbe Smith: I'm sorry, but I need to send it back to Sue Henry. Before I do, I should add that in researching this story I read that the recent decline in manufacturing employment in the U.S. was due not to imports, but to the recent recession and increases in U.S. labor productivity. In fact, most economists believe that expanding overseas markets–through free trade–would be a shot in the arm for American manufacturing.

Sue Henry: Thanks Abbe…We now go to David Richards who has a delegate from the WTO with him…

Group of Protesters: Hey Hey, Ho Ho…the WTO has got to go! Hey Hey, Ho Ho…the WTO has got to go!

David Richards: That's right Sue, I am joined by Mr. Singh, a delegate to the WTO conference–and a few very loud protesters. First, Mr. Singh, can you tell us what the WTO does?

Mr. Singh: Thank you. The WTO is an international organization dealing with the rules of trade between nations. The WTO has nearly 150 nations as members, and the WTO agreements among all of these nations are designed to lower and eventually eliminate all trade barriers. Ultimately that helps people all over the world get more goods and services to consume at the lowest possible prices. But WTO agreements also help producers of goods and services, including both exporters and importers, operate their businesses more efficiently.

David Richards: Mr. Singh, the WTO has been accused of being a tool of the rich nations and corporations, dictating to the poor countries, destroying jobs, and ignoring the environment. How do you respond?

Mr. Singh: The WTO does not tell nations how to conduct their policies. We are member-driven, with member nations voluntarily agreeing to participate and negotiating new agreements every decade or so. We are not for free trade at all costs, but we do aggressively support the reduction of trade barriers. And our agreements have many elements that take the environment and development of poorer nations into account…

Activity 2 (continued)

Board member, Ox-Fam International (breathlessly…) Here he is…we were told a delegate was giving an interview here. Let me say that the WTO is hypocritical. They claim that they want free trade, lower trade barriers, and yet they allow the United States to have the largest set of trade barriers of any nation–its agricultural subsidies. By subsidizing the cost of producing a bushel of corn, for example, the U.S. government allows U.S. farmers to produce corn at a net cost–it actually costs the farmer more to *make* it than the price in the market. But the government subsidies make U.S. corn much cheaper than Mexican corn, for example. The same is true for cotton farming in the United States. Poor nations, such as Chad and Burkino Faso, can't compete with subsidized U.S. cotton prices, so they can't export cotton. That costs them millions of dollars every year. The WTO continues to allow the U.S. and other wealthy nations, including Japan and the E.U. nations, to keep these unfair advantages.

Mr. Singh: This is a difficult problem, but we have begun negotiating on this…the issue was discussed at the Doha Round of talks…

Retiree (from large U.S. corporation): Hold on there…I want to say something in support of the WTO. It's through the WTO-negotiated agreements that my former company was able to build and buy factories in several Asian and Southeast Asian countries. Because of this, thousands of local employees had jobs, and earned wages many times the local rate. For the first time, some communities in these countries had income they could use to build schools and houses. The company prospered, too, of course, and so did my retirement account, which is what I live on now!

David Richards: This is obviously a very complicated issue. Perhaps we could pick this up a little later. Sue, I'm sending it back to you…

Sue Henry: Thanks David, I've read that the free-trade agreements that developing countries sign with the WTO make them more accountable to the people in those countries, more democratic. Some economists claim that the more economic freedom a country has, the more likely it will have political freedom as well…Let's see who Abbe's with…

Group of Protesters: People and planet before profits, the earth is not for sale! People and planet before profits, the earth is not for sale!

Abbe Smith: Thanks Sue. I am here with an art professor who is also an art gallery owner. You have a unique perspective on globalization, don't you?

Art Gallery Owner: Yes I do. I have devoted my life to promoting art from other countries and cultures, and I am very concerned that globalization has come to mean simply 'exporting American culture' to the developing world. We are shipping American tastes in food, music, art, and commerce around the world! What happens is that local cultures–their artwork, their language, their music–get pushed out by the big loud American culture. The same thing happens when a 'big box' retail store moves into a small town in this country. The superstores crowd out the local 'mom and pop' stores, including little galleries like mine, because it's impossible to compete with the low prices at the giant stores…

Activity 2 (continued)

Wall Street floor trader (on her way back to the NYSE with a carryout lunch): …I couldn't help but overhear this interview…let me get this straight. You're arguing against exporting lower priced, quality products to people in countries who want these products? It sounds like you are saying *you* know what's better for them than *they* do…

Art gallery owner:…No. I'm just saying that when local cultures have to compete with so-called American or western culture–you know, music, movies, media, and fashion from the U.S.–the local cultures are often lost, and that should not happen.

Floor trader (a bit agitated):…so you *are* saying that its better to keep the local culture, even if people would freely choose to drink American soft drinks or wear American-style jeans because they like the products, or because they are less expensive? It also sounds like you want to limit Americans' ability to buy lower cost products from the 'big box' stores you described, so that they would have to buy from 'mom and pop' stores, even if they have to pay more and have less to choose from…

Art gallery owner (a bit more agitated): …yes, we are losing the local flavor of regional foods, for example, because everywhere you turn there's a fast food place driving small restaurants out of business, or some national coffee chain forcing the local cafe to close its doors…

Abbe Smith: Once again, it sounds like we won't resolve this today…Sue, get me out of here…

Sue Henry: Glad to help out Abbe. David, I think you have a pair of interested spectators, don't you?

Group of Protesters: IMF, World Bank, WTO…all three have got to go! IMF, World Bank, WTO…all three have got to go!

David Richards: Sue, I am here with not one, but two delegates to the United Nations. Both represent developing countries in the eastern hemisphere, and both have very different views of globalization. Sir, I wonder if you can explain your point of view?

UN delegate 1: I am happy to explain. I believe that global trade, and the growth it helps create, is the best hope for the developing world and nations such as mine. Studies have shown that economic growth is closely linked to free trade. In fact, the freer a nation's economy, the more growth one can expect, and growth is good for the very poor. For example, more than 200 million people in Asia escaped poverty in the 1990s.

UN Delegate 2: These statistics are misleading…growth does not provide a solution to all problems. It has been said that a 'rising tide lifts all boats,' meaning that growth raises the standard of living for all; but from 1960-1989 the income inequality ratio between the richest 20% and poorest 20% of the world population *increased* from 30 to 1 to 59 to 1. Globalization and trade have increased the gap between rich and poor nations.

UN Delegate 1: …but if the poorest 20% are better off than they were before globalization, isn't that more important than how far behind other countries they are? In recent decades life expectancies in developing countries have increased from 41 years to 65 years. Of course this is still less than in the developed world, but that gap has closed greatly. You must also know that our own

Activity 2 (continued)

Secretary General Kofi Annan has said 'Personally, I do not believe that those [poor] people are victims of globalization. Their problem is not that they are included in the global market but, in most cases, that they are excluded from it.'

David Richards: As you can seen, even representatives of developing nations have differing views on globalization and free trade. Sue, I don't think we can settle this here today…

Sue Henry: David, I have to agree with you there. What our program today does tell us is that this is a complex topic and both sides believe strongly that they are right. That makes it difficult to have a reasonable discussion of the issues. Our coverage today has at least shown why the question of globalization is so controversial. I believe we have summarized the issues fairly well here today, and I encourage our listeners to use what they have heard today to make better-informed decisions about their personal positions on the question of free trade and globalization.

Activity 3
Summarizing the Arguments in the Globalization Debate

Reviewing your copy of the script for the readers theater activity on protests at the WTO meetings in New York, indicate whether each of the following characters is for or against globalization, and briefly indicate the supporting evidence you used to make this determination. The first example is done for you.

Character	For/against globalization?	Supporting evidence
Protester 1	*Against*	*Wearing "No More Sweatshops" T-shirt; "most people live on less than $1.00/day"*
Protester 2		
Manager 1		
Manager 2		
Protester 3		
Union representative		
IT employee		
Economics student 1		
Economics student 2		
Mr. Singh, WTO delegate		
Board member, Ox-Fam International		
Retiree		
Wall Street floor trader		

Activity 3 (continued)

Art gallery owner		
UN delegate 1		
UN delegate 2		

Now use these character descriptions to list and briefly describe *at least four* key arguments used by each side in the debate over globalization.

Key arguments of those who support free trade and greater access to markets (globalists)	Key arguments of those who oppose free trade and greater access to markets (anti-globalists)
1.	1.
2.	2.
3.	3.
4.	4.
5	5.
6.	6.

Activity 4
Representing the Debate: Making a Protest Sign

The class just "acted out" some of the arguments for and against globalization. Now, working in small teams, develop a poster or sign that represents (*circle one:* **supporters** or **opponents**) of globalization. Your poster or sign should communicate the position of this group accurately, be eye-catching and creative, and must contain the following elements:

1. An interesting slogan or saying that captures this side's argument.
2. Two images (these can be drawn or printed using clip-art) that support the slogan or statement.
3. A list (creatively incorporated into the poster or sign) of at least 4 additional arguments used by this side in the debate over globalization.

Sample:

Activity 5
Crossword: The Debate Over Globalization

ACROSS

8 Companies that do business in more than one nation.

9 The globalization debate centers on free trade's impact on________; critics say free trade increases it, supporters claim free trade reduces it.

10 Critics of globalization argue that all workers deserve a ________ wage.

DOWN

1 Supporters of globalization argue that the greater a nation's economic freedom, the greater its ________ freedom will be as well.

2 Term used to describe U.S. businesses hiring workers in foreign countries because they have lower wage rates.

3 Critics of globalization claim the U.S. is hypocritical in arguing for free trade and keeping its own agricultural ________, which act as trade barriers.

Activity 5 (continued)

DOWN (continued)

4 In order to attract the best workers, corporations often pay their local workers in developing countries a wage_______ , several times higher than the prevailing wage.

5 Supporters of globalization claim that free trade can result in greater _______ _______ for developing nations.

6 World merchandise trade has increased over the last 30 years, due in part to greatly reduced _______ costs.

7 Organization responsible for negotiating and maintaining trade agreements among member states: _______.

LESSON TWO
WHY PEOPLE TRADE, DOMESTICALLY AND INTERNATIONALLY

LESSON DESCRIPTION

Students participate in a trading game and discuss why people trade. Then they apply the concept of comparative advantage to two hypothetical situations involving individuals and countries. They learn why both parties in voluntary trades can benefit by specializing in the production of one good and trading for the other good, even in most cases in which one party can produce more of either good than the other party.

INTRODUCTION

Trade is the voluntary exchange of goods and services. When the expected gains from trade outweigh the expected costs, trade will occur. This is true for individuals and businesses trading within a country, or when they trade with people and organizations in other countries.

The fundamental reason to trade is comparative advantage, which means specializing in the production of goods and services that can be produced at a lower opportunity cost than the cost a trading partner would have to pay to produce the same products. Specialization based on comparative advantage increases the total output and consumption of the goods that are traded.

CONCEPTS

Absolute advantage
Comparative advantage
Opportunity cost
Production possibilities table

CONTENT STANDARDS

Voluntary exchange occurs only when all participating parties expect to gain. This is true for trade among individuals or organizations within a nation, and among individuals or organizations in different nations.

When individuals, regions, and nations specialize in what they can produce at the lowest cost and then trade with others, both production and consumption increase.

BENCHMARKS

People voluntarily exchange goods and services because they expect to be better off after the exchange.

Voluntary exchange among people or organizations in different countries gives people a broader range of choices in buying goods and services.

Like trade among individuals within one country, international trade promotes specialization and division of labor and increases output and consumption.

Individuals and nations have a comparative advantage in the production of goods or services if they can produce a product at a lower opportunity cost than other individuals and nations.

OBJECTIVES

Students will:

- Explain how overall levels of satisfaction increase when people and firms specialize and trade.
- Construct and interpret a production possibilities table.
- Determine when an individual or country has an absolute and/or a

comparative advantage in producing a good or service.

- Analyze data and conclude that trade promotes specialization and increases output and consumption.

TIME REQUIRED

120 minutes. In class periods of about one hour, the suggested coverage is: Period 1: Procedures 1 - 28; Period 2: Procedures 29 - 30, Closure, and Assessment.

MATERIALS

- Visual 1: Trading Chart
- Visual 2: Items Available for Trade, by Group
- Visual 3: Who Should Do What? (one copy per student)
- Visual 4: To Trade or Not to Trade? (one copy per student)
- Visual 5: Specialization and Trade (one copy per student)
- Activity 1: Trading Cards–Groups A, B, and C (each group run on a different color paper, cut apart. Make enough copies for each student in the group to have one card.)
- Activity 2: Production Cards–Country A (6 copies, with the 2 pages printed back to back on 1 sheet of paper)
- Activity 3: Production Cards–Country B (6 copies, with the 2 pages printed back to back on 1 sheet of paper)
- Activity 4: Assessment (one copy per student)
- Small sheets of paper (one sheet per student)

PROCEDURES

1. Ask students what types of trades they have made recently and why they traded. *(Answers will vary.)* Tell students they are going to participate in a trading activity to understand why people trade, and then extend the idea of individuals trading to international trade, which entails trades between individuals and organizations in different countries.

2. Divide students into groups of about eight. Distribute a set of the Activity 1 trading cards to each group. Tell students that each card shows an article of clothing or an accessory. Have each student in the group take one card. Tell students not to show the item on their card to others in the group.

3. Instruct students to look at their card. Tell them that the item on the card is theirs to keep or trade. Ask them to assess how happy they are with the item on the card, using a rating scale from 1 (lowest/worst) to 5 (highest/best). Distribute a small sheet of paper to each student. Ask them to record their ratings.

4. Have students show what they have to trade to other students in their group. Tell students they may trade the card they have with members of their group, but they do not have to trade. Allow 2 minutes for students to trade. Display Visual 1. Ask students to raise their hands if they have made a trade. Count the number of trades and record on the visual. Ask students for examples of trades they have made.

5. Ask students to rate the items they have now, after trading or not, using the 1 to 5 scale again, and record their ratings. Ask how many were happier after trading, and record the number on the visual.

6. Tell students that there will be one more trading round, and that in this round they may trade with any students in the class. Before the trading round begins display Visual 2 and explain that it shows what items are available in the other groups. Give students a minute or two to look at the visual, then allow 3 or 4 minutes for students to trade. Remind students that they are not required to make a trade.

7. After the trading period, ask students to once again rate their items on the 1 to 5 scale and record their ratings. Have students raise their hands if they made a trade and record the number on Visual 1. Ask how many were happier after trading in Round 2, and also record that number on Visual 1.

8. Ask students the following questions, and discuss their answers:

A. Did more people trade in Round 1 or Round 2? *(Usually more students will make trades in Round 2.)* Why did this occur? *(In each round students were able to trade for an item that they valued more than the item they had. In Round 1 trade was limited and students weren't allowed to trade outside their groups. In Round 2 there was a greater variety of items available to trade.)*

B. Were you required to trade? *(No. Trade was voluntary.)* Did anyone have a higher rating in Round 1 or 2 without trading? If so, how could that happen? *(Some students may not trade. Once they see what is available, they may decide the item they have is more valuable to them than any of the other items available for trade. While these students often do not change their ratings, sometimes they increase their rating because they feel that they were given the best item, compared to anything else they might have been given or acquired by trading.)*

C. Stress that the number of items to trade remained the same in each round, but overall people seemed happier with the items they had at the end of Round 2 than at the end of Round 1. How could this be? *(After the trading in each round the items were held by students who valued them more highly. Voluntary trade increased satisfaction by transferring items to the individuals who valued them more highly.)*

9. Review with students why they were willing to trade. *(They expected to be better off after trading.)*

10. Explain that, just as in the trading activity, people and organizations in different countries often trade goods and services because they value the things that they buy more than the things they sell. Importers and exporters in trading countries would not trade if they didn't expect to be better off.

11. Ask students if they think people and businesses in the United States should trade with people and businesses in other countries, or would it be better for people in the United States to make everything they consume for themselves? Why? *(Answers may well vary. Do not try to develop any class consensus at this point.)*

12. To explore this question further, tell students they are going to look at two problems. The first involves two workers in a pizza shop, and the second deals with two countries. In each case the class must decide if the students or countries should specialize and trade, or not. Point out that in these problems, unlike the earlier trading activity, a key effect of specialization and trade is to increase the amount of goods produced and consumed.

13. Display Visual 3, Who Should Do What?, and distribute a copy to each student. Ask students to read the information.

14. Explain that **comparative advantage** occurs when people or firms specialize in the production of a good or service for which they have a lower

opportunity cost. Tell students that **opportunity cost** is the highest valued alternative that is given up when a choice is made. Lead students through the calculations to determine who has the comparative advantage in producing pizzas and who has the comparative advantage in preparing salads.

A. Nino's opportunity cost of producing 9 pizzas is 36 salads. Therefore, his opportunity cost of producing 1 pizza is 4 salads.

B. Tony's opportunity cost of producing 6 pizzas is 12 salads. Therefore, his opportunity cost of producing 1 pizza is 2 salads.

C. Nino's opportunity cost of preparing 36 salads is 9 pizzas. Therefore, his opportunity cost of preparing 1 salad is 1/4 pizza.

D. Tony's opportunity cost of preparing 12 salads is 6 pizzas. Therefore, his opportunity cost of preparing 1 salad is 1/2 pizza.

E. Who has the lower opportunity cost for making pizzas? *(Tony)*

F. Who has the lower opportunity cost for preparing salads? *(Nino)*

G. Who has the comparative advantage in producing pizzas? *(Tony)* Salads? *(Nino)*

H. How will specialization affect the running of the pizza shop? *(It increases output and lowers the cost of making more pizzas and salads.)*

15. Tell students they are now going to apply the principle of comparative advantage to determine if two countries that produce cell phones and microwave ovens should specialize and trade.

16. Write Country A on one side of the board and Country B on the other. Ask for six student volunteers to stand next to the label for Country A. Give each student a card from Activity 2, Production Cards, Country A. Explain that this is a very small country, with only six workers.

17. Tell students that in one day each worker in Country A can produce 8 cell phones or 4 microwave ovens. Have students flip their cards to show 8 cell phones and then 4 microwave ovens.

18. Display Visual 4, To Trade or Not to Trade?, and distribute a copy to each student. Have all six students flip their cards to show cell phones. Ask one of the student volunteers to count the number of cell phones Country A can produce in a day if it uses all of its workers to produce cell phones. *($6 \times 8 = 48$)* Record 48 on the chart in column A. How many microwave ovens can it produce if all of its workers produce cell phones? *(0)* Record zero in column A.

19. Have the first student flip his card to show microwave ovens. Ask how many cell phones could be produced if Country A uses one worker to produce microwave ovens, instead. *(40)* How many microwave ovens would be produced? *(4)* Record these numbers in Visual 4.

20. Continue having students flipping their cards, one at a time, recording the number of cell phones and number of microwave ovens that can be produced [shading for Option B is explained in procedure 30]:

Country A	A	B	C	D	E	F	G
Number of Cell Phones	48	40	32	24	16	8	0
Number of Microwave Ovens	0	4	8	12	16	20	24

21. Discuss the following questions:

A. How does the number of cell phones that can be produced change as Country A produces more microwave ovens? *(decreases)*

B. How does the number of microwaves Country A can produce change as more cell phones are produced? *(decreases)*

C. What does the overall chart show? *(The possible combinations of microwave ovens and cell phones that can be produced given Country A's resources.)* Tell students this is called a **production possibilities table.**

D. Why is there a tradeoff in producing more of either good? *(Country A has a limited amount of resources for producing cell phones and microwave ovens. If more resources are used to produce cell phones there are fewer resources available to produce microwave ovens, and vice versa.)*

22. Ask for six volunteers to stand near the board labeled Country B. Explain that this is another very small country, also with only six workers. Give each student one card from Activity 3, Production Cards, Country B. Tell students Country B can also use its workers to produce microwave ovens or cell phones, but in Country B each worker can produce 1 cell phone or 2 microwave ovens in one day. Have the volunteers flip their cards to show 1 microwave oven and then 2 cell phones.

23. Have all the students representing Country B flip their cards to microwave ovens. Ask one of the volunteer students to count the number of microwave ovens Country B can produce in a day if it uses all of its workers to produce microwave ovens. *(6 × 2 = 12)* Record 12 on the chart for Country B in column A. How many cell phones can be produced if all its workers are used to produce microwaves? *(0)* Record zero in column A.

24. Have the first student flip his card to show cell phones. Ask how many microwave ovens could be produced if Country B uses one worker to produce 1 cell phone. *(10)* Record 10 microwave ovens and 1 cell phone in Column B.

25. Continue having students flip their cards, one at a time, recording the number of microwave ovens and number of cell phones that can be produced [shading for Option D is explained in procedure 30]:

Country B	A	B	C	D	E	F	G
Number of Cell Phones	0	1	2	3	4	5	6
Number of Microwave Ovens	12	10	8	6	4	2	0

26. Discuss the following questions:

A. What does the production possibilities table show you about making cell phones and microwave ovens in Country B? *(The possible combinations of microwave ovens and cell phones that can be produced using all of Country B's resources. As more resources are used to produce cell phones, fewer microwaves can be produced. If more resources are used to produce microwave ovens, fewer cell phones are produced.*)

B. Why does this occur? *(Like Country A, Country B has a limited amount of resources for producing cell phones and microwaves. If more resources are used producing cell phones there are fewer resources available to produce microwave ovens, and vice versa.)*

C. If each country only produces cell phones, which country can produce more cell phones? *(Country A*) If each country only produces microwave ovens, which country can produce more microwave ovens? *(Also Country A)*

27. Tell students that when a worker in a country can produce more of a good than a worker in another country, the worker in the first country has an **absolute advantage** in producing that good. In the example with cell phones and microwave ovens, workers in Country A have an absolute advantage in the production of both goods.

28. Ask students if they think that Country A should trade cell phones or microwave ovens with Country B, even though it has an absolute advantage in producing both goods? If so, what good should Country A produce? *(Answers will usually vary at this point.)* Country B? *(Again, answers will usually vary.)* Remind students that the pizza shop example looked at comparative advantage, not absolute advantage, by calculating the opportunity cost for Nino and Tony to make pizzas or salads. It is now time to calculate the opportunity cost for Country A and Country B in producing cell phones and microwave ovens.

29. Divide all of students in the class into pairs. Ask students to complete the questions on Visual 4 to determine which country has a comparative advantage in the production of cell phones and which in the production of microwaves. Review answers.

Country A

A. What is the opportunity cost of producing 8 cell phones? *(4 microwaves)*

B. What is the opportunity cost of producing 1 cell phone? *(½ microwave)*

C. What is the opportunity cost of producing 4 microwaves? *(8 cell phones)*

D. What is the opportunity cost of producing 1 microwave? *(2 cell phones*)

Country B

E. What is the opportunity cost of producing 1 cell phone? *(2 microwaves)*

F. What is the opportunity cost of producing two microwaves? *(1 cell phone)*

G. What is the opportunity cost of producing 1 microwave? *(½ cell phone)*

H. Which country has the lower opportunity cost of producing cell phones? *(Country A)* Microwaves? *(Country B)*

30. Remind students that Visual 4, To Trade or Not to Trade?, shows the combinations of microwave ovens and cell phones each country can produce in a day using all of its workers. Tell students that

before trading Country A was producing at combination B and Country B was producing at Combination D. Circle column B for Country A and column D for Country B. (These two columns are shaded above, in procedures 20 and 25.) Discuss the following questions:

A. At these combinations what is the total output of cell phones produced by the two countries? *(43, 40 in Country A + 3 in Country B)* Of microwave ovens? *(10, 4 in Country A + 6 in Country B)*

B. If Country A decides to put all of its resources into the production of cell phones, how many additional cell phones would be produced? *(8)* How many microwave ovens would be lost? *(4)*

C. If Country B decides to put all its workers into the production of microwave ovens, how many additional microwave ovens would be produced? *(6)* How many cell phones would be lost? *(3)*

D. How much would the total output of cell phones increase if these two countries specialize and trade? *(5, after subtracting the reduction of 3 in Country B from the increase of 8 in Country A)*

E. How much would the total output of microwave ovens increase if these two countries specialize and trade? *(2, after subtracting the reduction of 4 in Country A from the increase of 6 in Country B)*

F. How did specialization and trade affect the overall production levels for cell phones and microwave ovens? *(Both increased. Point out that if these were larger countries, with each student representing thousands or even millions of workers, the gains in production and consumption levels would be that much larger, too.)*

G. How would specialization and trade affect the overall consumption level for each good? *(Because more of both goods are produced and sold, at a lower cost in terms of the real or opportunity cost of the goods that are given up, the consumption of both goods would also increase.)*

H. What are some disadvantages of specializing and trading for goods you don't produce? *(The countries are more interdependent, and rely on each other to produce one of the products they consume. Wars and other kinds of disputes, including the imposition of trade barriers such as tariffs or quotas, might disrupt that trade. It would then require time to find another supplier for the product, or to start producing it again. But not trading means paying the higher opportunity cost and decreasing the overall level of production and consumption of the two products. In other words, living standards will fall.)*

CLOSURE

1. Why do individuals, organizations, and nations trade? *(They expect to be better off, by increasing production levels, reducing production costs, and transferring goods and services to the people who value the products most, and are willing and able to pay for them.)*

2. How does overall level of satisfaction increase when people trade? *(When people trade, they trade for a good or service that gives them more value or*

satisfaction than the item–or money–that they gave up to get it.)

3. How does specialization and trade affect production and consumption? *(Specialization allows more goods to be produced, which means that consumption levels increase.)*

4. What is absolute advantage? *(When an individual, organization or country can produce more of a good or service than another individual, organization or country with the same resources.)*

5. What is comparative advantage? *(When people or countries specialize in the production of a good or service for which they have a lower opportunity cost.)*

6. Display Visual 5.

Explain that the table shows how many units of cheese or wheat 1 worker can produce in a day.

Discuss the following questions:

A. Which country has an absolute advantage in the production of cheese? (*United States*) Wheat? (*United States*)

B. In the United States how many units of cheese does a worker give up to get one more unit of wheat? (*¼*)

C. In France how many units of cheese does a worker give up to get one more unit of wheat? (*½*)

D. In the United States how many units of wheat does a worker give up to produce 1 more unit of cheese? (*4*)

E. In France how many units of wheat does a worker give up to produce 1 more unit of cheese? (*2*)

F. Which country has a comparative advantage in the production of wheat? (*United States*) Explain. (*The United States has the lower opportunity cost in the production of wheat. It gives up ¼ unit of cheese for every unit of wheat; France gives up ½ unit of cheese for every unit of wheat.*)

G. Which country has a comparative advantage in the production of cheese? (*France*) Explain. (*France has the lower opportunity cost in the production of cheese. It gives up 2 units of wheat for every unit of cheese; the United States gives up 4 units of wheat for every unit of cheese.*)

H. Direct students' attention to the combinations of wheat and cheese that can be produced in each country with 100 workers. Tell students that each country has decided to produce at combination B.

Discuss the following questions:

1. At combination B what is the total output of wheat produced by the two countries? (*1100*) Of cheese? (*150*)

2. If the United States decides to put all its workers into the production of wheat, how many additional bushels of wheat would be produced? (*400*) How many pounds of cheese would be lost? (*100*)

3. If France decides to put all its workers into the production of cheese, how many additional pounds of cheese would be produced? (*150*) How many bushels of wheat would be lost? (*300*)

4. How much would the total output of cheese increase if these two countries specialize and trade? (*50 pounds for every 100 workers in the industry*)

5. How much would the total output of wheat increase if these two countries specialize and trade? (*100 bushels for every 100 workers in the industry*)

ASSESSMENT

Distribute a copy of Activity 4.

Review the problem and answer with students. *(Florida should specialize in the production of tomatoes. It can produce tomatoes at a lower opportunity cost than Idaho. Idaho can produce potatoes at a lower opportunity cost than Florida, so Idaho should specialize in potatoes. With specialization and trade total output and consumption of both tomatoes and potatoes will increase.)*

Visual 1
Trading Chart

Round	Number of trades	Number of students happier after trading
1		
2		

Visual 2
Items Available for Trade, by Group

<u>Group A (white cards)</u>
Pair of baggy jeans (male)
Pair of designer jeans (female)
T-shirt of favorite band (2)
Pair of athletic shoes (female) (2)
Pair of sandals (male)
Designer bag (female)

<u>Group B (yellow cards)</u>
Pair of basic jeans (male) (2)
Professional basketball team jersey
Pair of summer sandals (female)
Professional baseball team cap (2)
T-shirt of favorite sports team
Sports watch (female)

<u>Group C (green cards)</u>
Pair of low rise jeans (female)
Professional hockey team jersey (2)
Pair of carpenter pants (male) (2)
Professional football team jersey
Sweatshirt
Pair of athletic shoes (male)

Visual 3
Who Should Do What?

Nino owns a pizza shop. He is very good at what he does. In one hour he can make 9 pizzas or prepare 36 salads. His business is growing and he needs to hire someone to help prepare pizzas and salads. Tony has applied for the job and seems like a reliable individual. In 1 hour Tony can make 6 pizzas or prepare 12 salads. Nino plans to hire Tony. Since Nino can make more pizzas in an hour and prepare more salads in an hour than Tony, he has a dilemma. Should he have Tony make pizzas or prepare salads?

To answer this question, Nino should determine who can produce each good at a lower opportunity cost. Help Nino figure that out by filling in the blanks below for questions A–G, and then write a summary statement for question H.

A. The opportunity cost of producing 9 pizzas for Nino is _____ salads. The opportunity cost of producing 1 pizza is _____ salads.

B. The opportunity cost of producing 6 pizzas for Tony is _____ salads. The opportunity cost of producing 1 pizza is _____ salads.

C. The opportunity cost of preparing 36 salads for Nino is ______ pizzas. The opportunity cost of preparing 1 salad is _____ pizzas.

D. The opportunity cost of preparing 12 salads for Tony is ______ pizzas. The opportunity cost of preparing 1 salad is ______ pizzas.

E. Who has the lower opportunity cost for making pizzas? _______

F. Who has the lower opportunity cost for preparing salads?________

G. Who should produce pizzas? _________ Salads? _________

H. How will specialization affect the running of the pizza shop?

Visual 4
To Trade or Not to Trade?

Remember that comparative advantage means that people specialize in the production of a good or service for which they have the lower opportunity cost. To determine if Country A and Country B should specialize, you must first determine the opportunity cost in each country of producing cell phones and microwave ovens.

Country A

	A	B	C	D	E	F	G
Number of cell phones							
Number of microwave ovens							

Country B

	A	B	C	D	E	F	G
Number of cell phones							
Number of microwave ovens							

Country A

A. What is the opportunity cost of producing 8 cell phones?

B. What is the opportunity cost of producing 1 cell phone?

C. What is the opportunity cost of producing 4 microwave ovens?

D. What is the opportunity cost of producing 1 microwave oven?

Visual 4 (continued)

Country B

E. What is the opportunity cost of producing 1 cell phone?

F. What is the opportunity cost of producing 2 microwave ovens?

G. What is the opportunity cost of producing 1 microwave oven?

H. Which country has the lower opportunity cost for producing cell phones? Microwave ovens?

Visual 5
Specialization and Trade

	Cheese	Wheat
United States	3	12
France	2	4

Combinations of wheat and cheese that can be produced in one day in each country with 100 workers.

United States

	A	B	C	D
Cheese	0	100	200	300
Wheat	1200	800	400	0

France

	A	B	C	D
Cheese	0	50	100	200
Wheat	400	300	200	0

Activity 1
Trading Cards–Group A

Pair of Baggy Jeans (male)	Pair of Designer Jeans (female)
T-shirt of Favorite Band	Pair of Athletic Shoes (female)
Pair of Sandals (male)	Designer Bag (female)
T-shirt of Favorite Band	Pair of Athletic Shoes (female)

Activity 1 (continued)

Group B

Pair of Basic Jeans (male)	Professional Basketball Team Jersey
Professional Baseball Team Cap	Pair of Summer Sandals (female)
T-shirt of Favorite Sports Team	Sports Watch (female)
Professional Baseball Team Cap	Pair of Basic Jeans (male)

Activity 1 (continued)
Group C

Pair of Carpenter Pants (male)	Pair of Low Rise Jeans (female)
Professional Hockey Team Jersey	Pair of Athletic Shoes (male)
Professional Football Team Jersey	Sweatshirt
Pair of Carpenter Pants (male)	Professional Hockey Team Jersey

Activity 2
Production Cards–Country A

Cell Phones

Activity 2 (continued)

Microwave Ovens

Activity 3
Production Cards–Country B

Cell Phone

Activity 3 (continued)

Microwave Ovens

Activity 4
Assessment

Florida and Idaho both grow potatoes and tomatoes. One worker in Florida working 1 day can produce 15 pounds of potatoes or 60 pounds of tomatoes. In Idaho one worker can produce 10 pounds of potatoes or 20 pounds of tomatoes in a day.

If Florida and Idaho specialize and trade, what should Florida produce? What should Idaho produce? Why? How would specialization and trade affect total production of tomatoes and potatoes?

LESSON THREE FINDING A COMPARATIVE ADVANTAGE, INCLUDING YOUR OWN[*]

LESSON DESCRIPTION

Students examine trade data for U.S. exports to and imports from China, and use the data to identify both nations' comparative advantage in trading with each other. They discuss which of three possible sources of comparative advantage might lie behind these specific examples. Then they examine trade data for four "mystery countries," predicting what each nation's comparative advantage might be and trying to identity the nation. To apply the idea of comparative advantage students consider the specialized skills of a professional basketball player, Shaquille O'Neal, and discuss how these skills contribute to his success in basketball, but not necessarily to his success as a rap artist. Finally, students try to identify their own sources of comparative advantage by completing an inventory of skills they have (or will have when they complete their education), and comparing these skills to several job descriptions published by the U.S. Bureau of Labor Statistics.

INTRODUCTION

Nations and individuals have a comparative advantage when their opportunity cost of producing a good or service is lower than the opportunity cost of other nations or individuals. That is why trade between nations and individuals can increase the standard of living for both parties in a trade: By specializing according to comparative advantage fewer resources are used to produce goods and services, which means that more goods and services can be produced and consumed.

How do nations or individuals find their comparative advantages? Over time, trial and error can reveal what products or jobs offer the greatest possible rewards, in light of competition from other producers and workers. But trial and error is often an expensive way to learn, so to help predict the goods or services that they can produce successfully, workers and firms in all nations should try to understand the sources of comparative advantage.

In the introductory essay for this volume, David Hummels identifies three major sources of comparative advantage. First, endowments of key inputs may vary from nation to nation, just as endowments of talents, skills, and physical characteristics vary across individuals. For example, commercial farming uses large amounts of land, so if land is especially scarce in a country (Japan, for example), it is likely to import agricultural products, which can be grown at a lower cost in nations where arable land is more abundant.

Second, differences in government services and regulations can also result in different comparative advantages. For example, nations with compulsory public education that develop high literacy rates are likely to have more productive workers than countries in which many workers receive less education. And nations with less regulation of pollution may have a comparative advantage in "dirty" industries that produce high levels of pollution.

[*] Although not required, you may want to use Lesson 2 in this volume, which defines and illustrates comparative advantage and the gains from trade, before using this lesson.

Third, over time, a major source of comparative advantage comes from investments in technology. One reason the United States has a comparative advantage in space exploration and in manufacturing large commercial airplanes is because U.S. firms in these industries have invested in state-of-the-art production technologies. In some cases firms developed these technologies due to government incentives or contracts, such as those associated with U.S. space exploration and national defense programs.

CONCEPTS

Comparative advantage
Productive resources
Specialization
Exports
Imports
Human capital

CONTENT STANDARDS

Voluntary exchange occurs only when all participating parties expect to gain. This is true for trade among individuals or organizations within a nation, and among individuals or organizations in different nations.

When individuals, regions, and nations specialize in what they can produce at the lowest cost and then trade with others, both production and consumption increase.

BENCHMARKS

Free trade increases worldwide material standards of living.

Like trade among individuals within one country, international trade promotes specialization and division of labor and increases output and consumption.

Two factors that prompt international trade are international differences in the availability of productive resources and differences in relative prices.

Individuals and nations have a comparative advantage in the production of goods or services if they can produce a product at a lower opportunity cost than other individuals or nations.

OBJECTIVES

Students will:

- ♦ Examine U.S./China trade data to determine comparative advantages for both nations.
- ♦ Identify the sources of comparative advantage for several "mystery nations," and then predict the identity of those nations.
- ♦ Complete a personal skills inventory to help identify potential sources of their own comparative advantages, and investigate which of several jobs would require that kind of comparative advantage.

TIME REQUIRED

Two to three class periods. In class periods of about one hour, the suggested coverage is: Period 1: Procedures 1–15; Period 2: Procedures 16, Closure, and assign Assessment project; Period 3: Assessment project/group presentations. You may want to give students a day or two to work on Procedures 15 and 16, using the internet. At that time you may also want students to research Mali, for the Assessment activity.

MATERIALS

- Visual 1: Sources of Comparative Advantage
- Visual 2: What's My Comparative Advantage?

- Visual 3: Mali Background Data (one copy per student)
- Activity 1: Imports, Exports, and Comparative Advantage in the United States and China (one copy per student)
- Activity 2: Name that Comparative Advantage (one copy per student)
- Activity 3: Finding *Your* Comparative Advantage (one copy per student)– student access to the Internet is required for this activity.

PROCEDURES

1. Remind students that (as shown in Lesson 2 of this volume) individuals or nations have a **comparative advantage** in producing a good or service if they can produce it at a lower cost than other individuals or nations. That is what makes it possible to gain by trading, with people or firms producing and selling things that they can produce at a lower cost, and buying things that other people or firms can produce at a lower cost. Some of that trade is with people and firms from other countries, or in other words international trade. Announce that today the class will explore the sources of comparative advantage, or why some people and nations have a comparative advantage in producing some goods or services, but not others.

2. Explain that both nations and individuals specialize in producing goods for which they hold a comparative advantage. Economists define **specialization** as a person or nation producing fewer goods or services than they consume, and then trading some of the things they produce for the other things that are consumed. For example, a doctor does not produce food or build houses, but uses the income he or she earns as a doctor to purchase those products from farmers and home builders. Similarly, nations export some goods and services to other nations, and import other goods and services.

3. Point out that specialization makes it possible to produce more goods and services, and at lower costs. To illustrate this and provide an example of specialization, ask students how many in the room cut their own hair. (*A few hands may go up, but most will not.*) Next ask how many students have someone in their family cut their hair at home. *(A few more hands may go up, but most students pay to have their hair cut by barbers or beauticians.)* Ask students why most of them do not cut their own hair, or have it cut by a family member. (*Answers will vary.*) Ask if they *could* cut it themselves, or have it cut by someone in the family? (*Of course.*) Ask what skills they would have to acquire in order to successfully cut hair that they don't currently have. (*Scissor techniques, knowledge of hairstyles, using clippers, etc.*) Could they acquire these skills? (*Yes, in time.*) What would they have to give up in order to acquire these skills, and what would the opportunity cost be? (*The time and money for training, purchasing clippers and other equipment, etc. The opportunity cost would be what they would otherwise do with the time and money, etc.*)

4. Ask students: Did the early pioneers cut their own hair, or have a family member cut it. (*Usually.*) Why has that changed today? (*Unlike the early pioneers, few people today try to produce everything they consume because it is much easier for them to trade with other people than it was for the pioneers.*) Are the haircuts people get today of a better quality than the haircuts most of the early pioneers received? (*Yes, generally. Stress that specialization typically leads to greater skills and higher productivity. Today everybody can get better at some job, but nobody has to try to be good at doing everything.*)

5. Ask students to provide examples from several different sports of how athletes

in team sports, playing different positions, illustrate specialization. (*Many examples can be given. In soccer, players with "good hands" are often goalies, while in U.S. football they are often receivers. Boys and girls with strong arms are likely to be pitchers on baseball or softball teams, or quarterbacks in football. Larger and taller players are usually forwards and centers in basketball, or linemen in football; smaller and faster players are more often guards in basketball, or defensive backs in football.*)

6. The principle of comparative advantage suggests a team will be more successful when each player plays a position for which his or her contribution is, relatively speaking, the greatest. Put differently, the cost of having them play the position is lowest, in terms of what is given up by having them play some other position. Babe Ruth provided the classic example of this, because early in his career he was a very successful pitcher for the Boston Red Sox. His comparative advantage as a hitter soon became clear, however, so he moved to the outfield to play and hit every day, not just every fourth or fifth day as a starting pitcher. (Teachers can learn more about these concepts and Babe Ruth in Ed Scahill's 1990 article, "Did Babe Ruth Have a Comparative Advantage as a Pitcher?" in the *Journal of Economic Education,* 21 (4), 402-410. Students can learn more about these concepts at *EconEdLink*'s "The Economics of Professional Sports" http://www.econed link.org/lessons/index.cfm?lesson=NN104&page=comparative_part1.html

7. Remind students that nations as well as individuals have comparative advantages. Tell students that they are going to investigate recent data on trade between the United States and China to determine what types of goods each country exports to the other (indicating that the exporting country has a comparative advantage in the production of those goods), and which goods it imports (indicating that the other country has a comparative advantage in producing those goods). Explain that these data are just for goods, but services (such as tourism, education, and banking or other financial services) can also be imported or exported.

8. Distribute Activity 1 and ask students to read the opening paragraphs. Before giving students about 15 minutes to answer the questions on the activity using the trade data, briefly discuss the size and rapid growth of U.S.-China trade, telling students that by 2004 China had become the United States' third largest trading partner, surpassing Japan. [Students may also want to know that the largest trading partner with the U.S. is Canada ($466 billion in total trade for 2004; followed by Mexico ($266 billion); China; Japan ($184 billion); and Germany ($108 billion)]. Have students use the two tables at the end of the handout to answer the four questions in Activity 1, working individually. Lead a class discussion of the questions:

A. Does China export different types of goods to the United States than it imports from the United States? Specifically, how many categories of goods imported to the United States from China do not appear on the categories of goods exported from the United States to China? (*Explain that U.S. exports to China are China's imports from the United States, and vice versa. Then point out that the types of goods exported by the two countries to the other country are generally very different. Only two categories–21301, computer accessories; and 21400, telecommunication equipment–appear on both lists for trade between the two countries.*)

B. What kinds of goods does the United States most often import from China? What kinds of goods does China most often import from the United States? (*The U.S. exports large machinery, agricultural goods, computers, engines, and commercial aircraft to China; China send toys, footwear, and small appliances to the United States.*)

C. What types of goods are produced in the United States, and what types in China? (*The United States produces and exports certain types of agricultural goods–including cotton and soybeans–large machinery, computers, engines, and aircraft. China produces and exports textiles and apparel, toys, footwear, and small electronics and appliances.*) Help students see that the education and skills for workers who assemble airplanes or computer microprocessors is different from the education and skills required for workers who make toys, T-shirts, or shoes.

9. Display Visual 1 and quickly review the three key sources of comparative advantage. (Note to teacher: Review the discussion of these three factors on page 10 of the introductory essay.) Ask students which of the three sources is responsible for the U.S. comparative advantage over China? (*investment in capital/technology*) Which source is the most likely source of China's comparative advantage over the U.S.? (*factor endowments, including a large labor force*)

Have Students complete the following statement: "Generally speaking, the United States has a comparative advantage over China in producing products that use more (*high-skilled labor and more technology, such as computers, semiconductors, and industrial engines*), and China has a comparative advantage over the United States in producing products that use more (*low-skilled labor and less technology, such as shoes and textiles*).

10. Ask students to identify and discuss factors that underlie these differences in factor endowments and technology. (*Students should point to the size of the Chinese population, which means there is a large supply of unskilled labor, and therefore lower wages for these workers in China. They may also realize that China has only recently begun to industrialize, compared to the United States, which implies a lower level of technology and less capital. With less capital to work with, labor productivity is lower in China, and even more so because capital resources often embody technologies that further increase labor productivity.*)

11. Distribute Activity 2. Explain to students that they will now examine trade data from four "mystery" nations. The table at the end of the handouts shows the top U.S. imports from these nations in 2004, which are therefore exports of the mystery countries. As students learned in Activity 1, a nation exports goods if it has a comparative advantage in producing them. Using the tables at the end of Activity 2, have students answer the following questions:

Does the United States import the same types of goods from each of the "mystery" countries? (*Not always. There are some similarities, for example between Country A and Country C, but most are very different.*) What are the top five export goods categories for each of the four countries?

Country A	Country B	Country C	Country D
1. (40000) *Apparel and household goods–cotton*	1. (30000) *Passenger cars, new and used*	1. (42100) *Gem diamonds–uncut or unset*	1. (10000) *Crude oil*
2. (40020) *Apparel and household goods–other textiles*	2. (40100) *Medicinal, dental and pharma-ceutical prepara-tions*	2. (40000) *Apparel and household goods–cotton*	2. (10030) *Liquefied petroleum gases*
3. (00120) *Fruits and preparations, including frozen juices*	3. (30230) *Other parts and accessories*	3. (41310) *Jewelry (watches, rings, etc.)*	3. (10010) *Fuel oil*
4. (01000) *Fish and shellfish*	4. (21180) *Other industrial machinery*	4. (40020) *Apparel and household goods-other textiles*	4. (10020) *Other petroleum products*
5. (14270) *Non-monetary gold*	5. (21610) *Other scientific, medical and hospital equipment*	5. (14100) *Iron and steel mill products–semi-finished*	5. (10110) *Gas–natural*

12. When students complete Activity 2, display Visual 1 again and ask students to consider the different sources of comparative advantages for each of the countries in Activity 2. Ask if they can guess the identity of some or all of the "mystery" countries. Even if students do not pick the correct country, note whether they were able to guess a country with similar comparative advantage and export characteristics. Suggested answers for this part of Activity 2 are provided in the next column:

'Mystery' Country	Goods exported from this country to the US:			Source of comparative advantage:
Country A: Honduras	*A mix of agricultur-al and industrial goods*	*Require low-skilled labor*	*Require little capital invest-ment*	*Factor endowments (gold, fish, etc.) and large supply of low-skilled labor (cotton apparel production)*
Country B: Germany	*Mostly industrial and high tech goods*	*Require high-skilled labor*	*Require a great deal of capital invest-ment*	*Capital investment (industrial machines; automobiles)*
Country C: India	*A mix of agricultur-al and industrial goods*	*Require low-skilled labor*	*Require little capital invest-ment*	*Factor endowments (diamonds) and large supply of low-skilled labor (cotton apparel production)*
Country D: Nigeria	*Mostly natural resources*	*Require low-skilled labor*	*Require little capital invest-ment*	*Factor endowments (oil)*

13. Tell students that individuals have comparative advantages, just as nations do. Ask students to think of some examples and then display Visual 3 on the overhead, revealing just Individual A. Read each of the skills listed, and explain them if students have any questions. Point out that this individual has many talents. Ask students to guess who this might be. Reveal that this individual is Shaquille O'Neal, center for the Miami Heat of the NBA in 2005–06, and before that for the Los Angeles Lakers and Orlando Magic.

14. Now reveal Individual B. Point out that this individual has many talents as well. Ask students to guess who this individual might be? Reveal that it is Master P (aka Percy Miller), a rap artist who played college basketball and tried out for several NBA teams. Ask students if these two individuals have similar talents. (*Both have skills in basketball and in creating rap*

music.) Then ask students what comparative advantage, based on the information presented, each individual has. If necessary, remind students that comparative advantage means being able to do something at a lower opportunity cost. (*Shaq, an NBA all-star, has a comparative advantage in basketball, which makes it too expensive for him to spend more time doing rap music. Master P has more than 10 multi-platinum CDs, so he has a comparative advantage in rap music. Both have had some success in each area, but if Shaq had given up his NBA career to become a full-time rapper, he would give up his NBA salary of millions of dollars a year. After he retires from the NBA, things may change, of course. Master P has a comparative advantage in making rap music, because his opportunity cost as a basketball player is a very low salary in the minor leagues.*)

15. Distribute Activity 3. Tell students that they are going to explore their own comparative advantages by completing the Human Capital Inventory and comparing their skills and education (which economists call **human capital**) with the skills and education required in several careers. Ask students to be candid and honest in their self-assessment, but to consider not only skills they currently have but also the skills they are likely to acquire through education before they enter the job market. Students must have access to the Internet to complete the second part of the activity.

16. A day or two later, after students have completed the Human Capital Inventory and compared their skills to those required for these careers, ask them to share their results. Ask students to share where they feel their comparative advantages lie at this point in their lives.

CLOSURE

Nations and individuals have a comparative advantage when their opportunity cost of producing a good or service is lower than the cost for other nations or individuals. Three main sources of comparative advantage are:
(1) endowments of key inputs such as land and labor, (2) government services and regulations, such as compulsory public education or pollution controls, and
(3) investments in technology. Technology is a key reason why nations like the United States have a comparative advantage in such fields as space exploration and manufacturing large commercial airplanes. Less-developed and newly industrialized nations often find their comparative advantages in producing goods that require a great deal of unskilled labor, while industrialized nations hold comparative advantages in goods that require intensive capital investments. Individuals have comparative advantages based on skills and personal characteristics, some of which are different across individuals at birth, but which are usually developed even more by personal investments in human capital (education and training). Individuals and nations increase production, consumption, and standards of living by specializing in producing goods and services for which they have comparative advantages.

ASSESSMENT

Divide the class into groups of four. Explain to each group that they will be role playing a business consulting firm, and their first task is to develop a name for their firm. Then tell students that their firms have just been asked by the African nation of Mali to make a presentation on how to increase Mali's revenue from international trade. Display Visual 3 and give a copy of the visual to each student. In order to convince the government of Mali to "hire" their firm, students must use what they have learned in this lesson to develop a brochure that outlines recommendations for Mali. Included in the presentation should be a description of the theory of comparative advantage, Mali's potential sources of comparative advantage, and how specialization can lead to gains from trade. Students can begin researching Mali while completing the online portion of Activity 3.

Visual 1
Sources of Comparative Advantage

Both nations and individuals can consume more by specializing in producing things for which they have a comparative advantage, and then trading with others to get the other things they consume.

Different nations have comparative advantages in producing different things. Three key reasons for these differences in comparative advantage are:

1. **Investments in technology**
   Some nations invest more in research and technology, and in capital goods that incorporate new technologies. That increases labor productivity.

2. **Relative supply of key inputs**
   Nations may have relatively more (or fewer) resources in one or more areas, including:
   a. Natural resources (e.g., land for farming, deposits of crude oil and natural gas, and rivers that can be used to produce electricity).
   b. Labor (skilled or unskilled).
   c. Capital (e.g., factories and machines)

3. **Government services/regulations**
   a. Differences in the level and quality of public education provided to workers affect labor productivity.
   b. Transportation and communication infrastructures (e.g., highways, bridges, airports, ports, telephone services) affect costs of production for many goods and services.
   c. Laws and regulations affecting enforcement of contracts, product and worker safety, and environmental standards affect costs of production.

Visual 2
What's My Comparative Advantage?

Individual A

Skills/Characteristics:

- 7' 1" tall
- 310 lbs.
- Bench press: 450 lbs.
- Shoe size: 21 EEE
- NBA scoring average: 26.4 points per game
- Annual NBA salary: est. $27,000,000.00
- 5 rap CDs; 2,000,000 in CD sales

Individual B

Skills/Characteristics:

- 6' 4" tall
- 220 lbs.
- Invited to try out with NBA Toronto Raptors; cut after one week
- Cut by NBA Denver Nuggets summer league team
- Annual NBA salary: $0.00
- 11 rap CDs; more than 15,000,000 in CD sales
- Estimated net worth from music producing/sales: $56,500,000.00

Both individuals can rap, and both can play basketball. Who appears to hold the comparative advantage for rap? For basketball? Why?

Visual 3
Mali Background Data

Mali Background Data

Mali is among the poorest countries in the world, with 65% of its land area desert or semi-desert. About 10% of the population is nomadic and about 80% of the labor force is engaged in farming and fishing. Industrial activity is concentrated on processing farm commodities. Mali is heavily dependent on foreign aid and vulnerable to fluctuations in world prices for cotton (its main export) and gold.

- Population: 12.2 million (0–14 years: 47.1%; 15-64 years: 50%; 65 years and over: 3%)
- Arable land: 3.8% (cotton is the main export commodity)
- Endowments: Gold, granite, phosphates; hydroelectric power (Mali produced a net 50 million kilowatt-hours of electricity in 2003). Mali has large bauxite, iron ore, tin, and copper reserves, but these are not currently being mined.
- Literacy rate: 46.4% of the population

(Source: CIA World Factbook Online: http://www.cia.gov/cia/publications/factbook/geos/ml.html)

Activity 1
Imports, Exports, and Comparative Advantage in the United States and China

In 2004 the United States' total trade (exports and imports) in goods with China was more than $245 billion. Obviously the United States and China have developed an important trading relationship.

The theory of comparative advantage explains trade between nations and between individuals by saying both parties in a trade benefit if people and nations specialize in producing products that they can produce at a lower opportunity cost. In other words, products are produced by those who give up fewer other goods and services to produce them.

People and firms in different nations specialize in producing the goods and services they can produce at a lower cost, and trade some of those products to other people or firms, including people and firms in other nations. They trade for things that other people and countries can produce at a lower cost than they can. By having production done where fewer resources are used, specialization and trade increase the total amount of goods and services produced and consumed, raising the standard of living for both trading partners.

In this activity you will investigate whether the theory of comparative advantage explains the pattern of goods that were actually traded by the United States and China in 2004. Then you will try to determine why the costs of producing some kinds of goods is lower in China, but the costs of producing other kinds of goods is lower in the United States. In other words, you will try to determine the source of China's comparative advantage in producing some kinds of products, and the United States' comparative advantage in producing other kinds of goods and services.

The tables at the end of this handout show the dollar values of trade in 2004 for the top 15 goods exported from the United States to China, and from China to the United States. Use the information in those tables to answer the following questions:

1. Does China export different types of goods to the United States than China imports from the United States? Specifically, how many categories of goods imported to the United States from China do not appear on the categories of goods exported from the United States to China?

2. What kinds of goods does the United States most often import from China? What kinds of goods does China most often import from the United States?

3. Think about how these different kinds of goods are produced. For example, which goods are manufactured, or use resources that are manufactured when they are produced? Which types of goods require more skilled labor than others? Which types of goods require more technology (e.g., computer-controlled welding) than others? What types of goods are usually produced in China, and what types are usually produced in the United States?

4. Complete the following statement: "Generally speaking, the United States has a comparative advantage over China in producing products that use more ______________________, and China has a comparative advantage over the United States in producing products that use more __________________."

Activity 1 (continued)

U.S. Exports to China, 2004

By U.S. Dept. of Commerce 5-digit End-Use Code (shown in parentheses before each good). Values for exports are in thousands of dollars.

	Use-End Code	Value ($)
1	(21320) Semiconductors	2,938,303
2	(00100) Soybeans	2,328,833
3	(21180) Industrial machines	1,911,342
4	(22000) Civilian aircraft	1,617,532
5	(12540) Chemicals–organic	1,442,375
6	(10000) Cotton, raw	1,431,259
7	(12500) Plastic materials	1,381,725
8	(21301) Computer accessories	1,070,259
9	(21400) Telecommunications equipment	1,020,814
10	(21160) Measuring, testing, control instruments	996,202
11	(21100) Industrial engines	845,466
12	(20005) Electric apparatus	816,755
13	(21120) Metalworking machine tools	650,639
14	(21610) Medicinal equipment	581,798
15	(12770) Other industrial supplies	516,617
	Total U.S. Exports to China (2004)	**34,700,000**

U.S. Imports from China, 2004

By U.S. Dept. of Commerce 5-digit End-Use Code (shown in parentheses before each good). Values for imports are in thousands of dollars.

	Use-End Code	Value ($)
1	(21301) Computer accessories, peripherals and parts	23,794,210
2	(41120) Toys, shooting and sporting goods, and bicycles	17,844,052
3	(41050) Other (clocks, portable typewriters, other household gds)	17,336,897
4	(40020) Apparel and household goods–other textiles	10,601,204
5	(21300) Computers	10,052,085
6	(41000) Furniture, household items, baskets	9,709,247
7	(40040) Footwear of leather, rubber, or other materials	8,421,936
8	(41200) Television receivers, vcrs & other video equip.	7,905,474
9	(41030) Household and kitchen appliances	5,902,998
10	(21400) Telecommunications equipment	5,672,818
11	(41210) Radios, phonographs, tape decks, and other stereo	5,480,107
12	(40030) Nontextile apparel and household goods	4,636,983
13	(20005) Electric apparatus and parts	4,619,903
14	(40050) Sporting and camping apparel, footwear and gear	3,850,202
15	(40000) Apparel and household goods–cotton	3,848,721
	Total U.S. Imports from China (2004)	**196,700,000**

Source: *Source: FTDWebMaster, Foreign Trade Division, U.S. Census Bureau, Washington, D.C. 20233*

Activity 2
Name that Comparative Advantage

As you saw in the previous activity, analyzing a country's trade patterns helps to reveal a nation's comparative advantage. For example, the United States exports computer microprocessors to China. It has a comparative advantage in the production of microprocessors in part because these high-tech goods require skilled labor and major investments in capital resources that incorporate technologies developed through very expensive research and development programs.

Of course the United States trades with many other countries, too. The tables at the end of this handout provide data on the top 12 U.S. imports in 2004 from four "mystery" countries, listed only as Country A, B, C, and D. Use the data in those tables to answer the questions below.

In general terms, does the United States import the same types of goods from each of the four countries? Specifically, what are the top five import categories for each of the four countries? (List the top five import categories for each country below.)

Country A	**Country B**	**Country C**	**Country D**
1.	1.	1.	1.
2.	2.	2.	2.
3.	3.	3.	3.
4.	4.	4.	4.
5.	5.	5.	5.

Based on the information in the tables at the end of this handout, complete the following three-part assessment for each of the mystery countries (A–D). First circle one of the three bullet items in each column that best describes that country's exports to the United States, then select the most likely source of comparative advantage for that country (in its trade with the United States), and finally try to guess what country each mystery country might be. You will probably not be able to identify the specific mystery countries, but you probably can identify countries that have similar kinds of comparative advantages, and sources of that comparative advantage.

Activity 2 (continued)

Country A:

Goods exported from Country A to the United States (circle one in each column):

• Are mostly agricultural • Are mostly industrial/ technological • Are a mixture of both	• Require low-skilled labor • Require high-skilled labor • Require a mixture of both	• Require little capital investment • Require a great deal of capital investment

Country A's source of comparative advantage might be:

A. **factor endowments:** country may have high quantities of low-cost land, low-cost electricity, or abundant natural resources such as oil; or the country may have a favorable climate for goods that are exported.
B. **large supply of low-skilled labor:** country may have a large population; goods exported require low-tech production facilities.
C. **capital investment:** research and development increases productivity; goods produced require high-tech production facilities.

I think Country A might be ___________________________________

Country B:

Goods exported from Country B to the United States (circle one in each column):

• Are mostly agricultural • Are mostly industrial/ technological • Are a mixture of both	• Require low-skilled labor • Require high-skilled labor • Require a mixture of both	• Require little capital investment • Require a great deal of capital investment

Country B's source of comparative advantage might be:

A. **factor endowments:** country may have high quantities of low-cost land, low-cost electricity, or abundant natural resources such as oil; or the country may have a favorable climate for goods that are exported.
B. **large supply of low-skilled labor:** country may have a large population; goods exported require low-tech production facilities.
C. **capital investment:** research and development increases productivity; goods produced require high-tech production facilities.

I think Country B might be ___________________________________

Activity 2 (continued)

Country C:

Goods exported from Country C to the United States (circle one in each column):

• Are mostly agricultural • Are mostly industrial/ technological • Are a mixture of both	• Require low-skilled labor • Require high-skilled labor • Require a mixture of both	• Require little capital investment • Require a great deal of capital investment

Country C's source of comparative advantage might be:

A. **factor endowments:** country may have high quantities of low-cost land, low-cost electricity, or abundant natural resources such as oil; or the country may have a favorable climate for goods that are exported.
B. **large supply of low-skilled labor:** country may have a large population; goods exported require low-tech production facilities.
C. **capital investment:** research and development increases productivity; goods produced require high-tech production facilities.

I think Country C might be ____________________________________

Country D:

Goods exported from Country D to the United States (circle one in each column):

• Are mostly agricultural • Are mostly industrial/ technological • Are a mixture of both	• Require low-skilled labor • Require high-skilled labor • Require a mixture of both	• Require little capital investment • Require a great deal of capital investment

Country D's source of comparative advantage might be:

A. **factor endowments:** country may have high quantities of low-cost land, low-cost electricity, or abundant natural resources such as oil; or the country may have a favorable climate for goods that are exported.
B. **large supply of low-skilled labor:** country may have a large population; goods exported require low-tech production facilities.
C. **capital investment:** research and development increases productivity; goods produced require high-tech production facilities.

I think Country D might be ____________________________________

Activity 2 (continued)

U.S. Imports from Four Mystery Countries, 2004

U.S. Dept. of Commerce 5-digit End-Use Code (shown in parentheses before each good)
(Values for imports are in thousands of dollars.)

COUNTRY A		COUNTRY B		COUNTRY C		COUNTRY D	
End-Use Code	**Value ($)**	**End-Use Code**	**Value ($)**	**End-Use Code**	**Value ($)**	**End-Use Code**	**Value ($)**
(40000) Apparel and household goods–cotton	1,954,899	(30000) Passenger cars, new and used	20,349,301	(42100) Gem diamonds–uncut or unset	2,873,870	(10000) Crude oil	15,124,236
(40020) Apparel and household goods-other textiles	745,627	(40100) Medicinal, dental and pharmaceutical preparations	5,864,882	(40000) Apparel and household goods–cotton	2,274,154	(10030) Liquefied petroleum gases	510,451
(00120) Fruits and preparations, including frozen juices	174,916	(30230) Other parts and accessories	3,301,943	(41310) Jewelry (watches, rings, etc.)	1,494,271	(10010) Fuel oil	313,685
(01000) Fish and shellfish	132,447	(21180) Other industrial machinery	3,135,952	(40020) Apparel and household goods–other textiles	696,863	(10020) Other petroleum products	189,338
(14270) Nonmonetary gold	75,465	(21610) Other scientific, medical and hospital equipment	2,976,581	(14100) Iron and steel mill products–semifinished	579,112	(10110) Gas–natural	69,371
(40140) Other products (notions, writing and art supplies)	67,271	(30200) Engines and engine parts	2,441,503	(41040) Rugs and other textile floor coverings	506,375	(00200) Feedstuff and food grains	5,687
(00000) Green coffee	42,595	(20005) Electric apparatus and parts	1,857,216	(40100) Medicinal, dental and pharmaceutical preparations	462,808	(12050) Natural rubber and similar gums	4,766
(40050) Sporting and camping apparel, footwear and gear	34,909	(21150) Pulp and paper machinery	1,595,732	(01000) Fish and shellfish	407,142	(41320) Artwork, antiques, stamps, and other collectibles	3,234

Activity 2 (continued)

U.S. Imports from Four Mystery Countries, 2004

U.S. Dept. of Commerce 5-digit End-Use Code (shown in parentheses before each good)
(Values for imports are in thousands of dollars.)

COUNTRY A		COUNTRY B		COUNTRY C		COUNTRY D	
(41000) Furniture, household items, baskets	32,496	(21160) Measuring, testing and control instruments	1,569,105	(12540) Industrial organic chemicals	292,088	(00010) Cocoa beans	1,362
(00130) Vegetables and preparations	19,658	(21100) Industrial engines, pumps, compressors, generators	1,552,700	(13020) Stone, sand, cement, and lime	262,492	(00170) Tea, spices, and preparations	1,000
(40010) Apparel and household goods-wool	10,144	(50030) Minimum value shipments	1,487,020	(00140) Nuts and preparations	259,513	(16050) Other (synthetic rubbers, wood, cork, gums, resins, etc)	915
(00020) Cane and beet sugar	9,982	(12540) Industrial organic chemicals	1,412,986	(12070) Other (tobacco, waxes, nonfood oils)	206,890	(01000) Fish and shellfish	751

Source: *FTDWebMaster, Foreign Trade Division, U.S. Census Bureau, Washington, D.C. 20233*

Activity 3
Finding *Your* Comparative Advantage

Most workers specialize in producing goods or services, taking advantage of their individual comparative advantages. Individuals all have different skills, and experiences (economists call this **human capital**), and can find their comparative advantage by matching their human capital with particular careers that use that human capital. Think back to the Shaquille O'Neal and Master P example–both were somewhat successful in basketball and rap music. However, by using his specialized skills in basketball, Shaq was much better off than he would have been as a full-time rap singer.

Where, or what, is your comparative advantage? What special skills and human capital do you have (or want to acquire through education) that might lead you to a specialized career? Employers look for certain qualifications and technical skills, as well as general skills and attributes, such as motivation and a willingness to accept new assignments. And of course your own interests are also important.

One way to help find your comparative advantage is to complete a personal skills inventory, such as the Human Capital Inventory below. Fill in the chart for yourself, being as honest and candid about yourself as you can be, but also considering the education and training you are likely to complete before you start looking for a job and career.

Human Capital Inventory

Characteristic/Skill	Strongly Disagree	Disagree	Agree	Strongly Agree
I have strong oral communication skills	SD	D	A	SA
I have strong written communication skills	SD	D	A	SA
I am good at math	SD	D	A	SA
I have strong computing skills	SD	D	A	SA
I have strong research skills	SD	D	A	SA
I generally learn quickly	SD	D	A	SA
I have strong problem solving/applied reasoning skills	SD	D	A	SA
I have strong critical thinking skills	SD	D	A	SA
I work well with others	SD	D	A	SA
I enjoy working alone	SD	D	A	SA
I have strong leadership skills	SD	D	A	SA
I work well with customers	SD	D	A	SA
I have strong time management skills	SD	D	A	SA
I am a good planner	SD	D	A	SA
I am good at managing big projects	SD	D	A	SA
I can manage others under pressure	SD	D	A	SA
I am flexible/adaptable	SD	D	A	SA
I have great creativity/flair	SD	D	A	SA
I am strongly motivated/enthusiastic	SD	D	A	SA
I am very self-confident	SD	D	A	SA

Adapted from the University of Technology, Sydney's "Job Skills" Inventory; accessed at http://www.careerdevelopment.uts.edu.au/whatican/skills/ on August 12, 2005.

Activity 3 (continued)

On a computer with an Internet connection, use the results of the Human Capital Inventory to determine which of the six jobs/careers listed below fits most closely with your skills and interests. The URL for the Bureau of Labor Statistics (BLS) web site describing the skills and education needed for each job or career are provided. Go to that address for each career, and read the "Nature of the Work" and "Training, Other Qualifications, and Advancement" sections of the page. Complete the data retrieval chart as you read each job/career description.

Job/Career	**BLS web site**	**Which of your skills seem best suited for this job/career?**	**Which required skills do you lack?**
Bank teller	http://www.bls.gov/oco/ocos126.htm		
Office manager	http://www.bls.gov/oco/ocos127.htm		
Computer support specialist	http://www.bls.gov/oco/ocos268.htm		
Retail salesperson	http://www.bls.gov/oco/ocos121.htm		
Social worker	http://www.bls.gov/oco/ocos060.htm		
Air traffic controller	http://www.bls.gov/oco/ocos108.htm		

LESSON FOUR
GLOBALIZATION AND THE U.S. ECONOMY

LESSON DESCRIPTION

By comparing some of their own household items and clothing to those of an individual who lived in the late 1700s, and using a short reading to identify products widely sold in the United States today that are made in other countries, students recognize how international trade affects their daily lives. Analyzing data for the past century, they see how the kinds of goods traded has changed, leading to greater global interdependence and integration.

INTRODUCTION

Since 1960 both U.S. imports and exports have increased dramatically. As a percentage of GDP, imports grew from 4.2 to 13.8 percent, and exports increased from 4.9 to 9.3 percent. But compared to levels from nearly a century ago, during what economists call the first age of globalization, trade as a percentage of GDP is not substantially higher. And certainly international trade is not a new thing, as wrecks of merchant ships in the Mediterranean Sea, which are thousands of years old, make clear. What is different in today's new era of globalization is the kinds of things that are traded, and the much greater opportunity to move production of those products all around the world.

CONCEPTS

Interdependence
Globalization

CONTENT STANDARD

Voluntary exchange occurs only when all participating parties expect to gain. This is true for trade among individuals or organizations within a nation, and among individuals or organizations in different nations.

When individuals, regions, and nations specialize in what they can produce at the lowest cost and then trade with others, both production and consumption increase.

BENCHMARKS

Free trade increases worldwide material standards of living.

Voluntary exchange among people or organizations in different countries gives people a broader range of choices in buying goods and services.

Like trade among individuals within one country, international trade promotes specialization and division of labor and increases output and consumption.

Greater specialization leads to increased interdependence among producers and consumers.

OBJECTIVES

Students will:

- Analyze data to determine the share of international trade for the U.S. economy since the late 1800s.
- Analyze data to determine how the types of goods traded today are different from those traded in the late 1800s.
- Explain how increased globalization has made countries more integrated and interdependent.

TIME REQUIRED

120 minutes. In class periods of about one hour, the suggested coverage is: Period

1: Procedures 1 - 23; Period 2: Procedures 24- 27, Closure, and Assessment. Give students a copy of Visual 1 to complete a day or two before the lesson is taught.

MATERIALS

- Visual 1: Where Was It Made? (one copy per student)
- Visual 2: Which Companies are U.S. Firms?
- Visual 3: U.S. International Trade: Exports, Imports, Shares of GDP and Output of Goods
- Visual 4: Commodities Composition of U.S. Trade, 1890 vs. 1990
- Visual 5: Value of World Exports, by Sector (1950 = 100)
- Visual 6: A World of Many Parts, from Many Countries (one copy per student)
- Activity 1: What Mr. Charles Left Behind (one copy per student)
- Activity 2: An American Journey, or Is It? (one copy per student)
- Two decks of playing cards, each deck with a different color back, such as red and blue. Divide one deck into four stacks with the following cards:

  Ace through 9 of spades, 10 and jack of clubs, queen and king of hearts

  Ace through 9 of clubs, 10 and jack of hearts, queen and king of diamonds

  Ace through 9 of hearts, 10 and jack of diamonds, queen and king of spades

  Ace through 9 of diamonds, 10 and jack of spades, queen and king of clubs

PROCEDURES

1. Give each student a copy of Visual 1. As a homework assignment done a night or two before teaching this lesson, have students use this sheet to list five household items and five pieces of their own clothing, most of which were made in different countries. It is okay to have some items that are made in the United States, but try to find products made in other countries, too, and tell students they should only list items for which a label or tag indicates the country in which the product was made. Tell students to bring the completed form to class, to use in the class discussion.

2. Display Visual 1. With students referring to their own lists, record at least 10 examples of both household items and clothes, and the countries where they were produced.

3. Ask students if there are any general patterns shown by the lists. *(Individual answers may well vary, but a general summary should include a reference to the wide range of items that were made in many different countries.)*

4. Distribute a copy of Activity 1 to each student. Tell students this is an article about Mr. Charles, who lived in the late 18th and early 19th century in New England. Ask students to read the article and to compare Mr. Charles' wardrobe and household items with their own lists, as recorded on their copy of Visual 1.

5. Discuss the following questions:

A. How does the number and variety of items in your homes compare with those on Mr. Charles' list? *(There will be many more and different types of clothes and household items, suggesting that most people today have a higher standard of living than Mr. Charles, and certainly access to a greater variety of manufactured products and clothing.)*

B. Where were most of your clothes purchased? (*stores, catalogs, internet*)

C. Where were Mr. Charles' clothes purchased? *(If they were not made at home, they may have been purchased from a traveling salesperson, a neighbor, or perhaps a general store in a village.)*

D. How and where were Mr. Charles' clothes and household items produced? *(mainly at home, by hand)* Why were they made at home? *(Store-bought clothes and goods were too expensive and difficult to purchase for most people.)*

E. Where and how were your clothes and household items produced? *(Answers will vary, but include a variety of companies and countries. Most items are now manufactured/ mass produced, at a lower cost than people would pay to make the goods themselves.)*

F. How has international trade affected the production and consumption of clothes and household items? *(More products are available, with more things produced in other countries, at lower costs and sold at lower prices, compared to people's income levels.)*

6. Tell students that **globalization** refers to increases in the degree of integration between national economies, including the integration of production and consumption of goods and services, and the effects of public policies established in different nations and by international organizations. Ask students how their lists of household items and clothes reflect globalization. (*Many of their products were produced in other countries.*)

7. Distribute Activity 2. Give students a few minutes to read the short article. In the table below the story, tell students to place a check mark next to each company they believe is a U.S. company, but no check mark next to foreign companies.

8. Display Columns 1 and 2 of Visual 2. For each company, ask how many students checked that it was an American company. Record the number in Column 2.

9. Reveal Column 3 of Visual 2. Point out that all of the companies mentioned in the story are from other countries, but obviously conducting business in the United States. Discuss the following questions:

A. What surprised you about this article? (*the number of goods and services the family consumed that were made outside the United States, or by firms with a parent company located in another country; even the companies where Maxine and Melvin were employed were European-owned firms*)

B. How does this story of the journey illustrate globalization? (*Almost everything mentioned in the article is connected to a company from outside of the United States. That shows how Americans are connected to products made throughout the world.*)

10. Ask students if they think the United States engages in more trade today than it did a century ago. (*Most will say yes, because of the all the goods they have seen or personally use that are produced outside the United States, and because they may know that U.S. trade and world trade has increased dramatically over the past few decades.*)

11. Display the top half of Visual 3. Ask students what has happened to the volume of U.S. trade over time. (*Both U.S. exports and*

imports have increased from under 20 million dollars each in 1890 to $927.5 billion in exports and $1.727 trillion of imports in 2005.)

12. Display the bottom portion of Visual 3. Explain that column 2 of this chart shows exported merchandise goods as a share of U.S. GDP for each of the years shown. Discuss the following question: How much did exports of goods change as a percentage of GNP/GDP between 1889 and 2000? *(from 5.6% to 7.7%–not nearly the increase noted from 1950 to 2000, because of the drop in trade during the Great Depression and World War II)*

13. Tell students that international trade is not a new activity and, in fact, is one that has been carried on for thousands of years. Economic historians note that the first great era of globalization occurred at the end of the 19th century, when steamships made it much less expensive to carry larger loads of cargo all over the world. Despite that, many people claim that the United States and the rest of the world are experiencing an unprecedented era of globalization. Explain that there are two reasons for this. First, the kinds of things being traded today are very different from what was traded in the first era of globalization. Second, the higher levels of trade and the changes in the kinds of products that are traded have made countries far more **interdependent**.

14. Direct students' attention to the last column of Visual 3. Explain that these data show exported merchandise goods as a percentage of the total production of these goods. Discuss the following questions:

A. How did the share of the production of these goods that was exported change from 1889 to 2000? (*increased from 14.3% to 41.3%*)

B. How would that change affect U.S. goods producers? (*They became more integrated or connected to the world economy–concerned about sales to foreign consumers and competition from foreign firms.*)

15. Explain that in addition to the increase in exported merchandise goods as a percentage of the total production of these goods, another change in international trade over this period deals with changing the mix or kind of goods (in broad categories, agricultural, mining, and manufactured products) traded. Tell students they are going to participate in an activity to learn how things traded between different countries today are different from those traded in the late 1800s.

16. Divide students into four groups; designate each group as a country: A, B, C, or D. Tell the groups that they will play two rounds, and explain that at the end of round 1 each country must have 1 complete suit–13 cards, ace through king–from the deck of playing cards you will use in the activity. Country A will collect spades; Country B, clubs; Country C, hearts; Country D, diamonds. Tell the groups to keep track of the number of trades they make, the cards they traded, and the country with whom they traded.

17. Use only one, presorted deck of playing cards for this part of the activity. Distribute a set of cards from this deck to each group, as shown below:

Country A: Ace through 9 of spades, 10 and jack of clubs, queen and king of hearts

Country B: Ace through 9 of clubs, 10 and jack of hearts, queen and king of diamonds

Country C: Ace through 9 of hearts, 10 and jack of diamonds, queen and king of spades

Country D: Ace through 9 of diamonds, 10 and jack of spades, queen and king of clubs

18. Give students three minutes to make trades. Remind students to record the number of trades they make and the countries with which they traded.

19. Announce the end of round 1 and collect all cards. Divide students into eight groups and assign each group a country letter, this time A–H. Add the second deck of cards. Shuffle the two decks together several times, and randomly distribute 13 cards to each group/country. Announce that in this round the countries must trade to obtain the following cards:

A. Country A: Ace through the king of spades from the deck with blue backs

B. Country B: Ace through the king of clubs from the deck with blue backs

C. Country C: Ace through the king of hearts from the deck with blue backs

D. Country D: Ace through the king of diamonds from the deck with blue backs

E. Country E: Ace through the king of spades from the deck with red backs

F. Country F: Ace through the king of clubs from the deck with red backs

G. Country G: Ace through the king of hearts from the deck with red backs

H. Country H: Ace through the king of diamonds from the deck with red backs

As in round 1, have students keep track of the number of trades they make and the countries with which they trade. Allow 10 minutes for students to make their trades

20. Announce the end of round 2 and collect the cards. Begin the debriefing by discussing round 1:

A. Ask students how many trades were made in round 1 and with which countries. (*Each country should have made four trades, two with each of two different countries. Some may have made a few more trades, to get a deal done.*)

B. Tell students that in round 1, the cards Ace through 10 represented agricultural products; the jack and queen represented mined goods such as iron ore, copper, and coal; and the king represented manufactured goods. In other words, this deck represented an earlier century, when most production (and employment) was centered on agriculture. What kinds of goods were traded? (*Countries traded for one agricultural good, one manufactured good, and two mined goods.*)

C. What types of resources are needed to produce agricultural and mined goods? (*natural resources, and some capital and human resources, but generally not as much capital or skilled labor as required to make manufactured goods*)

D. To produce agricultural and mined goods, how many resources would be imported from other countries? (*typically not many, except for a few manufactured goods, such as agricultural and mining equipment*)

E. What determines where these kinds of goods are produced, not in the simulation but in real production and trade? (*For agricultural and mining products, production is based in countries that have the natural resource base used to produce these goods.*)

21. Explain that in round 2, the mixed decks of cards were used to represent each country producing manufactured goods, such as a cars, DVD players, laptop computers, or cell phones, with each card representing a different component of the final product that was produced. To produce the manufactured products, each country had to obtain all of the components for the product, or a complete suit of cards from one deck. Discuss the following questions:

A. How many trades were made in round 2 and with which countries? (*many more trades, most likely with all the countries*)

B. Why were so many trades made? (*The components of the final products were produced/available in many different countries.*)

C. Why would real manufacturing companies trade for so many resources? (*to be competitive, producers want to purchase resources from suppliers that can produce them at the lowest cost, which often means buying from companies in many different countries.*)

D. How does this type of trade make countries interdependent? (*To produce a product at the lowest cost, they rely on other countries for the inputs.*)

22. Tell students that round 1 represented the type of international trading that took place in the late 1800s. Make the following points:

- Most international trade in this period involved bulk commodities–such as wheat, cotton, beef, timber, and iron ore–and a few simple manufactured goods.

- The sources of the productive resources used to make the goods that were exported were usually at or close to the production site. Production relied primarily on the availability of natural resources and relatively unskilled labor. Producers did not rely on international trade for most of these inputs.

- Research and development costs involved in producing these goods were relatively low, compared to products that are traded today.

23. Display Visual 4. Discuss the following questions.

A. In 1890, what made up the bulk of U.S. trade? (*agricultural goods and raw materials*)

B. How had U.S. trade changed by 1990? (*most trade was in manufactured goods*)

24. Display Visual 5. Ask students what has happened to the value of manufactured goods exported worldwide since 1950? (*increased dramatically*) Explain to students that round 2 of the trading activity represented international trade that occurs today. The types of products being traded (including finished goods and components used to produce those goods) and the degree of global integration go far beyond the simple trading of agricultural and mined goods that characterized international trade a century ago, in the first age of globalization.

25. Display Visual 6 and distribute a copy to each student. Tell students again that most world exports and imports today are manufactured goods with components coming from many different countries. This chart shows some of the components that are used to produce the Mini automobile. Tell students the Mini is produced in Great Britain by BMW Group, a German company. They can see pictures of the car at miniusa.com or mini.co.uk. Tell students to study the chart and allow time for them to answer questions A-E.

26. Discuss the following questions:

A. In how many different countries are the parts listed for the Mini made? (*eight–Netherlands, Germany, Brazil, Japan, United Kingdom, Belgium, United States, and Italy*) How many continents are represented by these supplier nations? (*four–Asia, South America, North America, and Europe*)

B. Could the Mini be produced somewhere other than Great Britain? Explain. (*Yes. Unlike agricultural and mining products, where goods are produced in locations based largely on the availability of natural resources, manufactured goods today can be produced almost anywhere, using parts that come from many other nations.*)

C. Why might a company choose a particular production location? (*higher labor productivity, lower transportation and training costs, local taxes and government services, financial stability in the nation–all factors will be considered that affect the firm's profits in producing and selling the product*)

D. How does coordinating the production of a good made with components from all over the world compare to managing the production of agricultural products and mined goods, such as coal and iron ore, which made up a much larger part of international trade in earlier centuries? (*Products traded in the earlier period required relatively less coordination and global integration of production, trade, and government policies.*)

E. Globalization is sometimes defined as the increased degree of integration between national economies. How does the production of the Mini reflect increased globalization? (*The production steps illustrated in Visual 6 require coordination with eight countries on four continents. But in fact there are 2500 parts in the Mini, including some from still other countries, so the degree of integration required to produce the car is even greater than shown in Visual 6.*)

27. Explain that the production of the Mini illustrates several key characteristics of products that are traded internationally today:

- First, location of manufacturing production sites is not tied to the local availability of natural resources, as it was with agricultural and mining goods. Minis could be made almost anywhere in the world. Companies are not tied to a specific location, and choose to locate where they can produce and sell their products at a lower cost than their competitors.

- Second, one country or one company usually does not excel at producing every part of most complex manufactured products. Instead, parts and technologies used in the final products are likely to come from many labs, plants, and companies, from all over the world.

- Third, the value of the physical materials in the final products that are traded internationally today is often very small, compared to the value of the ideas and technology that goes into the production of the product, and to the skills and knowledge of the workers who design and make the products. For example:

  DVDs–expenses of paying recording artists, technicians, advertising, marketing, and legal fees outweigh the cost of physically producing the DVD.

  Laptop computers–nearly all the value comes not from the physical inputs (such as plastic and wires) but from the ideas incorporated into the central processing unit, disk drives, flat panel screen, etc. New technologies have to be researched and developed and intellectual property has to be protected from illegal copies. The protection of intellectual property with patents, copyrights, and legal enforcement must be global in scope.

- Fourth, unlike agricultural and mining products for which the final product is used up after it is sold, once they are developed technologies can be reused to produce more products, and new kinds of products. Therefore, discovering a new technology gives a firm an advantage over its domestic and international competitors, which can lead to very high profits.

CLOSURE

Review the key points of the lesson using the following questions:

1. How has international trade changed since the late 1800s, measuring imports or exports as a percent of GDP? (*modest increases*)

2. How has the dollar value of exports and imports changed? (*grown tremendously, as the GDPs of trading nations have grown rapidly, too*)

3. How has the percentage of manufactured goods that are produced for international trade changed over this time period? (*increased greatly*)

4. How has the share of manufactured goods as a percentage of all goods traded internationally changed since the late 1800s? (*A much greater portion of international trade involves manufactured goods today; agricultural goods and mining goods were a larger part of international trade in the late 1800s.*)

5. What characteristics of manufacturing goods affect international trade patterns today? (*Production is mobile, and usually does not have to be located near key supplies of natural resources. Components for a product come from many plants at many different sites, often from many different countries. The value of the physical materials in most final products has become much less significant. More value comes from technology and skilled labor services that are incorporated into the final product. Once a new technology is discovered it can be reused.*)

6. How does international trade affect producers, workers, and consumers today? (*increased interdependence, greater competition, wider variety of products available to consumers at lower cost/prices*)

ASSESSMENT

Ask students to respond to the following statement and question in a one-page essay, written individually or in small groups:

The level of U.S. trade today, measured by exports as a percentage of GDP, is not that much greater than it was a century ago. Nevertheless, we are said to be living in a period of unprecedented globalization. How can that be true?

Visual 1
Where Was It Made?

Household item	Where produced

Clothing item	Where produced

Visual 2
Which Companies Are U.S. Firms?

Company/Product	U. S. Owned (✓)	Owned by
Chrysler Mini Van		Germany's DiamlerChrysler
Shell Gas		Royal Dutch Shell
7 Up		Britain's Cadbury Schweppes
Nestlé's Crunch Candy Bar		Nestle SA of Switzerland
Bayer Aspirin		Bayer AG in Germany
Burger King Hamburgers and Fries		British Diageo
Crowne Plaza Hotel		British hotel firm Six Continents
Houghton Mifflin Book		French Vivendi Universal
Sony Television		Sony Japan
Snapple Ice Tea		Britain's Cadbury Schweppes
Taster's Choice Instant Coffee		Nestle SA of Switzerland
Lipton Tea		Unilever, Anglo-Dutch Company
Skippy Peanut Butter		Unilever, Anglo-Dutch Company
BP Gas		British Petroleum United Kingdom
ING DIRECT		Dutch Company
Barclays		United Kingdom

Visual 3
U.S. International Trade: Exports, Imports, Shares of GDP and Output of Goods

Value of U.S. Exports and Imports (in 2005 dollars)

Year	Exports	Imports
1890	$ 18,677,827	$ 16,892,144
1900	30,884,912	20,604,712
1950	83,843,609	70,735,293
1970	217,965,293	202,468,673
2005	$ 927,500,000,000	$ 1,727,000,000,000

Source: Bureau of the Census. *Historical Statistics of the United States Colonial Times to 1970, Bicentennial Edition, Part 2*. CIA Factbook: www.cia.gov/dia/publications/factbook. Nominal data for 1890, 1900, 1950, and 1970 were converted to 2005 dollars using the U.S. Inflation Calculator, http://www.westegg.com/inflation/.

U.S. Merchandise Exports as Percentages of Total Output, and Tradables Output, United States, 1889–2000

	Merchandise Exports	
Year	Percentage of GDP/GNP	Percentage of Goods Output
1889	5.6	14.3
1913	6.1	13.2
1929	5.2	13.9
1950	3.6	8.9
1960	3.8	11.0
1970	4.2	14.1
1980	8.3	29.2
1990	7.0	31.4
2000	7.7	41.3

Source: Douglas Irwin, "The United States in a New Global Economy? A Century's Perspective." *American Economic Review,* May 1996. James Gerber. *International Economics,* Third Edition, p 5, Pearson Addison Wesley, 2005.

Visual 4

Commodity Composition of U.S. Trade, 1890 vs. 1990

	1890	1990
	Percentage of Exports	
Agricultural Goods	42.2	11.5
Raw Materials	36.6	11.6
Manufactured Goods	21.2	77.0
Total	100.0	100.0

	1890	1990
	Percentage of Imports	
Agricultural Goods	33.1	5.6
Raw Materials	22.8	14.8
Manufactured Goods	44.1	79.6
Total	100.0	100.0

Source: Douglas Irwin, "The United States in a New Global Economy? A Century's Perspective," *American Economic Review*, May 1996.

Visual 5
Value of World Exports by Sector (1950 = 100)

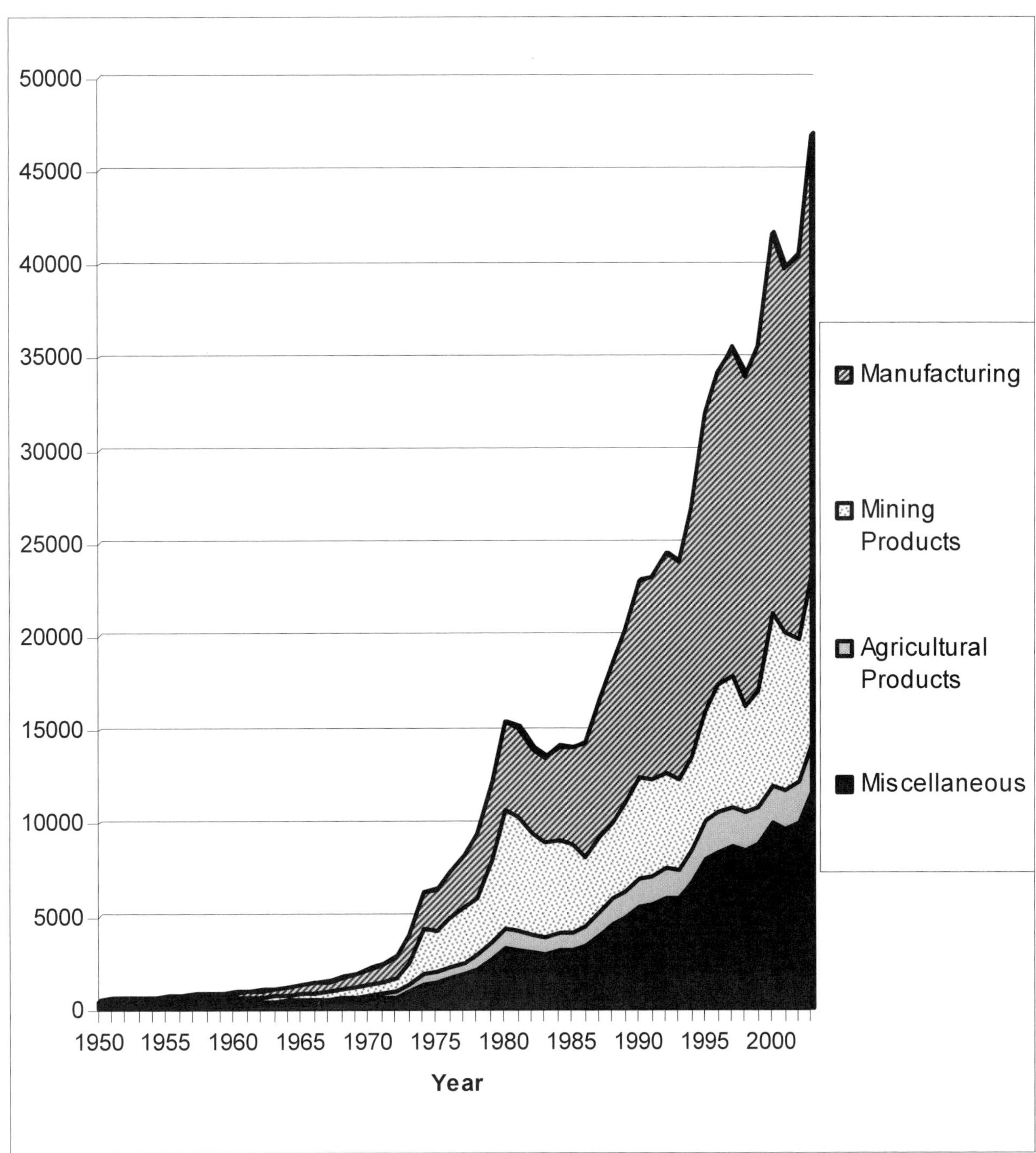

Visual 6
A World of Many Parts, from Many Countries

The BMW Group produces the Mini car in Oxford, England, using parts and supplies that come from companies based in Asia, North and South America, and Europe. The chart below shows only a few of the companies that supply the almost 2500 parts used to produce the car.

Car Part	Made in	Company Headquarters
Hood	Netherlands	Austria
Grille	Germany	Germany
Gasoline Engine	Brazil	Brazil
Diesel Engine	Japan	Japan
Front and Rear Bumpers	United Kingdom	Canada
Windshield	Belgium	France
Headliner	United States	Spain
Outside Mirrors	Germany	Canada
Seats	United Kingdom	United States
Exhaust System	United Kingdom	United States
Wheel bearings	United Kingdom	United States
Wheels	Italy, Germany	United States

Source: "A World of Parts," *National Geographic*, February 2005, pp. xxii-xxiv.

A. From how many countries do these parts for the Mini come? How many continents?

B. Could the Mini be produced somewhere other than Great Britain? Explain.

C. Why would a company choose to produce a product like the Mini at a particular location, instead of other possible locations?

D. How does coordinating the production of a product with components from all over the world compare to managing the production of goods such as agricultural products, coal, or iron ore, which represented a far larger part of the international trade in goods in earlier centuries?

E. Globalization is sometimes defined as the increased degree of integration between national economies. How does the production of the Mini reflect increased globalization?

Activity 1
What Mr. Charles Left Behind

Mr. Charles, a farmer, lived in New England in the late 18th century. When he died in 1804, the inventory of his estate included 3 junk bottles, 1 iron ring, a small tin cup, 1 old handsaw, 1 old brass kettle, 6 old chairs, and 15 old casks.

Mr. Charles had very few clothes: 4 pair of stockings, 1 wool shirt, three coats (1 old), 1 waistcoat, 2 pairs of pants, 2 silk handkerchiefs, 7 old handkerchiefs, 1 shirt, 2 gowns, 4 aprons, and 1 cloak.

In the early 19th century people worked hard but seldom had much to show for it. Basic hand tools and their own labor and skills largely determined what and how much could be produced.

Clothes were mainly made at home because store-bought goods were expensive. Even if cash was available, places to shop were limited. Occasionally a traveling salesperson might come to your home, or you might buy clothes from a neighbor who could make them faster or better, or on special trips you might go to a general store in a village, using roads and trails that were poor and often impassable. No matter how you made or bought them, clothes were expensive and the choices of styles and fabrics were limited.

Source: Federal Reserve Bank of Boston, *The Ledger*, Winter 2004, pp. 9-10.

Activity 2
An American Journey, or Is It?

Maxine and Melvin decide to take a day off from work so they can have a long weekend and drive upstate to visit friends. Melvin works for ING DIRECT and Maxine works for Barclays.

They fill up their Chrysler mini-van with gas at the local Shell station and begin their journey. They sip 7 Up and nibble on Nestlé's Crunch Bars until they stop for dinner at Burger King. That evening Maxine and Melvin spend the night at a Crowne Plaza Hotel. Melvin takes a Bayer aspirin for a headache and then watches a movie on the Sony television. Maxine reads a book published by Houghton Mifflin and drinks a bottle of Snapple Ice Tea.

The next day Maxine has a cup of Taster's Choice instant coffee and Melvin drinks a cup of Lipton Tea in their room. They make a snack of crackers with Skippy Peanut Butter, fill the car with gas at the BP station, and continue on their way.

How American was this journey?

In the chart below, place a check mark in the "Owned by" column for each company/product that you believe is owned or produced by a U.S. firm. Do not check companies you believe are from other countries, or products that you believe are produced by firms from other countries.

Company/Product	Owned by	Company/Product	Owned by
Chrysler Mini Van		Houghton Mifflin Book	
Shell Gas		Sony Television	
7 Up		Snapple Ice Tea	
Nestlé's Crunch Candy Bar		Taster's Choice Instant Coffee	
Bayer Aspirin		Lipton Tea	
Burger King		Skippy Peanut Butter	
Crowne Plaza Hotel		BP Gas	

Employers

ING DIRECT		Barclays	

LESSON FIVE
U.S. AND WORLD TRADE: PAST AND PRESENT

LESSON DESCRIPTION

Students conduct a class survey to learn which nations most people in their community believe are the leading U.S. trading partners, and what goods the United States exports and imports most. They then analyze current data on these questions and compare the data with the survey results. To learn about changes in patterns of trade over time, they examine U.S. trade data from 2005 and 1905, and draw conclusions about how and why trade patterns changed over that period.

INTRODUCTION

The five nations that trade more goods with the United States today than any others are Canada, Mexico, China, Japan, and Germany. Why does the United States trade more with these countries than others, when these five countries are so different in many key respects? Canada and Mexico are neighboring nations, which means transportation costs are low, and it is possible to ship some goods by rail or truck as well as by ships and airplanes. Like the United States, Japan, Germany, and Canada are industrialized countries with high average incomes. Many of the products produced in these countries, such as cars, electronic goods, and airplanes, are also produced in the United States, but with styles and models different enough from U.S. products to attract many U.S. consumers. At the same time, many people and firms in those nations often chose to buy some U.S. products instead of the similar products made in their own nations. China has become a major manufacturing nation in recent decades, reflecting the low cost of its labor and rapid growth in capital investments financed both by domestic savings and investments by international firms. All five of these U.S. trading partners have formal trade agreements with the United States that keep tariffs, quotas, and other barriers to trade low. Canada and Mexico signed the North American Free Trade Agreement (NAFTA) with the United States, and like the United States, all five of these countries are members of the World Trade Organization (WTO).

In more general terms, trade between people and firms in the same nation, or with people and firms in other nations, occurs because of comparative advantage. The United States imports goods and services when they can be produced at a lower opportunity cost by people or firms in other countries. It exports goods and services to other countries when people and firms in the United States can produce products at a lower opportunity cost. Over time, comparative advantage and trading patterns change, reflecting changes in technology, labor productivity, income, consumer tastes, and also political factors that affect different nations' stability and participation in world trade and trading agreements. That has been true for the United States and its major trading partners in the past, and will continue to be true in the future.

CONCEPTS

Exports
Imports
Trade
Comparative advantage

CONTENT STANDARDS

Voluntary exchange occurs only when all participating parties expect to gain. This is true for trade among individuals or organizations within a nation, and among individuals or organizations in different nations.

When individuals, regions and nations specialize in what they can produce at the lowest cost and then trade with others, both production and consumption increase.

BENCHMARKS

Imports are foreign goods and services purchased from sellers in other countries.

Exports are domestic goods and services sold to buyers in other countries.

Individuals and nations have a comparative advantage in the production of goods or services if they can produce a product at a lower opportunity cost than other individuals and nations.

Comparative advantages change over time because of changes in factor endowments, resource prices, and events that occur in other nations.

OBJECTIVES

Students will:

- Analyze data to identify the current major trading partners for the United States, and its major exports and imports to and from these countries.
- Explain why countries often import the same kinds of goods they export.
- Analyze data to explain how U.S. trading patterns have changed over the last 100 years.

TIME REQUIRED

90 minutes. In class periods of about one hour, the suggested coverage is: Period 1: Procedures 1 - 10; Period 2: Procedures 11 - 14, Closure, and Assessment. Students will have three adults complete a brief survey a day or two before the lesson is taught, and use the survey results in the lesson.

MATERIALS

- Visual 1: Survey Results
- Visual 2: Top Trading Partners for Selected Countries, 2003 (one copy per student)
- Activity 1: Survey on U.S. International Trade (three copies per student)
- Activity 2: U.S. International Trade Data, 2005 (one copy per student)
- Activity 3: U.S. International Trade Data, 1905 (one copy per student)
- Activity 4: Assessment (one copy per student)

PROCEDURES

1. At least a day or two before teaching this lesson, distribute three copies of Activity 1 to each student. Explain that each student is to find three adults to answer the questions on the survey. Tell students to explain that they are doing this as part of a class project. Set the deadline to complete the surveys and bring the completed forms to class, to be used in this lesson.

2. Divide students into small groups and ask them to tally the results of their surveys to determine which countries their survey respondents thought were the top three countries with which the United States trades, and what the top three U.S. exports and imports are.

3. Define **imports** as goods and services purchased from sellers in other countries and **exports** as goods and services sold to buyers in other countries.

4. Display Visual 1. Have groups share their results. As they do, record and tally the information on the visual.

5. Discuss the following questions, based on survey results:

A. What three countries did most people in the community say trade the most with the United States? (*Answers will vary.*)

B. What five products were most often named as the leading U.S. exports? (*Answers will vary.*)

C. What five products were most often named as the leading U.S. imports? (*Answers will vary.*)

D. Ask students if they agree with the survey results, or have other suggestions for leading trading partners, exports, or imports. (*Answers will vary.*)

6. Tell students they are going to examine actual **trade** data to determine which countries are the leading trading partners with the United States, and what products are the leading U.S. exports and imports. Then they will compare the data to the class survey results.

7. Distribute a copy of Activity 2 to each student. Working in the groups assigned in procedure 2 above, instruct students to use the data in the handout to answer the following questions:

A. What countries are the top five U.S. trading partners? (*Canada, Mexico, China, Japan, and Germany*)

B. How does this compare to the survey results? (*Answers will vary.*)

C. Why do you believe the survey responses were similar to or different from the actual list of U.S. trading partners? (*Answers will vary.*)

D. Why do you believe the United States trades more with these countries than it does with other countries? (Students will probably not suggest some important reasons. Be sure to cover all of the following points.)

- Canada and Mexico are neighbors with the United States. This geographic proximity results in lower transportation costs, and therefore lower costs of trade. The North America Free Trade Agreement (NAFTA) also reduced tariffs and other limits on trade between these countries. As a result, although the economies of Mexico and Canada are relatively small compared to the United States, in 2003 they purchased over a third of U.S exports and supplied a fourth of U.S. imports.

- Individuals and countries trade with other countries when they have different endowments in inputs such as labor (skilled and unskilled), capital goods and technology, and the quantity and quality of natural resources. Explain that individuals and nations have a **comparative advantage** in the production of goods or services if they can produce a product at a lower opportunity cost than other individuals and nations. For example, unskilled labor is less expensive in China and Mexico than in the United States, so goods made using unskilled labor are more likely to be produced in those countries.

- All of these countries, including the United States, are members of the World Trade Organization and other international organizations and agreements that promote trade and cooperation.

- Canada, Japan, Germany, and the United States are industrialized countries, with high incomes. Consumers in these countries often buy goods and services from other industrialized nations, or travel to those nations as tourists.

- China is a large country with a very large population and a rapidly growing economy. Wage rates are still very low compared to the United States and Western Europe, which keeps costs of manufactured goods low. High rates of saving in China and Asia, together with the rapid growth of international investments in the country, have rapidly increased capital resources and manufacturing output in the country.

8. Continue the discussion of question D on Activity 2 by asking the following questions, which do not appear on the activity, so allow students more time to consider their answers:

- What might be one explanation for the limited amount of trade between the United States and some European countries? (*One reason is the geographic distance between the United States and these countries, and their proximity to other European nations and membership in the European Union (EU), which promotes trade between the European nations. Many European nations are also very small, which makes them less likely to be major trading partners with the United States. The EU, considered as a block, is a major trading partner for the United States.*)

- Why are countries like Russia, India, and those on the continent of Africa not among our major trading partners? (*Geographic distances to the United States are a barrier, and most people in these countries have low incomes, which makes it difficult for them to buy products exported from countries like the United States. U.S. trade barriers for imported agricultural products, especially government subsidies to U.S. farmers, make it difficult for many of these nations to sell their agricultural exports.*)

9. Before discussing question E on Activity 2, display Visual 2 and distribute a copy to each student. Discuss possible reasons for these trading patterns, and to what extent those responses are similar to the reasons that explained U.S. trading patterns. (*Except for the United States and Israel, most of the trading partners are geographically close. The United States has trading agreements with Israel, and strong historical, cultural, and national security ties. Moldova tends to trade with other countries that were also formerly part of the Soviet Union. Industrialized countries such as Japan and the United Kingdom tend to trade with other industrialized countries, as seen earlier with the United States. China's rapid growth in trade and manufacturing capacity has made it a leading trading partner with several nations, both rich and poor, in virtually every part of the world.*)

10. Discuss the remaining questions on Activity 2, starting with question E:

E. What are the leading six categories of U.S. exports? (*In order by the value of exports: capital goods except automobiles; industrial supplies and materials; consumer goods except food and automobiles; automotive vehicles, parts, and engines; agricultural products; and foods, feeds, and beverages.*)

F. What are the leading six categories of U.S. imports? (*In order by the value of imports: industrial supplies and materials; capital goods except automobiles; automotive vehicles, parts and engines; consumer goods except food and automobiles; petroleum products; and agricultural products.*)

G. How do these data compare to the survey results? (*Answers will vary.*)

H. What is similar about the lists of exports and imports? (*In these broad categories, the United States imports many of the same goods that it exports.*) In Lesson 3 of this volume, students saw that in its trade with China, the goods that are imported are rarely exported, and vice versa. But China and the Unites States have very different economies, income levels, etc., so they usually specialize in producing different kinds of goods. The products considered in that lesson are also presented in much more specific categories than those presented here. Point out that for international trade between countries that have similar economies, such as the United States, Canada, Japan, Germany, the United Kingdom, and other nations in Western Europe, especially for broadly defined categories of goods, we often see that trade involves similar kinds of goods. Ask students to brainstorm for a few minutes about why that might be true, without approving or disapproving suggestions. You might ask students to consider some specific goods that are traded by those countries– including different brands of cars, music CDs, foods, etc.

11. To extend the discussion of item H in Activity 2, ask students if they would ever trade a bag of potato chips for a bag of corn chips or pretzels at lunch. (*Some have, or would.*) Point out that potato chips, corn chips, and pretzels are all similar kinds of snacks, but not exactly the same. "Snacks" is a broad category of these goods, and there are many different types of snacks, often sold by different companies. Explain that specialization within product categories also happens with trade between individuals and organizations in different countries. For example, two countries might import and export chemicals, with each country specializing in the production of one type of chemical. Similarly, the United States, Japan, and Germany all produce automobiles, with all three countries importing some brands and types of automobiles from the other countries, while exporting different brands and types of automobiles to those countries, too. Discuss the following questions:

A. Are the vehicles the United States imports different from those it exports? (*The U.S. tends to export larger vehicles, such as SUVs and pick-up trucks. It tends to import smaller, fuel efficient vehicles and luxury vehicles. In the market for high performance sports cars, differences in design and styling result in U.S. exports of cars such as the Corvette, but imports of cars including Porsches and Ferraris.*)

B. Why does the United States import airplanes when Boeing produces and exports commercial airlines to many other countries? (*The United States imports small jets from other countries, including Canada and Brazil. Some U.S. airlines have purchased large Airbus jets, which sometimes have different designs, components (such as engines) and other features than Boeing jets, or may simply have been available at a lower price in some years. Currently, Boeing and Airbus are about to compete in the market for even larger commercial jets, with plane designs that are markedly different.*)

12. Ask the last question in Activity 2, item I: Do you believe these trade patterns will remain relatively constant over periods of time? Why or Why not? *(Answers will vary.)* Remind students that individuals and nations have a comparative advantage in the production of goods or services if they can produce a product at a lower opportunity cost than other individuals and nations. As technology, the availability of resources, and other market forces change, the United States might find that it no longer has a comparative advantage in the production of some goods that it once exported. Discuss the following questions:

A. How might patterns of trade change as China's economy continues to grow? (*U.S. imports from and exports to China are likely to rise, but more production of goods that can be done by workers with less education and training is likely to move to China, including some manufacturing jobs, especially for products that can be shipped to other nations at relatively low costs.*)

B. How might patterns of trade between the United States and Mexico change if Mexico experiences a sharp, long-lasting depression? (*U.S. exports to Mexico would decline. Imports in most nations are "normal goods," which means that demand increases as income levels rise, but decrease when income falls.*)

C. How might patterns of trade between Japan and the United States change if Japan places a tariff on U.S. imported goods? (*U.S. exports to Japan would decline in the short run. In time, U.S. imports of Japanese products would also likely decline, with total trade between the two countries decreasing.*)

13. Ask students if trading patterns among nations remain constant, especially over long periods of time (for decades and even centuries)? *(No.)* Why not? (*New products are invented, and new ways of making old products are developed. In addition to technological changes, the availability of resources in different nations can also change, as well as labor productivity and training, and broader social factors such as political and economic stability.*) Discuss the following questions:

A. What countries do you believe were the leading trading partners with the United States 100 years ago? (*Answers will vary.*)

B. What do you believe the leading U.S. exports and imports were a century ago? (*Answers will vary.*)

14. Distribute a copy of Activity 3 to each student. Divide students into small

groups and ask them to study the data and answer the questions at the end of the Activity. Discuss the questions from the activity with the class:

A. What five nations were the leading trading partners with the United States in 1905? (*United Kingdom, Canada, France, Cuba, and Japan*)

B. How does this list compare with the leading U.S. trading partners today? (*Only Canada and Japan are still among the five leading trading partners.*)

C. What might have caused this change in trading patterns? (*Changes in technology and transportation costs decreased trading costs in general, resulting in a large increase in trade. Changes in technology, and in the quantity and quality of capital and labor resources, changed the mix of goods traded and produced by different countries.*) Ask: Why did Cuba fall from the list of leading U.S. trading partners, despite its geographic proximity to the United States? (*Because Cuba is a small and relatively poor nation, U.S. trade with other countries might have outpaced trade growth with Cuba in any case, but in 1962 the United Stated imposed economic and diplomatic sanctions on Cuba. A trade embargo prohibited exports and imports. Today, some shipments of medicines and other humanitarian products to Cuba are allowed, but for the most part the embargo is still in place.*)

D. What were the top five U.S. exports in 1905? (*cotton and cotton manufactures, meat, machinery, coal and related fuels, copper and copper manufacturers)*

E. What were the top five U.S. imports in 1905? (*sugar, coffee, hides and skins, raw silk, crude rubber, cotton manufactures*)

F. How do the lists of leading U.S. imports and exports in 1905 compare to the leading imports and exports in 2005? (*The lists are very different. In 1905 exports and imports were mainly simple commodities such as agricultural goods and mined goods. Today's traded goods embody much more technology and complex manufacturing. The pattern of changes from 1905 to 2005 are discussed at greater length in Lesson 4 of this volume.*)

CLOSURE

Review the lesson with students using the points below.

- The top five U. S. trading partners today are Canada, Mexico, Japan, China, and Germany.

- The United States trades with these countries for the following reasons:

  Geographic proximity with Canada and Mexico results in lower transportation costs

  Different comparative advantages based on differences in the relative availability of inputs such as skilled and unskilled workers, or in the quantity and quality of natural resources, capital goods, and technology

  Free trade agreements and membership in international institutions that work to lower trade barriers such as tariffs and quotas

- The major U.S. imports are industrial supplies and materials; capital goods except automobiles; automotive vehicles, parts, and engines; consumer goods except automobiles; and petroleum products.

- The major U.S. exports are industrial supplies and materials; capital goods except automobiles; consumer goods except automobiles; automotive vehicles, parts, and engines; and agricultural products.

- Specialization within different categories of trade results in the U.S. importing some of the same types of goods it exports.

- As technology, other resources, and prices change, countries often lose their comparative advantage in the production of some goods. This leads to a change in the mix of goods countries export and import.

ASSESSMENT

Distribute a copy of Activity 4 to each student. Working individually, have students prepare and turn in written responses to the questions.

Visual 1
Survey Results

Top Three U.S. Trading Partners

Country	# of Responses	Country	# of Responses
Brazil		Japan	
Canada		Malaysia	
China		Mexico	
France		Netherlands	
Germany		South Korea	
India		Taiwan	
Ireland		United Kingdom	
Italy		Venezuela	

Top Three U.S. Exports and Imports

Product	# of Responses	
	Imports	Exports
Computers, peripherals, and parts		
Civilian aircraft, engines, and parts		
Semiconductors		
Telecommunications equipment		
Electric generating machinery, apparatus, and parts		
Agricultural products		
Industrial supplies and materials		
Automotive vehicles, parts, and engines		
Consumer goods (nonfood such as clothes, furniture) except automotive		
Petroleum products		
Chemicals		
Building materials		

Visual 2

Leading Trading Partners for Selected Countries, 2003 (by value of total trade in millions of U.S. dollars)

Japan

Country	Total Trade
U.S.	$177,185
China*	164,420
Korea	52,754
Taiwan	46,584
Germany	30,639

United Kingdom

Country	Total Trade
U.S.	$87,234
Germany	84,118
France	60,298
Netherlands	45,371
Belgium	36,007

Moldova

Country	Total Trade
Russia	$491
Ukraine	365
Italy	199
Germany	192
Romania	188

Indonesia

Country	Total Trade
Japan	$17,831
U.S.	10,088
Singapore	9,555
China*	9,246
Korea	5,852

Israel

Country	Total Trade
U.S.	$17,349
Belgium	5,499
Germany	3,841
United Kingdom	3,523
Switzerland	2,590

Mexico

Country	Total Trade
U.S.	$249,807
China*	11,036
Japan	8,768
Germany	8,109
Spain	3,688

*Includes mainland China, Hong Kong, and Macao

Source: *Direction of Trade Statistics Yearbook 2004*, International Monetary Fund

Activity 1
Survey on U.S. International Trade

1. Circle the **three** countries below that you believe are the largest trading partners for the United States:

Brazil	Germany	Japan	South Korea
Canada	India	Malaysia	Taiwan
China	Ireland	Mexico	United Kingdom
France	Italy	Netherlands	Venezuela

2. Place a check mark (✓) in the imports (left) column in the table below to identify the **three** goods that buyers in the United States purchase most from sellers in other countries.

Goods	Imports	Exports
Computers, peripherals, and parts		
Civilian aircraft, engines, and parts		
Semiconductors		
Telecommunications equipment		
Electric generating machinery, apparatus, and parts		
Agricultural products		
Industrial supplies and materials		
Automotive vehicles, parts, and engines		
Consumer goods (nonfood such as clothes, furniture) except automotive		
Petroleum products		
Chemicals		
Building materials		

3. Place a check mark (✓) in the exports (right) column in the table above to identify the **three** goods you think sellers in the United States sell most to buyers from other countries.

Activity 2
U.S. International Trade Data, 2005

U.S. Trade (Goods) with Top 15 Countries, 2005 (millions of dollars)

Country	Exports $	Imports $	Total $, all trade*	Percentage of total trade
Brazil	15.3	24.4	39.8	1.5
Canada	211.3	287.9	499.2	19.4
China	41.8	243.5	285.3	11.1
Federal Republic of Germany	34.1	84.8	119.0	4.6
France	22.4	33.8	56.2	2.2
Ireland	9.3	28.6	38.0	1.5
Italy	11.5	31.0	42.5	1.7
Japan	55.4	138.1	193.5	7.5
Malaysia	10.5	33.7	44.2	1.7
Mexico	120.0	170.2	290.2	11.3
Netherlands	26.5	14.9	41.4	1.6
South Korea	27.7	43.8	71.4	2.8
Taiwan	22.0	34.8	56.9	2.2
United Kingdom	38.6	51.1	89.7	3.5
Venezuela	6.4	34.0	40.4	1.6
Total, Top 15 Countries	653.1	1,254.6	1,907.6	74.1
Total, All Countries	**904.3**	**1,671.4**	**2,351.3**	**100.0**

*Due to rounding, the sum of Exports $ and Imports $ does not always equal the Total $, all trade column.

Source: U.S. Census Bureau, *Foreign Trade Statistics* (http://www.census.gov/foreign-trade/statistics/highlights)

Activity 2 (continued)

Leading U.S. Exports and Imports, 2004
(millions of dollars)

Exports	Value
Foods, feeds & beverages	56,354
• Agricultural	50,742
Industrial supplies & materials (includes chemicals, paper & paper base stocks, textile supplies, building materials except metals, and metals)	203,582
• Agricultural	11,808
Capital goods except automobiles	331,091
• Civil aircraft & engine parts	50,322
• Computers, peripherals & parts	42,714
• Semiconductors	47,922
• Industrial, agricultural, & service machinery	52,710
• Electric generating machinery, electric apparatus, and parts	31,157
• Telecommunications equipment	24,481
Automotive vehicles, parts & engines	88,227
Consumer goods (nonfood), except automobiles	102,827
Petroleum products	16,661

Imports	Value
Foods, feeds & beverages	62,156
• Agricultural	46,510
Industrial supplies & materials (includes chemicals, paper & paper base stocks, textile supplies, building materials except metals, and metals)	412,220
• Agricultural	6,676
Capital goods except automobiles	343,736
• Civil aircraft & engine parts	24,554
• Computers, peripherals & parts	88,660
• Semiconductors	26,749
• Industrial, agricultural, & service machinery	62,047
• Electric generating machinery, electric apparatus, and parts	38,521
• Telecommunications equipment	29,437
Automotive vehicles, parts & engines	228,248
Consumer goods (nonfood), except automobiles	373,156
Petroleum products	180,491

Source: *Survey of Current Business*, April 2005, Vol. 85, Number 4 (www.bea.gov/bea/pubs/htm)

Activity 2 (continued)

Use the data on trading partners, exports, and imports to answer the following questions.

A. Which countries are the 5 leading U.S. trading partners?

B. How does this list compare with the list of countries from your class survey results?

C. Why do you believe the survey responses were similar to or different from the actual list of leading U.S. trading partners?

D. Why do you believe the United States would trade more with these countries than with other countries?

E. What are the leading six categories of U.S. exports?

F. What are the leading six categories of U.S. imports?

G. How do the lists of leading imports and exports compare to lists of imports and exports from the survey results?

H. What is similar about the lists of imports and exports from the trade data?

I. Do you believe these trade patterns will remain relatively constant over long periods of time? Why or why not?

Activity 3
U.S. International Trade Data, 1905

Total Trade (Goods), 1905
(millions of dollars)

Country	Exports $	Imports $	Total $, all trade	Percentage of total trade
Total, All Countries*	2,769	1,674	4,443	100.0
United Kingdom	912	256	1168	26.3
Canada	301	160	461	10.4
France	369	77	446	10.0
Cuba	76	186	262	5.9
Japan	41	99	140	3.2
Brazil	26	99	125	2.8
Germany	28	91	119	2.7
Mexico	34	78	112	2.5

***Total for all countries with which the United States traded**

U.S. Exports and Imports, 1905
(percentage of total selected commodities)

Exports	%	Imports	%
Cotton & Cotton Manufactures	39.0	Sugar	15.5
Meat	9.0	Coffee	13.6
Machinery	8.1	Hides & Skins	10.4
Coal and Related Fuels	8.0	Raw Silk	9.6
Copper & Copper Manufactures	8.0	Rubber, Crude	8.0
Petroleum and Products	8.0	Cotton Manufactures	8.0
Animal Fats and Oils	6.4	Wool & Mohair	7.4
Wheat & Wheat Flour	4.4	Fruits & Nuts	4.2
Iron and Steel Mill Products	4.1	Copper & Copper Manufactures	4.0

Source: *Historical Statistics of the United States: Colonial Times to 1970*, Part 2

Activity 3 (continued)

Use the data in the tables from Activities 2 and 3 to answer the following questions:

A. What five nations were the leading trading partners with the United States in 1905?

B. How does this list of nations compare with the leading U.S. trading partners today?

C. What might have caused this change in trading patterns?

D. What were the top five U.S. exports in 1905?

E. What were the top five U.S. imports in 1905?

F. How does this compare with the leading U.S. exports and imports today? Explain.

Activity 4
Assessment

German Trade (Goods) with its Leading Trading Partners, 2003
(millions of dollars)

Country	Exports $	Imports $	Total $, all trade
Austria	39,503	23,601	63,104
Belgium	37,477	28,939	66,416
China	20,453	28,094	48,547
France	78,504	54,764	133,268
Italy	54,757	37,795	92,552
Netherlands	46,035	49,858	95 893
Spain	36,515	18,429	54,944
United Kingdom	61,973	35,781	97,724
United States	69,009	43,626	112,635

Source: *Direction of Trade Statistics Yearbook 2004*, International Monetary Fund

Germany's Leading Exports and Imports, by Category, 2004

Exports	Imports
Machinery	Machinery
Vehicles	Vehicles
Chemicals	Chemicals
Foodstuffs	Foodstuffs
Textiles	Textiles
Metals and Manufactures	Metals

Source: www.photius.com

1. Which five nations are Germany's largest trading partners?
2. Why do you believe Germany trades more with these countries than it does with other nations?
3. Which products does Germany import and also export? Why does Germany import and export the same products?
4. What might cause Germany's trade patterns to change in the future?

LESSON SIX
THE IMPACT OF GLOBALIZATION ON TRADITION AND CULTURE

LESSON DESCRIPTION

In this lesson students investigate the impact of globalization–especially the effects of increased international trade–on local or national culture and traditions. Given a definition of culture as a shared system of behaviors and customs, students first provide examples of how their own culture has been affected by globalization. Then they explore the debate over the impact of globalization on cultures around the world, by considering a series of quotations from different observers and classifying them as either critical or supportive of greater openness to trade and globalization. Finally, students take and defend a position on this issue by writing a letter to the editor.

INTRODUCTION

Globalization has been defined as the emergence of an interdependent global economic system with growing political, technological, and cultural linkages connecting individuals, communities, businesses, and governments all around the world. Much of the debate over globalization tends to focus on its impact in the economic or political spheres. Both critics and supporters of globalization have recognized, however, that globalization has also had an impact on local and national cultures. This impact on culture is often harder to quantify than effects on prices, life expectancies, rates of economic growth, and material standards of living, but nevertheless these cultural effects can easily be identified, for good and/or ill.

Critics point to the rapid loss of local languages, art, and music as a direct consequence of globalization. They claim that local and national cultures have been "crowded out" by the proliferation of western popular culture, as typified by American music and film. They condemn the resulting homogenized world culture, in which international trade and globalization lead all nations to more closely resemble the United States.

Supporters of free trade and globalization counter that, rather than replacing local and national cultures with one, monolithic world culture, by removing barriers to the flow of goods, services, ideas, and people, globalization increases the variety of products and cultures available in all nations. That allows local and national cultures to extend beyond geographic and political boundaries that were always, in some sense, artificial. For example, when it becomes easier to trade with Morocco, or to travel to and from Morocco, people around the world are able to purchase and enjoy Moroccan art, which allows Moroccan artists to prosper and reach new audiences.

CONCEPTS

Culture
Gains from trade
Voluntary exchange
Interdependence

CONTENT STANDARDS

Voluntary exchange occurs only when all participating parties expect to gain. This is true for trade among individuals or organizations within a nation, and among individuals or organizations in different nations.

Effective decision making requires comparing the additional costs of alternatives with the additional benefits. Most choices involve doing a little more or a little less of something; few choices are all or nothing decisions.

Different methods can be used to allocate goods and services. People, acting individually or collectively through government, must choose which methods to use to allocate different kinds of goods and services.

BENCHMARKS

Voluntary exchange among people or organizations in different countries gives people a broader range of choices in buying goods and services.

To determine the best level of consumption of a product, people must compare the additional benefits with the additional costs of consuming a little more or a little less.

National economies vary in the extent to which they rely on government directives (central planning) and signals from private markets to allocate scarce goods, services, and productive resources.

OBJECTIVES

Students will:

- ♦ Define culture.
- ♦ Provide examples of the impact of globalization on students' own consumption, recreation, and other cultural activities.
- ♦ Identify arguments describing the positive and negative impacts of globalization on local and national cultures, and prepare a summary list of the arguments on both sides of the issue.
- ♦ Compose a letter to the editor in which they take and defend a position on the impact of globalization on local and national cultures.

TIME REQUIRED

90 minutes, spread over two class periods. A homework assignment is distributed in Procedure 8, and discussed in the next class period (Procedure 9).

MATERIALS

- Visual 1: What Is Culture?
- Visual 2: Universal Components of Culture
- Visual 3: Format for Letter to the Editor
- Activity 1: Defining Culture (one copy per student)
- Activity 2: Your School Culture (one copy per student)
- Activity 3: A Global Impact on Youth Culture (one copy per student)
- Activity 4: Is It Truly a Brave New McWorld? Scholars Debate the Impact of Globalization on Local Cultures (one copy per student)
- Activity 5: Quotation Cards, Part I, The Impact of Globalization on Culture (one copy per student); Part II: *Negative* Impact of Globalization on Culture (one copy per student); Part III: *Positive* Impact of Globalization on Culture (one copy per student)
- Activity 6: (Extension Activity) Information Retrieval Assignment from *Travels with Charley: In Search of America*
- Scissors and Scotch tape for each group of four students

PROCEDURES

1. Explain to students that they will be studying the impact of globalization–particularly international trade–on local and national cultures. Tell students that first,

however, it is important to define and discuss the concept of culture.

2. Display Visual 1, revealing just the word *Culture*. Ask students to suggest their own definition of culture.

3. After a reasonable number of student comments have been taken, reveal each bullet point on Visual 1 in succession, discussing each item with the students. For example, after revealing the first bullet, ask students to give some examples of cultural practices (from their families perhaps) that are passed down from generation to generation. After the third bullet, ask students what else besides language might be a "cultural universal."

4. Display Visual 2. Reiterate that anthropologists have identified a large number of components that are present in all cultures. These "universal components of culture" are:

- MATERIAL CULTURE (things a culture values, such as housing, clothing, consumer goods, etc.)
- ARTS, PLAY, AND RECREATION (celebrations, leisure activities, the arts)
- LANGUAGE AND NON-VERBAL COMMUNICATION (forms of communication unique to, or understood only by members of, the culture)
- SOCIAL ORGANIZATION (groups within the culture, including family, clans, clubs, and other organizations)
- SOCIAL CONTROL (methods used by a culture or society to maintain order, including peer pressure, government, laws, and enforcement agencies)
- CONFLICT AND WARFARE (both within the culture, such as between generations, and outside the culture, such as wars with other cultures or nations)
- ECONOMIC ORGANIZATION (firms, financial organizations, co-operatives, communes; in general terms, how a society allocates scarce resources)
- EDUCATION (how the culture passes on its customs and prepares its youth for adult roles in the society)
- WORLD VIEWS/RELIGIOUS BELIEFS (views of individual and world purpose or faith that the culture holds)

5. Distribute Activity 1. Ask students to read the introduction silently. Briefly review the universal components of culture from Visual 2 again, and explain that examples of each of these components can be found in all cultural groups. Tell students that their school could be classified as a cultural group. Ask students for an example of each of the various components. *(For example, the school's material culture might include sweatshirts or T-shirts with the school logo, and notebooks on which the school name is emblazoned. Social organizations might include school athletic and academic teams, clubs, or even the different grade levels–freshman, etc.–for different students and activities, such as junior or senior proms.)*

6. Distribute Activity 2. Ask students to work with a partner to find at least one example of each of the universal components for their school culture. Once students have identified examples for each component, ask for volunteers to provide examples for each component and use Visual 2 to record examples.

7. Distribute Activity 3. Give students several minutes to read "Global Impact on Youth Culture." Once completed, ask students how many recall the Pokemon™ craze of the late 1990s. Ask how many had (or still have) Pokemon cards or video games. Explain that, as the Pokemon example illustrates, the more the world becomes economically **interdependent**, the more likely local cultures are to be affected by products and ideas from other countries and cultures. Interdependence is the reliance on people in other places for information, resources, goods, and services.

8. Have students complete the blank chart at the bottom of Activity 3 as a homework assignment. Ask students to think about how their culture (especially music and material culture, such as clothing) has been affected by international trade and ideas from other nations and cultures. Encourage students to ask their parents to think of some examples as well, especially from earlier decades (for example, imported cars, such as the VW "bug" and many other brands of automobiles from Japan and other Asian nations).

9. Begin the next class session with a brief review of the definition of culture and the universal components of culture, and ask students to recall some specific examples from their discussion of their school culture in the previous class. Then ask students to share the results of their homework assignment. You may have to prompt students to think beyond obvious examples and explore additional examples of food, music, art, and entertainment. *(Answers might include foods such as tofu or sushi from Asian cultures, or kabobs and gyros from the Middle East and Greece; clothing such as women's fashion boots modeled after Inuit mukluks; or rave music from England.)*

10. Explain to students that many critics of globalization claim that the United States has more cultural exports that are adopted by other nations (e.g., music, language, clothing, movies, etc.) than it has cultural imports from other nations. They argue that local cultures all around the world are being crowded out by a Western, consumer culture. Other commentators strongly disagree with that view, and see globalism as a way to expose people in all nations to the different cultures of the world, through the free exchange of goods, services, and ideas.

11. Distribute Activity 4. Tell students this fictional newspaper article is based on several real publications, to provide an overview of the debate over the impact of globalization on local and national cultures. Tell students to read the article carefully, paying close attention to the arguments used by both sides. When students have completed the reading, have them answer the questions at the end of the Activity. Potential answer to these questions might include:

A. What are cultural exports? *(products from one nation that influence the culture of another)* What are some examples of cultural exports? *(music, food, clothing, movies, television programs)*

B. What are the major arguments of those who oppose cultural exports? *(Culture is becoming more homogenized, leading to a single global culture; small ethnic and national groups are losing their cultural identity; Western–primarily American–economic power is crowding out local cultures.)*

C. What are the major arguments of those who view cultural exports as positive? *(In addition to raising material standards of living, free trade provides all nations with greater access to cultural exports/imports; trade is voluntary, allowing individuals to make choices about their own culture and cultural practices with fewer constraints imposed by their geographic location (or sometimes isolation); limiting or banning cultural imports subsidizes local cultural goods, such as movies, that local consumers apparently view as inferior to the competing imported products.)*

D. In his book, *Into Thin Air*, Jon Krakauer discusses both sides of these arguments. Based on your reading of the excerpts from his book, and the rest of this article, which side of the debate do you believe Krakauer would most likely support? Defend your reasoning. *(Answers may vary, but students should draw directly on the reading to defend their responses.)*

12. Distribute Activity 5, Parts I, II, and III, and divide students into groups of four. Distribute scissors and Scotch tape. Have each group separate the quotation cards by cutting along the lines. Once the statements are cut apart, have each student read each card carefully and then, in their groups, determine whether the statement on the card was made by a critic of globalization or by someone who views its impact on culture as positive. When a majority of students in the group have reached agreement, have them tape the card to the appropriate sheet: either "*Positive* Impact of Globalization on Culture" or "*Negative* Impact of Globalization on Culture." Once this is completed, discuss results–and student reasoning–with the entire class.

Quotes for Negative Impact: 1, 2, 6, 7, 10
Quotes for Positive Impact: 3, 4, 5, 8, 9

13. When the discussion of individual quotations is completed, ask some groups to provide a summary of the arguments on the "*Positive* Impact" sheet. *(Trade increases access to cultural exports; increased access can mean increased standards of living; trade allows individuals to freely choose their cultural practices; preventing cultural exports subsidizes inferior local cultural goods.)* Ask other groups to provide a summary of the argument on the "*Negative* Impact" sheet. *(Culture is more homogenized, becoming a single global culture; people in many parts of the world, and especially in small ethnic groups or nations, are losing their cultural identity; Western–primarily American–economic power is crowding out local cultures.)*

CLOSURE

Briefly review the definition of culture and the cultural universals. Remind students that culture is often associated with a particular location or place, but it can also be influenced–as they have seen–by external forces such as trade. Ask students to think about whether their own culture (school or otherwise) has been significantly affected by globalization. Then ask them to think about how their answers might be different if they lived in France, Nepal, or some other country they chose to discuss.

EXTENSION ACTIVITY

Tell students that much like the debate over globalization, concerns have been raised in the United States about the loss of local culture–local characters and local character –stemming from the proliferation of "big box" retail stores and fast food restaurants. Tell students that, as with concerns over globalization, these debates are not new. For example, John Steinbeck wrote about these same issues more than 40 years ago in his Pulitzer Prize winning book, *Travels with Charley: In Search of America.* In it Steinbeck described his early 1960s trek across America using the then-developing interstate highway system. Steinbeck's descriptions include examples of the impact of the highway system on local cultures.

Secure a copy of Michael Watts (ed.), *The Literary Book of Economics.*[1] After distributing Activity 6, read pp. 69-74, which contains several excerpts from

[1] Michael Watts, ed., *The Literary Book of Economics*, ISI Books, Wilmington, DE: 2003.

Travels with Charley, aloud. As students listen, tell them to identify and record examples of this impact using the blank chart provided. For instance, the highway system brought access to more and better cultural products, as seen in the quote: "Even while I protest the assembly-line production of our food, our songs, our language, and eventually our souls, I know that it was a rare home that baked good bread in the old days. Mother's cooking was with rare exceptions poor, that good unpasteurized milk touched only by flies and bits of manure that crawled with bacteria…" (Watts, p. 72). The highway system also led, to some extent, to the elimination of local culture and the emergence of a single, national culture. Steinbeck described this as well: "And in their place will be a national speech, wrapped and packaged, standard and tasteless. Localness is not gone, but it is going… Traveling west along the northern routes, I did not hear truly local speech until I reached Montana" (Watts, p. 72).

ASSESSMENT

Explain to students that they will now be asked to demonstrate their understanding of the key arguments concerning the impact of globalization on local and national cultures by taking and defending a position on these issues. Tell students they must write a five-paragraph letter to the editor, following a particular format. You may want to encourage some students to send their letters to the local newspaper.

Display Visual 3 and review the format with students:

- First paragraph: *Describe the problem– in this case, the impact of globalization on local and national cultures.*

- Second paragraph: *Summarize the arguments of one side.* What arguments do critics of globalization's effects on local and national cultures use?

- Third paragraph: *Summarize the arguments of the other side.* What arguments do supporters of globalization's effects on local and national cultures use?

- Fourth and fifth paragraphs: *Outline and defend your own position on this issue.*

Visual 1
What Is Culture?

Culture

- A shared system of behaviors and customs passed from one generation to the next.
- Includes the type of language, religion, family systems, recreation, and education that a group of people share.
- Anthropologists have developed lists of cultural universals found in every culture. For example, all cultures have some unique forms of communication.
- Cultures are complex and evolving; they change over time.
- External forces can also have powerful influences on culture, including economic and political forces.

Visual 2
Universal Components of Culture

1. MATERIAL CULTURE
2. ARTS, PLAY, AND RECREATION
3. LANGUAGE AND NON-VERBAL COMMUNICATION
4. SOCIAL ORGANIZATION
5. SOCIAL CONTROL
6. CONFLICT AND WARFARE
7. ECONOMIC ORGANIZATION
8. EDUCATION
9. WORLD VIEWS/RELIGIOUS BELIEFS

Visual 3
Format for Letter to the Editor

Your Letter to the Editor must consist of a minimum of 5 paragraphs, and *follow this format:*

- First paragraph: Describe the problem–in this case, the impact of globalization on local and national cultures.
- Second paragraph: Summarize the arguments of one side. What arguments do critics of globalization's effects on local and national cultures use?
- Third paragraph: Summarize the arguments of the other side. What arguments do supporters of globalization's effects on local and national cultures use?
- Fourth and fifth paragraphs: Outline and defend *your own* position on this issue.

Activity 1
Defining Culture

Anthropologists define culture as a shared system of behaviors and customs passed from one generation to the next. These customs may include the type of language, religion, family systems, recreation, and education that a group of people share. Anthropologists have also described a set of universal components of culture, found in all cultures. For example, all cultures have customs and habits related to food and meals.

Culture is rooted in tradition, and is often associated with a particular place or location where, for example, a unique language is spoken. Cultures are complex and change over time. Some anthropologists estimate that thousands of languages have become extinct over the course of human history, and that as many as half of the 6,000 languages spoken today are in danger of becoming extinct. External forces can exert powerful influences on this type of cultural change, including economic and political forces related to increased globalization, and particularly trade with other groups and nations.

UNIVERSAL COMPONENTS OF CULTURE

1. MATERIAL CULTURE
   - housing, clothing, consumer goods, things a culture values

2. ARTS, PLAY, AND RECREATION
   - celebrations, leisure activities, the arts

3. LANGUAGE AND NON-VERBAL COMMUNICATION
   - forms of communication unique to, or understood only by members of, the culture

4. SOCIAL ORGANIZATION
   - groups within the culture, including family, clans, clubs, organizations

5. SOCIAL CONTROL
   - methods used by culture or society maintain order, including social pressure, governments, laws, and enforcement agencies

6. CONFLICT AND WARFARE:
   - within the culture (e.g., between generations) and outside the culture (e.g., wars with other cultures or societies)

7. ECONOMIC ORGANIZATION
   - firms, financial organizations, cooperatives, communes; in general terms, how a society allocates scarce resources

8. EDUCATION
   - how the culture passes on its customs and prepares youth for adult roles in the society

9. WORLD VIEWS/RELIGIOUS BELIEFS
   - views of individual and world purpose or faith that the culture holds

Activity 2
Your School Culture

On a small scale, your school represents a culture with its own customs and ways of behaving. In the chart below, identify at least one example of your school culture for each of the universal components of culture that are listed.

Universal Component of Culture	Example from Your School Culture
Material Culture	
Arts, Play, and Recreation	
Language and Non-Verbal Communication	
Social Organization	
Social Control	
Conflict and/or Warfare	
Economic Organization	
Education	
World Views/Religious Beliefs	

Activity 3
Global Impact on Youth Culture

Economic forces such as international trade can have a powerful impact on local or national cultures. For example, the Pokemon™ craze began in 1996, when a Japanese company released a Pokemon™ video game in Japan. The name comes from a shortened version of the Japanese phrase for "pocket monsters." The popularity of the video game led to a Japanese television series and a Pokemon Collectible Trading Card Game™, which also became tremendous successes in Japan.

The Pokemon phenomenon hit the United States in 1998 with the release of the original video games, the debut of the animated Pokemon television series, and the release of the English-language version of the Pokemon Trading Cards. By 2001 the Pokemon television show was the top-rated U.S. program among children aged 2 to 11. In 1999, the first of three big screen animated Pokemon™ feature films was released in North America. According to Galil Tilden, Nintendo's Vice President, "Pokemon is much more than a phenomenon. It's now a children's entertainment staple here in America and globally.... From the video games, to the toys, to the TV series, Pokemon's staying power is evident in its multifaceted appeal to its broad fan base." [2]

Clearly Pokemon, and more recently Yu-Gi-Oh™, became a major part of American youth culture. What started as a Japanese video also became a U.S. cultural phenomenon.

Think about your own school culture and the current U.S. teen culture. Can you provide an example like Pokemon of how global trade and ideas have affected these cultures? For example, have music, fashion, or other parts of these cultures been influenced by other nations or cultures?

Example:	**From (Nation or Culture):**

[2] Source: http://pokemonaholic.com/pokehistory.html

Activity 4

Is It Truly a Brave New McWorld? Scholars Debate the Impact of Globalization on Local Cultures[3]

by Staff Reporter, *The Global Courier*

Michael Jordon's famous jersey with the number 23. A McDonald's™ on a street corner in Tokyo. The latest *Spider-Man* movie shown with subtitles in Cairo. American popular music played on stereos on a street in Katmandu. Teenagers in Beijing wearing Gap™ jeans. What do these scenes all have in common? They are examples of what critics call the "exporting of American culture."

Globalization has led to a more interdependent economic system that now reaches every nation in the world. The volume of world merchandise trade increased by more than 25% between 2000 and 2004 alone. And while debate over increased globalization often focuses on economic or political spheres, critics and supporters alike have recognized that globalization has also had a major impact on local and national cultures.

In spite of improvements in life expectancies, economic growth, and material standards of living, critics argue that globalization comes with a high cost: threatening to turn the world's distinctive cultures into "one big, cheap, and gaudy strip mall."

Some scholars believe that local cultures (including native music, foods, and languages) are being "crowded out" by Western–and primarily American–cultural imports. These imports are often American popular music or clothing, or Western-style fast food restaurants.

Why is this a problem? Maude Barlow, writing in the *Earth Island Journal,* stated, "Many societies, particularly indigenous peoples, view culture as their richest heritage, without which they have no roots, history or soul. Its value is other than monetary. To commodify it is to destroy it."[4]

Jeremy Rifkin, another prominent critic of globalization, says that, "organizations representing the cultural sphere–the environment, species preservation, rural life, health, food and cuisine, religion, human rights, the family, women's issues, ethnic heritage, the arts and other quality-of-life issues–are pounding on the doors at world economic and political forums and demanding a place at the table."[5]

---

[3] Sources for this fictional newspaper article are: http://www.cato.org/pubs/policy_report/v25n3/globalization.pdf, http://www.nyu.edu/classes/stephens/Globalization%20page.htm, http://washingtontimes.com/op-ed/20051025-101032-6114r.htm, and Jon Krakauer, *Into Thin Air,* New York, Villiard. 1997

[4] See: http://www.earthisland.org/eijournal/new_articles.cfm?articleID=270&journalID=48

[5] See http://www.globalization101.org/index.php?file=issue&pass1=subs&id=119

Activity 4 (continued)

The debate itself has made it into popular culture. For example, Jon Krakauer, in his award-winning book *Into Thin Air,* described some of the cultural crowding out he observed while climbing Mt. Everest in Nepal:

> Longtime visitors to Khumbu [in Nepal, near Mt. Everest] are saddened by the boom in tourism and the change it has wrought on what early Western climbers regarded as an earthly paradise, a real-life Shangri-La.... Teens hanging out in Namche carom parlors are more likely to be wearing jeans and Chicago Bulls T-shirts than quaint traditional robes. Families are apt to spend their evenings huddled around video players viewing the latest Schwarzeneggar opus. (p. 45)

However, the impact of globalization is not all negative, as Krakauer goes on to write:

> The transformation of Khumbu culture is certainly not all for the best, but I didn't hear many Sherpas [Nepalese who work as guides] bemoaning the changes. Hard currency from trekkers and climbers, as well as grants from international relief organizations supported by trekkers and climbers, have funded schools and medical clinics, reduced infant mortality, built footbridges, and brought hydroelectric power to Namche and other villages. It seems more than a little patronizing for Westerners to lament the loss of the good old days when life in Khumbu was so much simpler and picturesque. Most of the people who live in this rugged country seem to have no desire to be severed from the modern world or the untidy flow of human progress. The last thing Sherpas want is to be preserved as specimens in an anthropological museum. (p. 46)

Krakauer summarizes the primary argument of those who view globalization as a positive force for change: that open markets and trade represent a vehicle for individuals to choose their own path, including their own culture. Similarly, Tyler Cowan, an economist at George Mason University, sees culture as a process of choices, and therefore the more choices individuals have, the better: "Markets support diversity and freedom of choice…[and] trade gives artists greater opportunity to express their creative inspiration."[3] Cowan views cultural exchanges in a gains-from-trade model, and believes that "when two cultures trade with each other, they tend to expand the opportunities available to individual artists." For example, he notes that people in London now enjoy Indian tandoori and that residents of New York eat French crepes.

Cowan also believes that, rather than leading to a single, Western-based global culture, globalization increases cultural differences. Globalization encourages trade, which means cultural imports such as music and art can be enjoyed by more people around the world. So while more people in other countries listen to American music, more people in America listen to music from other countries, too. Cowan claims trade liberates culture from geography, so that people can enjoy music, art, and food from other regions that, before globalization, were often not available.

[3] See: http://www.cato.org/pubs/policy_report/v25n3/globalization.pdf

Activity 4 (continued)

Historian Benjamin Barber believes this argument is too simplistic, because America's immense economic power makes cultural exchange inherently unequal. Barber says, "you've got to imagine the American armed with…all of the goods and brands of modern technology (and) modern commerce" as well as American military power over the globe. "That's the culture that's meeting up with some little Third World culture that's got some Navajo blankets or some fusion music that we'd kind of like to collect."[4]

Others argue that the issue is less about protecting local cultures and more about protecting local trade. The Convention on the Protection and Promotion of the Diversity of Cultural Expressions, passed by UNESCO's General Conference in October 2005, is a case in point. Helle Dale, Director of the Douglas and Sarah Allison Center for Foreign Policy Studies at The Heritage Foundation, writes that the convention agreement would "give other countries the right to keep out American cultural exports in the name of preserving their own cultures." Dale argues that, rather than protecting cultures, this agreement mainly protects European economic interests. According to Dale, "Negotiations leading to the [Convention] were inspired by desperate French efforts to keep American culture at bay," in this case movies, music, and the printed word. "The problem with globalization," Dale writes, "is that it allows French and Canadian citizens to watch American movies and buy CDs with American bands, which they do in droves like other consumers the world over." Some French and Canadian groups don't like that, and Dale reports, "my stepson asked 'Why don't they just make better movies themselves?' getting to the heart of the matter. Consumer choice and a globalized international trade means competition on a scale with which the French are deeply uncomfortable."[5]

What is the real impact of globalization on local cultures? Will a single global culture reign supreme? While the answers to these questions continue to unfold, one thing is certain: this hotly contested debate will rage on.

A. What are cultural exports?

B. What are the major arguments of those who oppose cultural exports?

C. What are the major arguments of those who view cultural exports as positive?

D. In his book, *Into Thin Air*, Jon Krakauer reports both sides of the argument. Based upon your reading of the excerpts from his book, and the rest of this article, which side of the debate do you believe Krakauer would most likely support? Defend your reasoning.

[4]See: http://www.cato.org/pubs/policy_report/v25n3/globalization.pdf
[5]See: http://washingtontimes.com/op-ed/20051025-101032-6114r.htm

Activity 5
Quotation Cards

Part 1: The Impact of Globalization on Culture

1. For Americans, cultural industries are industries like any others. For Canadians, cultural industries are industries that, aside from their economic impact, create products that are fundamental to the survival of Canada as a society. For Canada and other countries, globalization has been a phenomenon within which their distinct, non-American cultures must struggle to survive.

Source: http://www.globalization101.org/issue/culture/3.asp

2. Many governments around the world have attempted to protect their native cultures by imposing bans on what they declare to be foreign cultural intrusions. For example, the French Academy routinely scours the land for invasive words from other languages, most notably English ones. Words such as "walkman," "talk show," and "prime time" have been declared unwelcome foreigners, and the government has attempted–with rather limited success–to replace them with French substitutes.

Source: http://www.global ization101.org/issue/culture/3

3. For Paris and its friends in Ottawa, the problem with globalization is that it allows French and Canadian citizens to watch American movies and buy CDs with American bands, which they do in droves like other consumers the world over. "Why don't they just make better movies themselves?" asked my teenage stepson, getting to the heart of the matter. Consumer choice and a globalized international trade means competition on a scale with which the French are deeply uncomfortable.

Source: http://washingtontimes.com/op-ed/20051025-101032-6114r.htm

4. In most other countries, however, American cultural products are not as widespread as they are in Canada. In most cases, two general trends can be observed. First, many American cultural products tend to be popular with people of very different societies. Second, despite the popularity of American cultural products, other countries still produce a substantial number of films, music, books, and TV shows.

Source: http://www.globalization101.org/issue/culture/3.asp

5. The homogenizing influences of globalization…are actually positive; globalization promotes integration and the removal not only of cultural barriers but of many of the negative dimensions of culture. Globalization is a vital step toward both a more stable world and better lives for the people in it. – David Rothkopf, "In Praise of Cultural Imperialism," *Foreign Policy,* June 22, 1997

Source: http://www.globalpolicy.org/globaliz/cultural/globcult.htm

6. It is likely that in the future our survival and our further development will depend in an equally crucial way on the maintenance of cultural and biological diversity, but …we are seducing and trampling down other cultures all over the world. It is, in a way, monstrous.

Source: http://www.nyu.edu/classes/stephens/Globalization%20page.htm

Activity 5 (continued)

Part 1: The Impact of Globalization on Culture (continued)

7. The influence of American companies on other countries' cultural identity can be seen with regard to food, which matters on two levels. First, food itself is in many countries an integral aspect of the culture. Second, food chains can influence the mores and habits in societies where they operate. The French are proud of having a unique cuisine that reflects their culture, such as crepes and pastries. Because of their pride in their cuisine, some French people are concerned that U.S. food chains crowd out their own products with fast food. Some French people would argue that fast food does not belong in the French society and is of lower quality than their own.

Source: http://www.globalpolicy.org/globaliz/cultural/globcult.htm

8. Governments from countries like France have attempted to intervene in the functioning of the market to try to protect their local cultural industries, by taking measures such as restricting the number of foreign films that can be shown. But if a government imposes domestic films, TV shows, or books onto its people, it limits their choice to consume what they prefer. In other words, the government is effectively saying that it does not trust its people to make the choices that are right for them.

Source: http://www.globalpolicy.org/globaliz/cultural/globcult.htm

9. "There isn't any culture in the world today," says Frederic Wakeman, a UC Berkeley professor of Chinese history, "that is hermetic, sealed off by itself." It should therefore come as no surprise that we fellow *Kojak* and *Alf* watchers are also starting to think alike: about politics and economics, for example. Democratic capitalism seems very much in vogue…for the moment at least, democratic ideas do seem to be spreading along with blue jeans and *Who's the Boss?*

Source: http://www.nyu.edu/classes/stephens/Globalization%20page.htm

10. The United Nations Educational Scientific and Cultural Organization (UNESCO) has almost unanimously approved the Convention on the Protection and Promotion of Diversity of Cultural Expressions. The document, which will go into effect as soon as 30 countries ratify it, allows countries to put in place "policies and measures" to defend their cultural expressions (music, art, language and ideas) from foreign competition. The convention has met strong opposition from the United States, which fears barriers for its profitable export of music and films.

Source: http://washingtontimes.com /op-ed/20051025-101032-6114r.htm

Activity 5 (continued)

Part 2: *Negative* Impact of Globalization on Culture

Read all 10 quotation cards. In the spaces below, tape in the quotation cards you believe were written by those who view globalization's impact on local and national culture as negative.

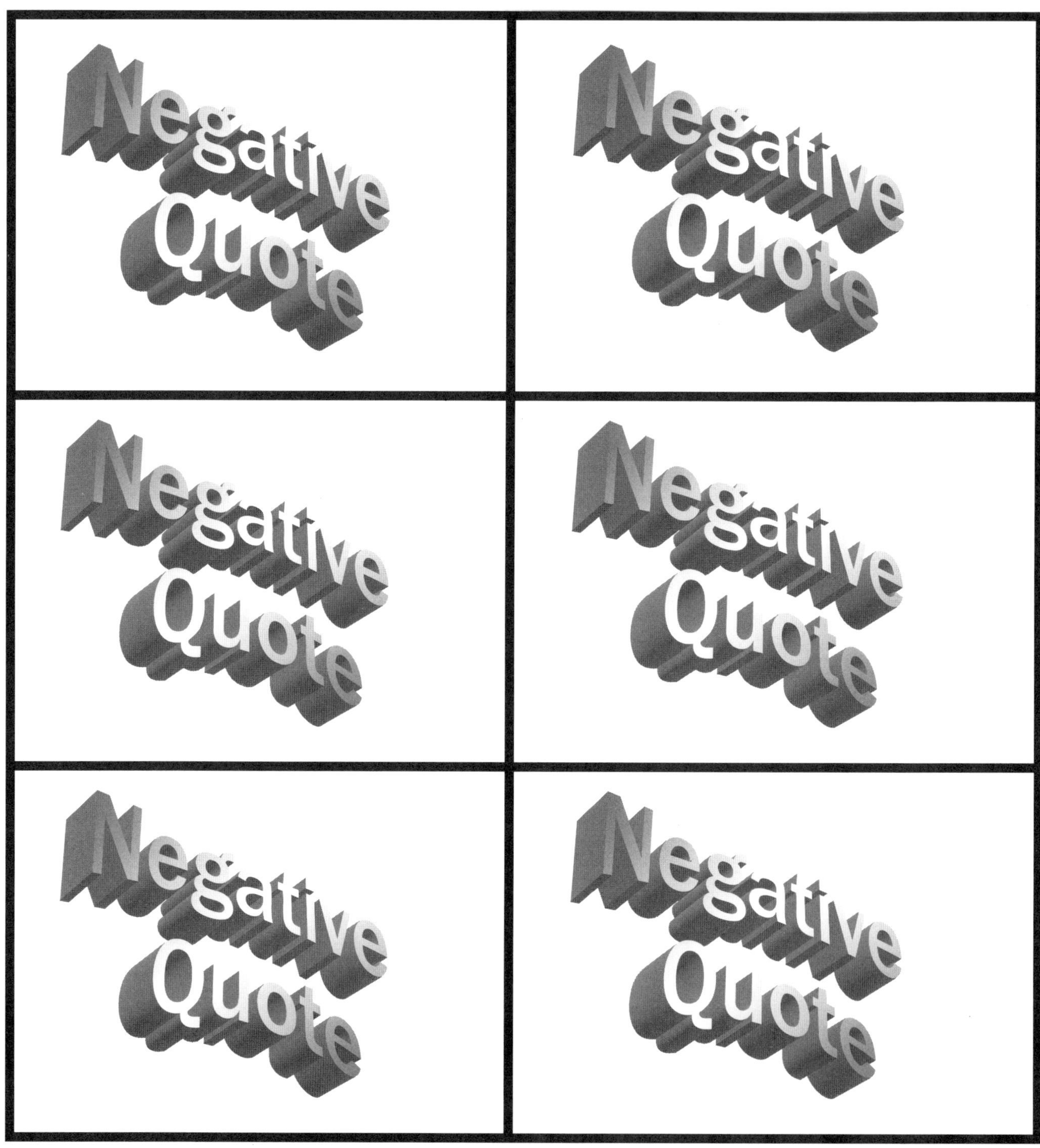

Activity 5 (continued)

Part 3: *Positive* Impact of Globalization on Culture

Read all 10 quotation cards. In the spaces below, tape in the quotations you believe were written by those who view globalization's impact on local and national culture as positive, or that are critical of arguments made by those who view the impact of globalization as negative.

Activity 6

Travels With Charley: In Search of America

The blank table below lists both positive and negative effects of globalization, as you developed in Activity 4. As you listen to the excerpts from Steinbeck's *Travels with Charley,* list at least one example or short passage dealing with the same kinds of effects of economic growth and development in the United States in the early 1960s.

Positive Impact	Example(s) from *Travels with Charley*
Increased standard of living	
Increased number of cultural choices	
Access to more and better cultural products	
Negative Impact	**Example(s) from *Travels with Charley***
Loss of local institutions (e.g., stores, restaurants, coffee shops)	
Emergence of a single, homogenized culture	

LESSON SEVEN
GLOBALIZATION AND THE ENVIRONMENT

LESSON DESCRIPTION

A demonstration activity in which teams of students simulate a production process by shelling peanuts illustrates how "spillover" problems can affect people who are neither producers nor consumers of the product, sometimes including people who live in other countries.

Dealing with international environmental problems is difficult for many reasons: national governments from many countries must agree on how to measure and deal with the effects of pollution, recognizing differences in national levels of output/income, in the amount and kind of pollution created, and in the amount of pollution people in different nations are willing to accept to maintain or increase employment and income levels. The idea that some nations may choose to become "pollution havens" is illustrated in the demonstration and analyzed.

Market-based solutions to global environmental problems are discussed in the context of the Kyoto Protocol, which deals with emissions of greenhouse gases. The lesson concludes with a review of the idea that environmental quality is a normal good, which people and nations demand more as their income levels rise.

INTRODUCTION

Pollution is a classic example of a negative externality, which imposes costs on "third parties"–people who are neither producers nor consumers of the product. If these costs are not recognized, there will be too much production of goods and services that result in pollution, and the products will be sold at too low a price. That is a difficult problem to address within a single nation, but some forms of pollution have global effects, which makes dealing with the problems even more difficult and expensive, and frequently more controversial.

Many international agreements have been proposed or adopted to deal with these issues by controlling the supply of pollutants, such as the Kyoto Protocol and the Basel Convention. Ultimately, calls for environmental quality are also affected by people's and nation's demand for cleaner air, water, and other resources that are typically not privately owned. As income in a nation rises, citizens usually demand a cleaner environment, and are willing to pay more to get it.

Policies that reduce pollution at lower costs also help, of course, and economists have long supported market-based policies for reducing pollution as more effective than across-the-board bans or limits on most forms of pollution.

CONCEPTS

Externalities
External costs
GDP
GDP per capita
Developed countries
Developing countries
Pollution havens
Market-based policies for
environmental quality

CONTENT STANDARDS

There is an economic role for government in a market economy whenever the benefits of a government policy outweigh its costs. Governments often provide for national defense, address environmental concerns, define and protect property rights, and attempt to make markets more competitive. Most government policies also redistribute income.

Voluntary exchange occurs only when all participating parties expect to gain. This is true for trade among individuals or organizations within a nation, and among individuals or organizations in different nations.

Investment in factories, machinery, new technology, and the health, education, and training of people can raise future standards of living.

BENCHMARKS

Externalities exist when some of the costs and benefits associated with production and consumption fall on someone other than the producers or consumers of the product.

When a price fails to reflect all the benefits of a product, too little of the product is produced and consumed. When a price fails to reflect all the costs of a product, too much of it is produced and consumed. Government can use subsidies to help correct for insufficient output; it can use taxes to help correct for excessive output; or it can regulate output directly to correct for over- or under-production or consumption of a product.

Economic growth is a sustained rise in a nation's production of goods and services. It results from investments in human and physical capital, research and development, technological change, and improved institutional arrangements and incentives.

Demand for a product changes when there is a change in consumers' incomes or preferences, or in the prices of related goods or services, or in the number of consumers in a market.

OBJECTIVES

Students will:

- ♦ Identify pollution as an external cost associated with the production or consumption of products, but harming people who are not producers and consumers of the product.
- ♦ Understand how market-based policies for achieving overall limits on pollution emissions, both internationally and within a nation, can reduce pollution at a lower cost than across-the-board limits on emissions by firms or nations.
- ♦ Review provisions in two international treaties that address international environmental problems.
- ♦ Explain why citizens in developing nations may accept higher levels of pollution, but over time demand a cleaner environment as average incomes rise.

TIME REQUIRED

Two one-hour class periods. In class periods of about one hour, the suggested coverage is: Period 1: Procedures 1–25; Period 2: Procedures 26–39, Closure, and Assessment.

MATERIALS

- Visual 1: International Trade in Waste and Scrap
- Visual 2: The Basel Convention on the Control of Transboundary Movements of Hazardous Wastes and Their Disposal
- Visual 3: Pollution Havens
- Visual 4: Evaluating the Pollution Haven Hypothesis (optional, for more advanced classes)
- Visual 5: Key Features of the Kyoto Protocol
- Visual 6: Kyoto Protocol Emission Targets

- Visual 7: The Three Kyoto Protocol Mechanisms
- Visual 8: Income Levels and Environmental Quality, Part I
- Visual 9: Income Levels and Environmental Quality, Part II
- Visual 10: Assessment
- A large bag of unshelled peanuts (at least 180 peanuts for each class)
- Masking tape
- Three small (8 oz.) cups
- A large blue bowl or container
- Two small tables, large enough to have 3 students sitting on one side of the table. (Push two or three student desks together to make each table, if necessary.)
- Game board money
- Small rewards to sell or auction

PROCEDURES

1. Tell the class that in recent decades international trade and globalization have led to increased production levels in many nations around the world.[1] Ask students if this increased production is entirely a good thing, or if it creates some problems, too. *(Students often see many problems, including using up nonrenewable resources –sometimes to make what they see as frivolous products–and creating more pollution, global warming, or other environmental problems.)* Tell students you will now conduct a classroom demonstration to illustrate some of the environmental issues associated with globalization.

2. Ask for or select six volunteers. Seat these students on one side of two tables facing the class so that other students can watch their actions, three at each table. On each table, mark out a square with masking tape, just large enough to hold about 50 unshelled peanuts and one of the small cups (about 6 inches square). Place one cup in each square. Tell the class the taped area represents a nut processing factory, and that each table represents a different country.

3. Tell two students in each country they will be the owners and operators of a peanut factory in their countries. Their final product is shelled peanuts, and their job is to shell peanuts and put the finished products in the cup. Tell the producers they will receive one dollar (in game board currency) for every peanut seed they shell, and that they will be able to buy rewards with the dollars they earn at the end of the lesson. Note that because each peanut shell usually contains two nuts, they will usually earn two dollars for each peanut they shell. Explain to the class that the third student at each table represents people in the country who live near the peanut factory, including many people who do not like or buy peanuts. These students will be called "the bystanders." Have the bystanders sit between the two peanut producers.

4. Give one country approximately 50 peanuts, but the other country only 10 peanuts. Ask students what this might represent. (*Different countries have different amounts of resources, including both natural resources and resources that have been produced in earlier years.)* Tell students that **gross domestic product (GDP)** is the value of all final goods and services produced in the country in one year. Final goods and services means that intermediate products used to produce other goods and services are not counted–for example a loaf of bread is the final product counted in GDP, but the value of the flour, salt, and water used to make the bread are not added to the value of the bread, because that would constitute double counting. Ask students to identify which country has the potential to produce a higher level of GDP. *(the country with 50 peanuts)*

[1] Lesson 2 of this volume illustrates this point.

5. Explain that in this demonstration, the table with 50 peanuts represents a **developed country**, characterized by high levels of production, income, and **GDP per capita** - GDP divided by the nation's population. The table with only 10 peanuts represents a **developing country**, characterized by low levels of production, income, and GDP per capita.[2]

6. Remind the peanut producers that they must shell the peanuts and put the shelled nuts into the plastic cup. Explain that they must dispose of the peanut shells somewhere on the table *outside* the factory, because peanuts shells can be hazardous to workers or to consumers who buy the shelled nuts. Tell producers in both countries they will have two minutes to shell peanuts in round 1. Conduct the production period.

7. After the production round, pay the producers with game board money. Record the amount paid in each country on the board or an overhead, under the heading Round 1.

8. Tell students they did a great job of shelling, but note that their table/country is "polluted." Tell the bystanders that if they want a cleaner environment they can collect the shells and throw them away in an "approved waste disposal unit"–which can be the classroom wastebasket. Whether the bystanders do that or not, ask the class if the bystander is being treated fairly. (*Students should recognize that the bystanders are bearing costs because of the peanut production, either in cleaning up the mess or in having to live with it, even though the bystanders are not paid as peanut producers and may not be consumers of peanuts.)*

9. Explain that this is an example of an **external cost**. An **externality** occurs when the production or consumption of a product imposes a cost or provides a benefit to a third party or bystander, who neither produces nor consumes the product. In this case an external cost was imposed by the production of the shelled peanuts, illustrating the general issue of pollution. Ask the class to discuss what could be done to correct this kind of environmental problem. (*Answers will vary–guide students toward the general idea of establishing rules or fees to reduce the amount of pollution, represented here by the peanut shells. But also point out that this will make it more expensive to produce shelled peanuts, which may mean fewer peanuts will be shelled, with production and employment levels in the peanut shelling industry decreasing.)*

10. Tell producers there will now be another round to produce peanuts, with some things remaining the same but other things changing. Remove the peanuts that were shelled in round one from the cups, and also any peanuts that were not shelled in the first round. Reset the demonstration by giving each country the same number of peanuts they had in the first round, 50 at one table and 10 at the other. Explain to the entire class that the number of unshelled peanuts the two countries are starting with has not changed, and that the production round will again be two minutes long.

11. Tell the peanut producers with 50 unshelled peanuts (and the entire class) that because of the big mess they left for the people living around the factory in the first round, their government has imposed a new regulation. For each shell the producers dispose of in their country, they must pay the bystander $1 at the end of the round. Stress to the peanut producers in this country that they only pay this "tax" if the shells are disposed of in their own country. Also remind the producers they must keep

[2] Lesson 9 in this volume covers this topic in greater depth.

the factory clean, so they cannot leave the shells in the factory to avoid the tax.

12. Tell peanut producers in the country with only 10 peanuts that because incomes are low in their country, and every manufacturing job is highly valued, they still face no tax on any pollution.

13. Ask the class what that means about the costs of producing peanuts in the two countries. (*It is now less expensive to produce peanuts in the nation where pollution is not taxed.)* Ask the class if that suggests that peanut producers in the developed country might make some kind of deal with the peanut producers in the developing nation? Give students–especially those playing the roles of peanut producers–time to think about this, and to perhaps negotiate a deal. *(Two outcomes are most likely: some unshelled peanuts could be "shipped" to the low-income country and shelled there, as long as that costs less than the tax on pollution. Or a deal might be made to ship the peanut shells to the low-income country, paying two or perhaps all three students in that country to get them to agree. As long as the peanut producers in the high-income country pay less than the tax, they gain. If the producers do not think of any solutions, ask other students in the class if they can make suggestions that at least a majority of people in both countries would accept. If necessary, offer some hints. For example, because the tax on pollution in the country with 50 peanuts is basically 50%, the developed-country producers might send 2 unshelled peanuts–containing 4 nuts–to the other country if 3 shelled nuts are returned. That reduces their cost of shelling from 50% to 25%. Or peanut shells might be shipped from the developed country to the developing country in return for almost any amount of nuts or money, as long as that costs producers in the developed country less than the tax* **and** *people in the developing country are willing to take the shells in exchange for some payment. The exact amounts will depend in part on the negotiating skills of the two groups.)*

14. Before conducting the second production round, and whether or not an agreement is made between the two countries, point out that this round illustrates the idea of globalization, with more trade between countries and policies adopted in one country affecting people in other countries, too. Many different kinds of trading agreements can take place between firms and people in different countries, as long as the parties in both countries get terms that they believe will make them better off.

15. Conduct the second production round, pay the peanut producers for what they have produced, and collect and distribute the pollution tax to the bystander in the developed country. If an agreement for payments was made between the two countries, make sure those payments are made as agreed. Record the payments to producers on the Board under the heading Round 2.

16. Ask students to compare the results of overall production and income in the two rounds. What happened? *(It may have increased, decreased, or remained the same. The number of peanuts did not change, so if all peanuts were shelled in both rounds the total production and income will be the same. The tax on pollution and the costs of negotiating deals between the two countries might lead to lower production. On the other hand, if producers learn how to shell peanuts faster and did not shell all of their peanuts in the first round, production may increase.)*

17. Was either country better off or worse off in round 2 than it was in round 1? *(Peanut producers in the developed country*

probably ended up with fewer dollars in round 2 because they either had to pay a tax or pay people in the developing country to take some of the waste. On the other hand, the bystander in the developed nation may well have less pollution to deal with in round 2, and in the real world there are more bystanders than producers of any particular product. Peanut producers in the developing country may end up better off in round 2 if they receive payments from the producers in the developing country. All three people in the developing country are likely to face more pollution, however, and the bystander may well not have been paid for that, although it is possible they were.)

18. Ask students if it is fair for people in a developing country to end up with more pollution because they are making it less expensive to produce products for consumers who live in developed nations. (*Answers will vary. Trades will occur only if there are expected gains to at least some people in both countries, but a big part of the issue is whether everyone in the developing country receives a payment or employment from the agreement, or some remain as pure bystanders. Point out that in the demonstration all three people in the developing country may receive some form of compensation, but in the real world there will almost certainly be many bystanders who do not receive direct compensation or employment. Other students may say that even if everyone in the developing country receives some compensation it is not equitable for them to live with more pollution simply because they were born in a poorer country. The question of whether people can really determine what a reasonable payment is to accept greater environmental and health risks may also arise.)*

19. Explain to the class that sometimes (but not always) in the demonstration a waste product (peanut shells) is traded. If that did not happen in your class, briefly explain how that might work, and then ask students if that kind of trade is a good thing or not. As a follow-up question, ask if developing countries should accept waste materials, or even hazardous wastes, from developed nations. *(Again, some students may note that there are gains from trade to people in both countries, while others may see that trade in hazardous waste can result in international externalities–imposing costs on some people in the country that imports the waste who were not paid to accept or employed to work with these products. In the peanut demonstration, peanut producers in the developing country may receive all of the payments for accepting the unshelled peanuts or peanut shells, which imposes costs on the bystander in the developing nation but actually benefits the bystander in the developed nation.)*

20. Explain to the class that trade in waste really does take place. Display Visual 1, which lists some examples of trade in wastes and hazardous wastes. Note that some countries recycle what would become landfill waste in another country, which generates both economic and environmental benefits. In other cases there are special problems with hazardous wastes, such as those found in computer monitors.

21. Display and discuss Visual 2, which describes the objectives of the Basel Convention, an international effort to control the flow of hazardous waste from developed to developing countries. The United States signed this agreement in 1990, but the Senate has not yet ratified the agreement.

22. Ask students why, in the peanut demonstration, the developing country might have weaker pollution control standards. *(Poorer countries may accept higher levels of pollution because they care more about jobs and incomes, which are very low.)* Display the top paragraph of

Visual 3, and explain that the term **pollution haven** is used to describe countries that accept polluting firms and industries, including some that move into the country to avoid strict and more expensive (to the firms) pollution control laws in developed nations.

23. Remind students that in round 2 of the peanut demonstration the country that tolerated more pollution and had less stringent regulations was likely to end up with more peanut shells. Review the statements on the rest of Visual 3 to explain various reasons why a country might become a pollution haven.

24. Tell students that economists today are trying to determine whether the pollution haven hypothesis is true–that is, do developing countries with lower environmental standards attract "dirty" industries. Explain that this is not as easy to determine as it might sound, because there are many reasons other than lower environmental regulations for firms that pollute to locate in developing countries, including lower wage costs.

25. (Optional step, for more advanced classes.) Display Visual 4, which explains some of the difficulties of proving or disproving the pollution haven hypothesis. Discuss each of the reasons listed, and conclude with the general point that pollution control costs are often only a small portion of firms' total costs, so decisions about where to produce a good are based on many criteria, not just pollution regulations and controls.

26. Tell students there will be a third round of peanut production to illustrate policies proposed under the Kyoto Protocol, which you will then discuss in more detail. Empty the cups of shelled peanuts and remove any remaining unshelled peanuts. Push the two tables together so that the blue container, placed on one of the tables, is easily reached by either country's producers. Give the developed country 50 peanuts and the developing country 10 peanuts.

27. Tell students that in this round you will use the peanut shells only as a symbol of an airborne pollutant that is released into the atmosphere, which is represented by the blue container. Explain that in this round all waste will be released into the atmosphere, with no tax on the waste and no trading of unshelled peanuts or peanut shells between the two countries.

28. Tell students they will again have two minutes in this round. Conduct the production round, make the payments for the production, and record the results on the board or transparency. This is the last production round, so when the class discussion is ended let students use their game board money to purchase small prizes or rewards, perhaps in an auction.

29. Focus the discussion in this round on the pollution that was released into the atmosphere. Ask the class which country created more pollution. (*the developed nation*) Ask students if allowing everyone to dump as much pollution as they want into the atmosphere/bowl is a good idea, and if not why that can happen. *(Property rights for the atmosphere, oceans, etc. are poorly defined. Resources that are owned publicly are, in some ways, not really owned by anyone. That creates an incentive to overuse and pollute those resources–sometimes called the "tragedy of the commons"–unless governments take steps to correct the problem.)* Tell students that with some pollutants everyone bears some costs, no matter where the pollution was originally created. To illustrate that, as you dump roughly equal amounts of shells on each team's table, say "What goes up must come down." Let the bystanders clean up the shells by carrying them to the wastebasket if

they choose, after reminding them that the shells are hazardous. Ask the class if it is fair for the bystanders, and especially bystanders in the developing country, to either pay to clean up or be harmed by half the pollution. *(Life is often unfair.)*

30. Ask what can be done to address these problems, and why more is not done. (*Let the discussion go on for a time in general terms.)* During the discussion, or following it, remind students that cleaning up pollution is costly, and may lead to lower production and employment levels in polluting industries. Point out that it is especially difficult and expensive to negotiate and enforce international agreements involving hundreds of different countries. People in very poor countries have few resources to devote to pollution clean up, and may well care more about increasing production, employment, and income than they do about a cleaner environment.

31. Tell students that one recent groundbreaking but controversial international agreement dealing with pollution and global warming is the Kyoto Protocol. Display Visual 5, which summarizes several key features of the treaty. Additional information on the treaty is available on webpages for the United Nations Framework Convention on Climate Change (http://unfccc.int). Review the key points listed in Visual 5:

- The Kyoto Protocol places limits (targets) on pollution levels for developed countries, which release most greenhouse emissions into the atmosphere (as shown in the last round of the peanut activity).

- Developing countries are not assigned specific limits, but are encouraged to control their emissions. That is one of the controversial features of the treaty, because some developing nations, such as China and India, are rapidly industrializing and releasing more pollutants. One reason developing countries were not given specific limits was that the limits would have make it even more difficult for those countries to grow and raise income levels for their citizens.

- The Protocol allows countries to buy or sell emission quotas. That is done by having a country that will exceed its target purchase additional emission rights from countries that will be under their targets for the year. Emissions trading is an example of **market-based policies for environmental quality.** That allows pollution to be reduced more in places where it is less expensive to do so, and in that way achieves the overall goal for pollution reduction at the lowest possible cost. Across-the-board regulations requiring the same level of pollution reduction in all countries are more expensive, because the costs of reductions are almost always higher in some nations than in others.

32. Display Visual 6. This table lists by country all the emission targets/limits that were negotiated under the Kyoto Protocol. The overall reductions average 5% of 1990 levels, and are scheduled to be attained during the period from 2008 to 2012. Explain that the United States and a few other countries (including Australia and Croatia) have signed but not ratified the treaty, so the targets are not binding in those countries.

33. Display Visual 7. Explain that the Kyoto Protocol allows and even encourages countries to work together in meeting the target level of pollution. For example, under

the joint implementation procedures of the treaty, countries can receive additional credits for reducing pollution in another developed country (for example, by updating a power plant so that it pollutes less). These credits may be earned by governments that support such projects, or by private firms. As with buying and selling pollution credits from other countries, or firms in other countries, that allows the country to pollute more in its own borders, as long as the pollution is offset by pollution reductions in the other developed country. The clean development mechanism of the treaty works in a similar way, but in this case the pollution reductions take place in a developing country. A developed country or a firm from that nation might assist a developing country by, for example, installing solar power plants in rural areas in the developing country, and receive credits that allow the developed country to pollute more at home because it has reduced pollution in the developing country.

34. Conclude the discussion on the Kyoto Protocol by noting that many environmentalists believe it does not go far enough, while many economists believe it is not the most efficient method of reducing emissions. For example, some economists recommend a tax on carbon (specifically, taxing oil or coal based on its carbon content) to discourage the use of fossil-fuels.

35. Ask students to recall what happened in the peanut shelling activity when one country taxed shell pollution and the other country did not. *(Pollution and/or waste moved to the country with no pollution controls.)*

36. Ask students what countries in the world today might be choose to become pollution havens under the terms of international environment agreements such as Kyoto and Basel on the one hand, and free trade agreements such as NAFTA and the WTO on the other. (*When the United States signed free trade agreements with Mexico, many critics of that treaty were concerned that Mexico would become a pollution haven. Today, many environmentalists are concerned about weak provisions for environmental protection in China.)*

37. Display Visual 8. Explain to the class that this curve shows a possible relationship between per capita income and pollution (environmental degradation), at income levels found in developing nations such as China. The curve suggests that as a developing country begins to grow and increase its industrial production, the quantity of pollution increases.

38. Display Visual 9. Tell students that up to the point E this is the same graph shown in Visual 8. Beyond point E, however, as per capita GDP increases, pollution levels fall.[3] This may happen for several reasons. First, as income increases public demand for higher environmental standards increases. In response, elected officials enact stricter environmental legislation. Second, as income levels rise, production in the country may move more to the production of personal and professional services. Production of basic manufactured goods often moves to other countries. Third, pollution caused by higher production levels may be offset at later stages of development if a country adopts cleaner production technologies, some of which may have been developed due to more rigorous enforcement policies for pollution.

39. Tell students that the level of per capita income at which point E lies (which may be different in different countries, and for different kinds of pollution) is something many economists have tried to estimate.

[3] Many economists call this curve the Environmental Kuznets Curve.

Generally, estimates indicate that point E lies between $5,000 and $8,000 of annual per capita GDP.[4] Stress that these are only estimates, which vary considerably, but they do suggest that environmental quality is a normal good. In other words, as income increases the public demand for a cleaner environment rises, too. But the debate continues on whether this increased demand for a cleaner environment will eventually offset the increased pollution generated by economic growth and higher production and consumption levels.

CLOSURE

Review the following key points:

- Pollution is an external cost, especially likely to affect air, water, or other resources that are not privately owned.

- Government policies can be adopted to reflect the external costs associated with pollution, but that is more difficult and expensive to do when the sources and effects of pollution are international or even global, rather than national.

- Developing countries may accept waste or produce goods that create more pollution than products produced in developed countries, because they put more emphasis on expanding employment and income to address low income levels.

- International agreements, including the Kyoto Protocol and the Basel Convention, have been developed to address some global environmental problems.

- As countries develop, they often use more resources to promote environmental quality.

ASSESSMENT

Display Visual 10, and have students write a two-page essay supporting or opposing the statement as a homework assignment.

For more advanced students, an essay could be written either supporting or opposing a famous memo written by economist Lawrence Summers when he was at the World Bank, which supported sending waste products to developing countries. The text of the memo is available at http://en.wikipedia.org/wiki/Summers_Memo.

Alternatively, have students write a paper after reading more about the provisions of the Kyoto Protocol or the Basel Convention. Information for the Kyoto Protocol can be found on the website http://unfccc.int. Information on the Basel Convention can be found at www.basel.int.

---

[4] S. Dasgupta, B. Laplante, H. Wang, and D. Wheeler, "Confronting the Environmental Kuznets Curve," *Journal of Economic Perspectives*, Winter 2002, p. 147.

Visual 1
International Trade in Waste and Scrap

The United States exported $10.5 billion and imported $3.2 billion in waste and scrap materials in 2005.

The United Kingdom exported 1.7 million tons of wastepaper to China in 2004.

Nigeria imported 400,000 used computers a month in 2005–most used only for salvage and scrap parts.

Is there a problem with trading waste and scrap?

- Some waste and scrap is recycled and turned into useful things.
- Other items, such as some electronics, contain hazardous materials that may harm the environment if not properly disposed.

Sources: U.S. data from the U.S. Census Bureau website, http://censtats.census.gov, in NAICS category 910000, Waste and Scrap. "Niche Firms Show How China Can Offer Export Opportunities," *Wall Street Journal*, Eastern Edition, November 1, 2005, p. A15. "Poor Nations Are Littered With Old PC's, Report Says," *New York Times*, Late edition, East Coast, October 24, 2005, p. C5; the report referred to is "The Digital Dump" by the Basel Action Network.

Visual 2
The Basel Convention on the Control of Transboundary Movements of Hazardous Wastes and Their Disposal

The Basel Convention is an international effort to monitor the flow of hazardous wastes. The Convention took effect in 1992, to address concerns that developed countries (or companies from developed countries) would dump hazardous waste in developing countries or the transition economies.

The main objectives* of the Convention are:

1. To reduce transboundary movements of hazardous wastes, and other wastes, to a minimum level consistent with the environmentally sound management of these wastes.

2. To treat and dispose of hazardous wastes, and other wastes, in an environmentally sound manner, as close as possible to their source of generation.

3. To minimize the generation of hazardous wastes and other wastes, both in terms of quantity and potential hazards.

The Basel Convention has been signed by 168 countries. Of these countries, only three had not ratified the agreement by February 2006: Afghanistan, Haiti, and the United States.

For more information on the Basel Convention, see www.basel.int.

* Taken from the Basil convention *Manual for Implementation*, accessed at www.basel.int/meetings/sbc/workdoc/manual.doc.

Visual 3
Pollution Havens

A **pollution haven** is a country that attracts firms and industries by allowing them to release more pollution into the environment, with low or no fines or taxes on the pollution. That reduces pollution control costs for firms, and leads to more domestic and foreign investment in "dirty" industries.

Pollution control costs for firms can be lower in some countries than others because of:

- Lower pollution control standards
- Less enforcement of pollution control standards
- Physical features (including climate and geography) or population density in some countries may result in more natural absorption of pollution, which means the costs of pollution and pollution controls will be lower

Some opponents of globalization argue that pollution-intensive industries locate their operations in nations that are pollution havens, increasing the amount of pollution released into the global environment and undermining attempts by other countries to achieve better environmental standards, controls, and enforcement programs.

Visual 4
Evaluating the Pollution Haven Hypothesis

The pollution haven hypothesis is difficult to confirm or refute because:

- Pollution control costs are, for most industries, only a small share of their total costs.

- Countries with weaker pollution control standards or enforcement programs often have lower wages or lower material costs, too. That makes it difficult to determine whether companies locate there because of less pollution control, lower wages, or both.

- Many other factors are considered when deciding where to locate a firm's international facilities, including political stability, proximity to customers or suppliers, and protection of intellectual property (such as copyrights, patents, and trademarks).

- New factories built in pollution haven countries often use modern technologies that are not as "dirty" as older factories in that country, or even in other parts of the world. That makes it harder to determine how much effect weak environmental policies really play in firms' location decisions.

Visual 5
Key Features of the Kyoto Protocol

The Kyoto Protocol is an international agreement designed to reduce greenhouse gas emissions to 5% below 1990 levels. The Protocol went into effect on February 16, 2005. As of February, 2006, over 160 countries had ratified the Protocol.

Main points:

- The Protocol covers six greenhouse gases–carbon dioxide, methane, nitrous oxide, hydrofluorocarbons, perfluorocarbons, and sulphur hexafluoride–which are believed to contribute to global warming.

- The Protocol assigns targets for developed countries, limiting their emissions of greenhouse gases, or imposing penalties if they exceed those limits.

- Developing countries are not assigned emission targets, but are encouraged to develop technologies and practices that reduce emissions of greenhouse gases.

- Countries can receive credits that count in meeting their pollution emission limits for other activities that reduce greenhouse gases, such as planting trees (to absorb carbon dioxide).

- The Protocol allows emissions trading and encourages international cooperation to help countries meet their targets for reducing greenhouse gases.

For more information on the Kyoto Protocol see: UNFCCC, *A Guide to the Climate Change Convention and the Kyoto Protocol* (revised edition), Climate Change Secretariat (UNFCCC): Bonn, Germany, 2005.

Visual 6
Kyoto Protocol Emission Targets

Countries	Target (stated as the percentage of reduction in greenhouse gasses from 1990 levels by 2008/2012)
European Union-15*, and Bulgaria, Czech Republic, Estonia, Latvia, Liechtenstein, Lithuania, Monaco, Romania, Slovakia, Slovenia, Switzerland	– 8
United States+	– 7
Canada, Hungary, Japan, Poland	– 6
Croatia+	– 5
New Zealand, Russian Federation, Ukraine	0
Norway	+ 1
Australia+	+ 8
Iceland	+ 10

\+ Countries that have not ratified the treaty as of February 2006, and are therefore not bound by the targets.

* The fifteen members of the EU prior to 1996: Belgium, France, Germany, Italy, Luxembourg, Netherlands, Denmark, Ireland, United Kingdom, Greece, Portugal, Spain, Austria, Finland, Sweden.

Source: http://unfccc.int/essential_background/kyoto_protocol/items/3145.php

Visual 7
The Three Kyoto Protocol Mechanisms

1) Joint Implementation:

Allows credits for developed countries that undertake projects to reduce greenhouse gases in other developed or transition economies. For example, the government of a developed country, or a firm in a developed country, may pay for a more efficient power plant in another developed or transition country. The country or firm is then issued credits that allow them to emit more greenhouse gases, because they have reduced emissions in another country.

2) **Clean Development Mechanism:**

Allows developed countries to help developing countries reduce their emissions. As with joint implementation, a credit is issued to the developed country or its firms, equal to the reductions in greenhouse gas emissions achieved in the developing nations.

3) Emissions Trading:

If countries release fewer emissions than their protocol target, they may sell the remaining allowances to other countries.

For more information on the Kyoto Protocol, see http://unfccc.int/, the United Nations Framework Convention on Climate Change.

Visual 8
Income Levels and Environmental Quality, Part I

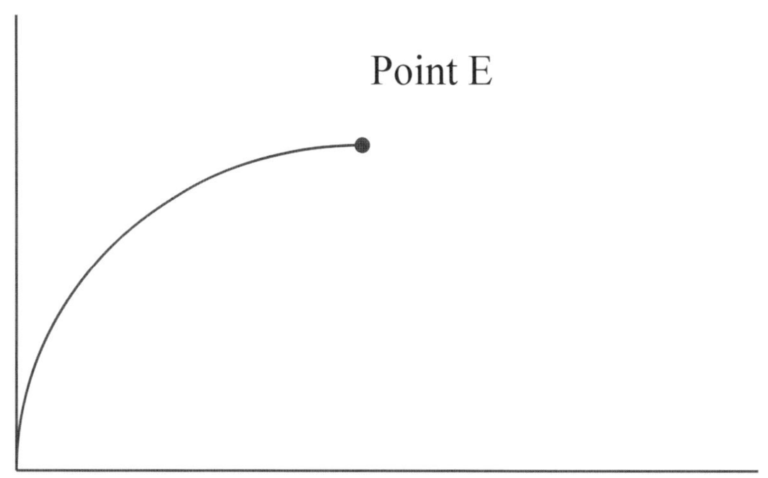

As income levels rise in developing nations, pollution may increase and environmental quality decline because:

- ⇨ Higher production levels lead to more pollution
- ⇨ There are weak environmental protection laws, regulations, and enforcement agencies (such as the U.S. Environmental Protection Agency).

Visual 9
Income Levels and Environmental Quality, Part II

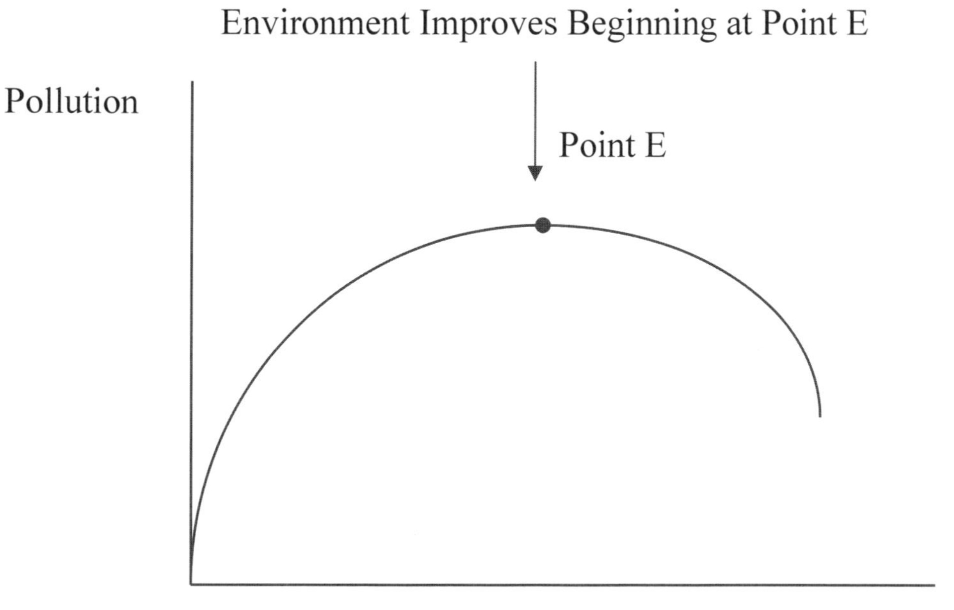

As income levels in a nation continue to rise, and living standards improve beyond some point (shown as point E above), environmental quality may begin to improve because:

- ⇨ Public demand for stronger environmental policies and enforcement increases as income levels rise
- ⇨ "Dirty" industries move to other countries
- ⇨ Technologies are developed to reduce pollution, and to dispose of remaining pollutants and wastes more safely.

Visual 10
Assessment

Write a two-page essay supporting or opposing the following statement:

"Developing countries should have the same level of pollution control standards and enforcement as the United States."

LESSON EIGHT
MIGRATION

LESSON DESCRIPTION

In an introductory activity students take the roles of people who are affected–some positively and some negatively–by the migration of skilled and unskilled workers. The economic causes and effects of migration are analyzed and discussed in relation to several important public policy issues, including the impact of immigration on wages in the United States and "brain drain" in developing nations.

INTRODUCTION

Workers' decisions to migrate to other countries, and the effects of migration in countries that experience net inflows or outflows of workers, often depend on the level of education and training of those workers. Immigration by large numbers of workers with low levels of education and training may decrease wages for unskilled workers, increasing public expenditures for programs that assist low-income families. The United States and other developed nations also experience immigration of highly educated and skilled workers. When those workers come from poorer, developing countries that raises questions related to the issue of "brain drain." With both types of immigration, native-born workers face increased competition in labor markets.

As shown in other lessons in this volume, international trade in goods and services increases overall levels of production, consumption, and the standard of living, but hurts some groups who face increased competition from foreign producers, at least in the short run. The same general pattern holds true for the immigration of both skilled and unskilled workers.

CONCEPTS

Human capital
Skilled workers
Unskilled workers
Emigration
Immigration
Brain drain

CONTENT STANDARDS

People respond predictably to positive and negative incentives.

Prices send signals and provide incentives to buyers and sellers. When supply or demand changes, market prices adjust, affecting incentives.

Income for most people is determined by the market value of the productive resources they sell. What workers earn depends, primarily, on the market value of what they produce and how productive they are.

BENCHMARKS

Acting as consumers, producers, workers, savers, investors, and citizens, people respond to incentives in order to allocate their scarce resources in ways that provide the highest possible returns to them.

A wage or salary is the price of labor; it usually is determined by the supply of and demand for labor.

People's incomes, in part, reflect choices they have made about education, training, skill development, and careers. People with few skills are more likely to be poor.

Changes in the prices for productive resources affect the incomes of the owners of those productive resources and the combination of those resources used by firms.

As a result of growing international economic interdependence, economic conditions and policies in one nation increasingly affect economic conditions and policies in other nations.

OBJECTIVES

Students will:

- Explore the economic incentives that lead to migration, and also identify some non-economic factors, such as armed conflicts, persecution of minority groups, or reuniting families.
- Describe the difference between skilled and unskilled workers, and compare and contrast the effects of immigration by skilled and unskilled workers.
- Explain who is harmed and who is hurt by the migration of skilled and unskilled workers, and analyze the overall economic effects of immigration and emigration on national economies.
- Define and discuss the causes and effects of "brain drain."
- Illustrate the impact of immigration on wages using a supply and demand diagram in an optional extension activity.

TIME REQUIRED

Two one-hour class periods: Period 1: Procedures 1 – 19; Period 2: Procedures 20 – 34 and Closure. The assessment may be done as a homework assignment. If it is done using a debate format that is also described in the lesson, an additional 30 minutes of class time is required.

MATERIALS

- Visual 1: U.S. Immigrants by Class of Admission, 2004
- Visual 2: U.S. Annual Caps (Limits) and Total Admissions on Temporary Worker Visas
- Visual 3: Effects of Immigration on U.S. Wages in the 1980s and 1990s
- Visual 4: Brain Drain: Costs and Potential Benefits to Source Countries of Emigration by Skilled Workers
- Visual 5: Brain Drain Data for Selected Countries
- Visual 6: Physicians: Have Visa, Will Travel
- Visual 7: Numbers of Skilled Migrants in OECD Countries, 2000

Note: Visuals 8 and 9 are used in an optional extension activity:

- Visual 8: Supply and Demand of Labor in Host Country, Before and After Immigration
- Visual 9: Supply and Demand of Labor in Source Country, Before and After Emigration

- Activity 1: Migration and My Story: Part I, Instructions and Interview Information Form (one copy per student); Part II, Role Cards: one or two copies of 24 role cards, cut apart, to give one role card to each student

PROCEDURES

1. Ask students if they or anyone they know were born in a different country. *(It is very likely that at least one of the students, or a student's parent, or someone the students know was born in another country. Even if that is not the case, point out that for the vast majority of families living in the United States today, their ancestors came to this country from other parts of the world.)*

2. Explain that the United States is often described as a nation of immigrants, or as a melting pot, salad bowl, or some other image representing a mix of people from different backgrounds and many nations. That is not true in many other countries, and in fact the United States has the largest migrant population of any nation in the world, with over 31 million people who were born in other countries. That represents over 11 percent of the U.S. population.[1] Define **immigration** as a person entering a nation different from their native country, to live and possibly work in the new nation permanently, or at least for a long period of time. Define **emigration** as a person leaving their native country to take up residence in another country.

3. Ask students why people migrate to the United States. *(Answers may include higher wages, political or religious freedom, reuniting with family members who migrated earlier, or other reasons.)*

4. Display Visual 1, which shows the number of people who became legal, permanent residents of the United States in 2004, categorized by their class of admission. Note that for many categories there are legal limits on the annual number of immigrants allowed to become permanent residents in the United States. The categories in the table indicate some of the different reasons immigrants are allowed into the United States. But point out that while some immigrants may be allowed to enter the country for "family" reasons, there may well still be an economic motivation for their migration. Provide the official definitions for some of the terms used in table: An immediate relative is a spouse, parent, or minor child. Family-sponsored immigration uses a wider definition of family than immediate relatives, including the adult children of citizens, spouses and children of permanent residents, and the brothers and sisters of adult U.S. citizens. The diversity program is also referred to as the lottery, because those who receive permanent resident status under this program are chosen at random from all eligible applicants. Asylees are refugees already in the United States. Refugees are people living outside their native countries who are unable to return to those countries because of persecution, or fear of future persecution.

5. Explain that it is difficult for people from other countries to become a permanent resident of the United States, or many other developed nations, such as Canada and countries in western Europe. To immigrate to the United States, you must be related to a U.S. citizen or resident, or be one of a limited number of immigrants allowed for other reasons. Ask students why immigration to the United States is limited and so difficult. *(Students may answer to protect jobs or keep wages high, or for national security reasons. Others may say to protect American culture.)* Reinforce that there are many reasons, but that loss of jobs or lower wages concerns many kinds of workers and their families.

6. Ask students which of the following people should be allowed to immigrate to the United States: a doctor, a computer programmer, a construction worker, or an agricultural worker. *(Answers will vary. Some students will say none, some will say all. Some will say the doctor and the computer programmer.)* Ask students who say they would admit the doctor or computer programmer why they would allow immigration for workers with these occupations. *(Doctors and computer programmers are well educated, with skills that allow them to find jobs that pay well.)*

---

[1] Nolan Malone, Kaari F. Baluja, Joseph M. Costanzo, and Cynthia J. Davis, *The Foreign-Born Population: 2000.* U.S. Census Bureau: Washington D.C., Document C2KBR-34. December 2003.

7. Tell students that most countries have adopted immigration policies that are at least partly based on workers' occupation or skill level. Define **skilled workers** as workers with "some special knowledge or (usually acquired) ability in [their] work."[2] In many contexts, and as used in this lesson, the definition implies education beyond high school. Define **unskilled workers** as workers with no special knowledge or ability.

8. Display Visual 2, which shows the number of temporary worker visas issued by the United States in 2006, and the number of actual admissions in 2004 based on the admission class. Explain that these visas allow workers to enter the United States and work for a limited period of time, but not to establish permanent residence. These visas may allow workers to work in the United States for more than one year but generally no more than 3 years. The visas may be extended, but not indefinitely (up to 6 years in total for the H1-B visa, for example). Admissions are higher than the cap limits because visa-holders can enter the country more than once in a year, and frequently do.

9. Stress the difference between permanent residence status for immigrants, shown in Visual 1, and the Temporary Worker Visas shown in Visual 2. Explain that the H1-B visa is for highly paid workers, including many with advanced levels of education (college professors or engineers, for example). The H2 visa (H-2A for agricultural workers and H2-B for non-agricultural workers) is for workers in U.S. industries or occupations facing shortages of workers, either year round or in certain seasons of the year (such as construction and agriculture). Like the permanent workers shown in Visual 1, the numbers of these temporary workers allowed into the United States are limited by law. (Note: U.S. immigration policies and related information can be found at the website for U.S. Citizenship and Immigration Services, http://uscis.gov.)

10. Tell students that although family reunifications and other reasons for migration are important, in this lesson you will be focusing on economic reasons. Ask students to identify again the key economic reasons people migrate to the U.S. *(Higher wages, benefits, public services, etc–in general terms a higher standard of living.)*

11. Ask students why some immigrants–such as doctors–earn high salaries in the United States while others–such as agricultural workers–earn very low wages. *(Doctors have extensive education and specialized skills, so they earn more than workers with less education and fewer skills, whether they were born in the United States or some other country.)*

12. Tell students that immigrants bring with them different amounts of human capital. Define **human capital** as the knowledge or skills acquired by workers through education or on-the-job training and experience. Tell students that the loss of any worker represents a loss of resources to a country, but if a worker has a high amount of human capital (is skilled), this represents a particularly large loss to the worker's home country, and a large gain to the host country.

13. Explain that immigration and emigration are increasingly important in today's global economy. Many people are affected by migration, including those who migrate and other workers in countries that experience net inflows or outflows of workers due to immigration or emigration. At the heart of the economic impacts of migration is the effect migration has on the wages of workers. Immigrants move to seek higher wages, but workers in countries that

[2] From en.wikipedia.org.

experience immigration do not like competing with immigrant workers because their wages are lower than they would be without the immigration. Migration also affects tax revenues and public expenditures in countries that experience significant levels of immigration or emigration. And of course illegal immigration is a controversial issue in many countries, for both economic and national security reasons.

14. Give each student a role card from Activity 1. There are 24 role cards, so in larger classes duplicate two copies of some of the cards, as necessary, and let two students represent the same kind of worker. Each card contains a brief description of someone who is affected by migration in a particular way. Tell students that they will act out that role in the following activity.

15. Distribute copies of the instructions and interview sheet from Activity 1. Explain that in the activity, in addition to taking their assigned roles in talking with other students, each student is also expected to interview five other students whose cards are different from theirs. When students are interviewed, they should describe who they are and how migration has affected their lives. If the person being interviewed is a migrant, the reasons for their migration should be investigated. Explain that not every card for migrants provides detailed statements on the person's reasons for migrating. In those cases, students should be prepared to improvise a story to explain why they migrated, with the explanation related to employment opportunities in the country they left, or the country they entered, or both.

16. Tell the class that each time an interview is conducted the interviewer should record the card # and the home country of the person being interviewed in the first column of the Interview Information Form. Summarize the most important statements made by the person being interviewed relating to the effects labor migration has had on their lives in the middle column of the Interview Information Form. There are five rows on the form, with one row for each person who is interviewed.

17. Immediately after completing each interview, the interviewer should write Yes or No in the third column of the Interview Information Form, to indicate whether they believe the person they just interviewed would support or oppose laws, regulations, and other public policies that would make it easier for people to migrate to the United States

18. Tell students they will have about 20 minutes to do the interviews. Remind them that during this time other students will be interviewing them, too. Conduct Activity 1.

19. Based on what they learned from their interviews, ask students to discuss who gains and who loses from immigration. Either before the discussion begins or as it unfolds, provide definitions of the following terms:

> Host country–the nation in which an immigrant resides.
>
> Home, source, or native country–the nation from which an immigrant came.
>
> Remittances–money sent by migrants to their home countries. This idea is mentioned on cards #9 and #14. Remittances are an important form of financial transfer payments in many developing countries.
>
> Returnees–immigrants who return to their home country, a process also known as reverse migration.

Returnees are mentioned on card #13.

Summary of activity cards showing those helped or hurt by migration:

People helped *(card numbers are shown in parentheses):*

- *Immigrant workers, both skilled (#1, #3, #15) and unskilled (#4, #5, #20)*
- *Family, employers, workers, and others in home country who benefit in some way from those who emigrate (#9, #11, #12, #13, #14)*
- *Employers of immigrant workers in host countries (#6, #10, #23)*
- *Consumers of goods produced in host countries by immigrant workers (#18)*
- *Businesses in host countries that benefit from expanded production and sales due to immigration (#21, #22)*

People harmed *(card numbers are shown in parentheses):*

- *Native-born workers in host countries who compete for jobs with immigrant workers (#2, #7, #16, #17, #24)*
- *People in home countries of emigrants who are harmed by the departure of workers, especially skilled workers (#8)*
- *Governments in host countries that must provide extra services for growing populations (#19)*

20. Again based on their interviews in the activity, ask students to discuss the main reasons that immigration is restricted in the United States. *(Lower wages for some native-born workers is the most frequent economic issue mentioned in actual surveys, but costs of government services and security or cultural issues may also be mentioned. Remind students that this activity focuses on economic issues.)*

21. Display Visual 3, which shows estimates of how immigration affected U.S. wages during the 1980s and 1990s. Explain that the percentages shown are estimates of how much lower wages in the United States were with the immigration that occurred in this period than they would have been if no immigration at all had been allowed. That does not mean that wages actually decreased for all of these groups–the estimates suggest that wages would have been this much higher if the supply of labor in these occupations had not been increased by immigration.

22. Ask students why the United States allows any immigration if the result is to lower wages of native-born workers. *(In some cases there were shortages of labor in occupations filled by immigrant workers, as depicted on cards #10 and #23. But even in occupations where there were not shortages, the decrease in wages is not the only effect of immigration. Lower wages also mean that firms' costs of production fall, which leads firms to increase output and lower prices for the goods and services consumers buy, as noted on card #18. The decrease in wages from immigration may be only a short-run effect, which might be completely or at least partially eliminated in the long run by economic expansion and growth. Some of the positive effects of more employment and production are noted on cards #10, #21 and #22. This expansion increases the demand for labor over time, which increases wage rates and employment of native-born workers.)*

23. Tell students that now you will focus on the migration of unskilled workers. Thinking about the examples in the role-playing interviews involving unskilled immigrants, ask students to list the advantages and disadvantages of the United

States allowing more unskilled immigration. *(Advantages include lower wages and perhaps higher profits for firms hiring these workers, as on card #23 and possibly #6. Another advantage is lower prices for consumers who buy goods produced by these firms, as on card #18. Disadvantages may be lower wages or fewer jobs for native unskilled workers, as on cards #7, #17, and #24. Card #24 describes a worker who is close to retirement, who may not have time to acquire skills for another job or occupation. Another disadvantage is increased spending for government services for a larger population, as on card #19.)* Point out again that although immigration may lower wages for some workers in the short run, it also promotes economic growth, which increases future production, consumption, and income, including wages.

24. Now ask students to focus on the immigration of skilled workers. Explain that because skilled migrants take a large quantity of human capital with them when they leave their home country, the issues of skilled worker migration have become more important with globalization in recent decades. Many countries have become more active in trying to attract skilled workers as immigrants, or in trying to keep skilled workers from emigrating. Ask students to list the advantages and disadvantages of the United States allowing more skilled immigration. *(Skilled native workers may face lower wages, as depicted on card #2 and Visual 3. But skilled workers also provide valuable services and other benefits to the economy, as shown on card #10. Even the underutilized skilled worker on card #15 is providing a service. Expansion of industries that hire skilled workers may also benefit other businesses, as described on cards #21 and #22.)*

25. Ask students if they believe the benefits of immigration by skilled workers are greater than the benefits of immigration by unskilled workers. *(Students will probably note that skilled workers are paid more. They produce more valuable services, and so they increase production, consumption, and income levels more. Also, because skilled workers are usually in occupations featuring more use of technology, a country may find that immigration by skilled workers helps it expand in high-tech industries.)*

26. Contrast the benefits of the immigration of skilled workers with the costs of emigration by skilled workers, particularly from developing countries. In those nations, where skilled workers are already scarce, emigration on a large scale can have a serious impact. Tell students the popular term for skilled workers leaving a country is **brain drain**. Ask students if any of their roles were examples of brain drain or examples of people adversely affected by brain drain. *(Cards #1, #3, and #8)*

27. Ask students if there are any benefits to the source country of having skilled workers emigrate. *(Actually, yes. Based on their cards, students may point out that emigrants sometimes provide remittances to their home countries [card #14], that some may eventually return to their home country with even more human capital [card #13], that skilled emigrants may facilitate business relations between the home and host countries [card #11], or that the economic benefits of emigration may inspire more people to invest in education–including some who may not emigrate [card #12].)*

28. Display Visual 4. Summarize the idea of brain drain and review the costs and potential benefits.

29. Point out again that, despite some potential benefits from emigration of skilled workers, brain drain can be a serious problem in developing countries. Display

Visual 5, and explain that it illustrates the high proportion of a developing country's skilled workers who may chose to leave their home countries.

30. Display Visual 6, which lists countries that have lost a high percentage of physicians to emigration. Ask students why people and political leaders in these countries might be especially concerned about the loss of physicians. (*Many developing countries face shortages of doctors, which affects the availability and cost of health care, and the treatment of many diseases that have basically disappeared in many developed nations [card #8].*) Ask students if they believe that the potential gains to brain drain might offset the losses. *(With skilled workers, the loss to the source country is significant and immediate. However, some students might suggest that over time remittances and business opportunities fostered by emigrants working in other nations may eventually offset the initial losses.)*

31. Ask students to speculate which countries are most likely to experience immigration by skilled workers. *(Answers will vary.)* Display Visual 7, which shows that the United States has the largest net immigration (in absolute numbers) of skilled workers, defined in this case as workers with more than 12th grade education.

32. Ask students why the United States and other developed nations attract skilled and unskilled workers from other nations. *(Higher wages, more opportunity, greater security.)* Ask why wages are so high in the United States, Western Europe, etc. *(High wages are based on high levels of labor productivity. Labor productivity is high in nations where technology and capital resources–including both physical capital and human capital from education and training–are highly developed. Stable government policies and public infrastructures–such as roads, schools, and legal systems–are also important.)*

33. If you choose to show the effects of migration using a simple graphical (supply and demand) framework, do the Extension Activity that appears below, following the Assessment section, at this time.

34. Conclude the discussion by noting that some people benefit from migration, but others do not, in both host and home or source countries. That often makes immigration a contentious issue in both kinds of countries, even though the overall effects of immigration are to provide more resources in the economies of the host countries, raising overall levels of production, consumption, and income.

CLOSURE

Review the lesson with students using the points below.

- Many immigrants move to another country to seek higher wages or income. Some also move for other reasons, such as greater political freedom, personal safety, or reuniting families.

- Native-born workers in host countries compete with immigrant workers in both skilled and unskilled occupations, which results in wages lower than they would be with no immigration, at least in the short run.

- In part because immigration can lower wages, the United States restricts the number of immigrants.

- Businesses in host countries gain from immigration by having a larger supply of workers (skilled and unskilled) and paying lower wages.

- Consumers in host countries gain from immigration. More output is produced because of lower labor costs, which lowers prices.

- Developing countries are hurt by brain drain–the loss of skilled workers. Some of these costs are offset by remittances, returnees, and an increase in the number of people who pursue post-secondary education, including some who chose not to emigrate.

ASSESSMENT

Option 1: Short essay. Have students choose one of the three topics listed below and write a one-page essay on the subject. Tell students to take one side of the argument or the other and defend their position.

Option 2: Debate. Divide the class into teams of four. Assign the teams topics to debate. In each team of four have two students support the statement, while the other two oppose the statement. Give teams time to outline their ideas. Give each team member one minute to express their point of view, beginning with a student on the team that supports the statement and then alternating sides until all four students have spoken.

Topics:

Topic A: Bill Gates advocates allowing more migration of skilled workers. He believes the 2006 cap on the H1-B visas of 65,000 is too low: "The whole idea of the H1B visa thing is, don't let too many smart people come into the country. The thing, you know, basically doesn't make sense. And you can't imagine how tough it is to plan as a company where we say, 'OK, well, let's have this engineering group and staff it.' Well, the visas run out." Bill Gates in a panel discussion on April 27, 2005 (www.microsoft.com/billgates/speeches/2005/04-27MSRTechPanel.asp).

Based on the class interview activity and discussion of migration, explain why you agree or disagree with Bill Gates on this issue.

Topic B: Based on the class interview activity and discussion of migration, explain why you agree or disagree that the United States should allow more unskilled workers to enter the United States as immigrants, especially to help the U.S. agricultural and construction industries.

Topic C: Based on the class interview activity and discussion of migration, explain why you agree or disagree with the idea that the United States should restrict the number of foreign-trained physicians entering the United States, considering the effects in the United States and the issue of brain drain in developing countries.

EXTENSION ACTIVITY

The basic framework for this lesson can be shown easily using simple supply and demand models, as presented in Visuals 8 and 9. To illustrate the concern about wages decreasing in host countries that experience immigration inflows, display Visual 8. Point out that initially immigration will increase labor supply and decrease the wage rate. Total employment increases because employers hire more workers at the lower wage, but some native-born workers will drop out of the labor market. In Visual 8, the difference between the 130 million workers hired at the wage of 8 and the 100 million jobs that are supplied by native workers will be filled by immigrants.

To consider the effects of migration on source or home countries, display Visual 9 and explain that emigration reduces the supply of labor. Wages increase, so firms hire fewer workers. In developing countries, these effects may be substantially different for skilled and unskilled workers. The wage increase is likely to be quite small for unskilled workers, and in extreme cases where wages are at or near subsistence levels they might not rise. For skilled workers, a higher wage may not increase the number of workers who have the necessary training, so quantity supplied may increase very little and very slowly after wages rise. But note that in most cases, over time, migration will tend to reduce wage differences in host and source countries.

Visual 1
U.S. Immigrants by Class of Admission, 2004

Class of Admission	Number of Immigrants
Classes with Annual Numerical Limits:	
Family-sponsored preferences	214,355
Employment-sponsored preferences	155,330
Diversity programs	50,084
Asylees	10,016
Others	2,588
Total with Numerical Limits:	**432,373**
Classes not Subject to Annual Numerical Limits:	
Immediate relatives of U.S. citizens	406,074
Refugees	61,013
Others	46,682
Total without Numerical Limits:	**513,769**
TOTAL	**946,142**

Source: United States Department of Homeland Security, *Yearbook of Immigration Statistics: 2004*. Washington, D.C.: U.S. Department of Homeland Security, Office of Immigration Statistics, 2006, p. 16.

Visual 2
U.S. Annual Caps (Limits) and Total Admissions on Temporary Worker Visas

Visa Class	Annual Cap 2006	Total Admissions 2004
H1 - B: Occupations with highly skilled workers	65,000	394,686
H2: Occupations in industries with peak load or seasonal employment demands	66,000	109,099

Actual admissions are larger than the cap (limit) because:

* **Workers may enter the country more than once in a year**

* **Visas are often issued for multiple years, and may be renewed**

* **Caps for H1-B visas were higher in years before 2004**

Source: United States Department of Homeland Security, *Yearbook of Immigration Statistics: 2004*. Washington, D.C.: U.S. Department of Homeland Security, Office of Immigration Statistics, 2006, p. 101.

Caps information from U.S. Citizenship and Immigration Services website at http://uscis.gov/graphics/services/tempbenefits/cap.htm.

Visual 3
Effects of Immigration on U.S. Wages in the 1980s and 1990s

Education Level	Percentage Change in Wages
High School Dropout	-8.9
High School Degree	-2.6
Some College	-0.3
College Degree	-4.9

Source: George Borjas, "The Labor Demand Curve Is Downward Sloping: Reexaminining the Impact of Immigration on the Labor Market," *Quarterly Journal of Economics*, November 2003, p. 1369.

Visual 4

Brain Drain: Costs and Potential Benefits to Source Countries of Emigration by Skilled Workers

I. Costs

- The loss of services of a highly skilled worker. For example, emigration by physicians creates significant losses in some developing nations.
- The cost of training replacement workers is very high, especially considering low income levels in developing nations.

II. Potential Benefits

- Remittances sent by emigrants provide income for households and may be used to promote enterprises within the country.
- Emigrants may provide information, ideas, or other opportunities for businesses in their home countries to do business with firms in their host countries.
- Returnees may start businesses in their home country after acquiring skills and business experience abroad.
- Opportunities to emigrate provide stronger incentives for people to pursue education and training, including some who then chose not to emigrate.

Visual 5
Brain Drain Data for Selected Countries

Countries with Highest Percentage of College-Educated Citizens Living Abroad*

Country	Percentage
Haiti	83.6
Ghana	46.9
Mozambique	45.1
Kenya	38.4
Laos	37.4
Uganda	35.6
Angola	33.0
Somalia	32.7
El Salvador	31.0
Sri Lanka	29.7

*** Considers only countries with populations of more than 5 million people.**

Source: Frederic Docquier and Abdeslam Marfouk, "International Migration by Educational Attainment," in Caglar Ozden and Maurice Schiff, eds., *International Migration, Remittances and the Brain Drain.* Washington, DC: The International Bank for Reconstruction and Development (World Bank): 2006, p. 176.

Visual 6
Physicians: Have Visa, Will Travel

Country or Region	Emigration Effect
Sub-Saharan Africa	**13.9**
Ghana	30.0
South Africa	18.5
Indian Subcontinent	**10.7**
Sri Lanka	27.5
Pakistan	11.7
India	10.6
Caribbean	**8.4**
Jamaica	41.4
Haiti	35.4
Dominican Republic	17.2
Middle East and North Africa	**5.2**
Lebanon	19.3

The emigration effect is calculated as the number of physicians from the listed country or region who are currently working in one of four nations (the United States, United Kingdom, Australia, or Canada), divided by the total number of physicians from that country (working either in their home country or as immigrants in the four developed nations). It therefore suggests the percentage of a country's physicians who are working abroad, although some physicians might have emigrated to other countries.

Source: Fitzhugh Mullan, "Metrics of the Physician Brain Drain," *New England Journal of Medicine*, October 27, 2005, pp. 1810-1818.

Visual 7
Numbers of Skilled Migrants Working in OECD Countries, 2000*

Country	Number of Skilled Immigrants (in millions)
United States	10.3
Canada	2.7
Australia	1.5
United Kingdom	1.2
Germany	1.0
France	0.6

*Skilled workers are defined here as those with more than a 12th grade education. The member nations of the OECD (Organization for Economic Cooperation and Development) are Australia, Austria, Belgium, Canada, Czech Republic, Denmark, Finland, France, Germany, Greece, Hungary, Iceland, Ireland, Italy, Japan, Korea, Luxemborg, Mexico, Netherlands, New Zealand, Norway, Poland, Portugal, Slovak Republic, Spain, Sweden, Switzerland, Turkey, United Kingdom, and the United States.

Source: Frederic Docquier and Abdeslam Marfouk, "International Migration by Educational Attainment," in Caglar Ozden and Maurice Schiff, eds., *International Migration, Remittances and the Brain Drain.* Washington, DC: The International Bank for Reconstruction and Development (World Bank), 2006, pp. 182-183.

Visual 8

Supply and Demand of Labor in Host Country, Before and After Immigration

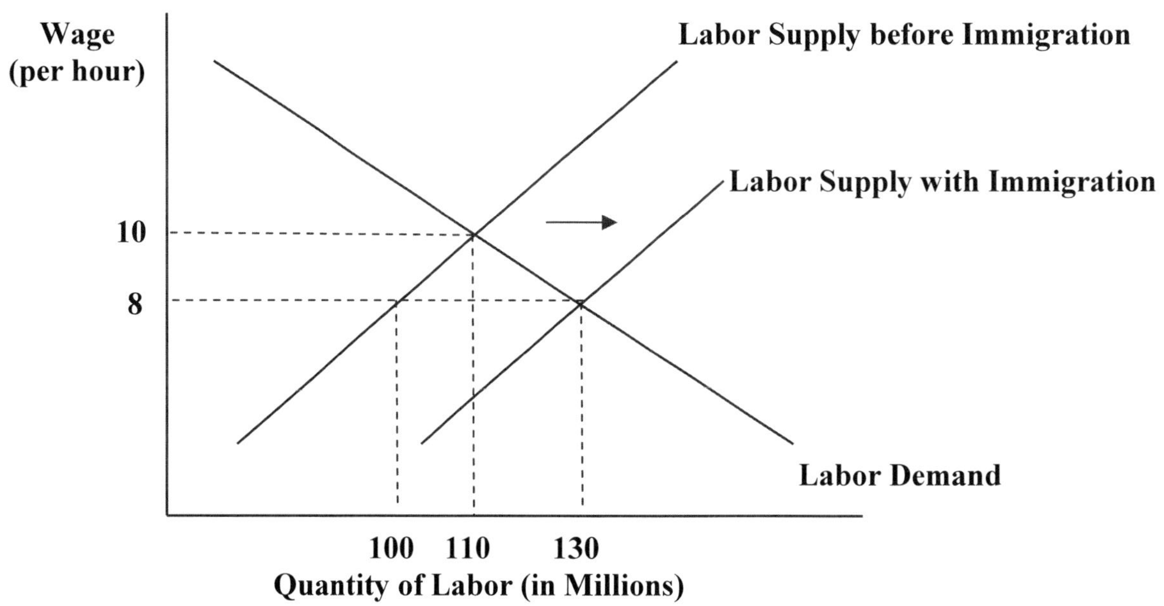

- When immigrants enter the labor market, the supply of labor increases (shifts right). The wage rate decreases from 10 to 8.

- At the lower wage, the total number of workers hired increases from 110 million to 130 million, but the number of native workers willing to work decreases from 110 million to 100 million. The "gap" between the 130 million workers hired at the new wage and the 100 million native workers willing to work is filled by 30 million immigrant workers.

- Firms that hire these workers benefit because the lower wage means their production costs have decreased.

- With more total workers employed, more output is produced and sold at lower prices. Consumers benefit from the lower prices.

Visual 9

Supply and Demand of Labor in Source Country, Before and After Emigration

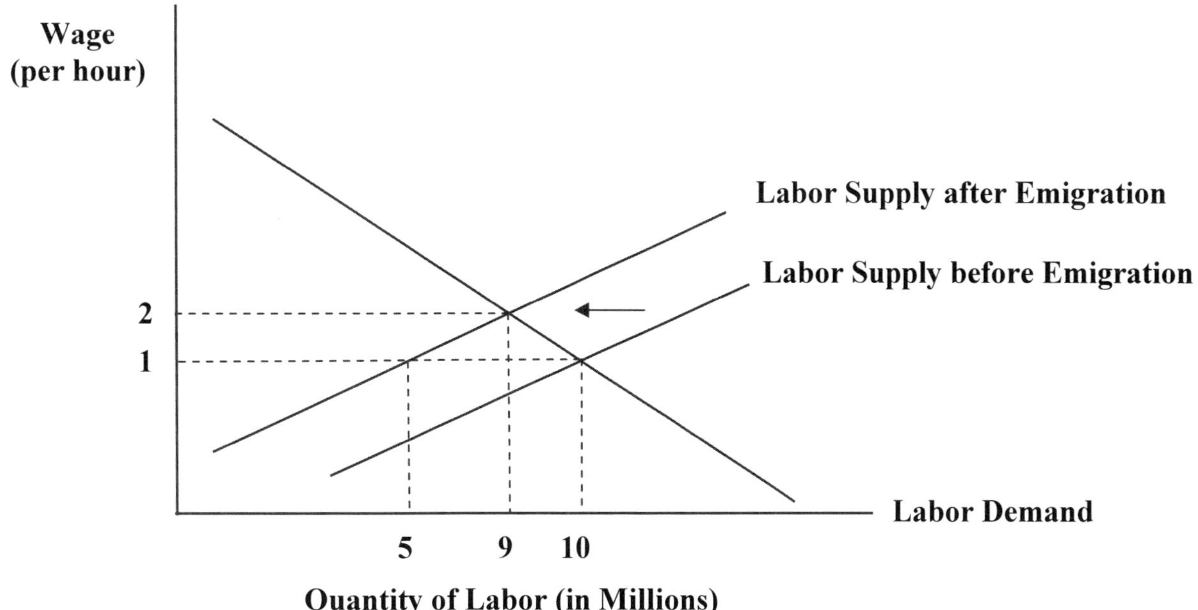

- When emigrants leave the labor market, the supply of labor decreases (shifts left). The wage rate for workers who remain in the country increases from 1 to 2.
- Firms that hire these workers are hurt by the wage increase, and hire fewer workers.
- With fewer workers employed less output will be produced, resulting in higher prices for consumers.

Activity 1
Migration and My Story
Part I: Instructions and Interview Information Form

Part 1:

Instructions

1. You will receive a card that describes a person affected by migration, and play the role of that person in this activity. The card gives some important information about the person, but you can improvise more details about the person's life during the activity. Do that when other students interview you, to find out how you have been affected by migration and whether you would favor or oppose laws that would make migration easier.

2. In addition to playing the role of the person described on your card, during the activity you will interview 5 other members of the class. Once again, the goal of the interview is to determine how each person has been affected by migration, and whether the person would favor or oppose laws to make migration easier. There are five rows on the interview form. Use one row for each person you interview.

3. At the start of each interview, record the card number and the home country of the person being interviewed in the first column of the Interview Information Form. Do not interview anyone who has the same card number that you hold.

4. After each interview, summarize the most important statements made by the person about the effects migration has had on their life in the middle column of the Interview Information Form. These statements might deal with why the person migrated or, if the person is not a migrant, how the person has been affected by the migration of other people.

5. Based on your interviews, decide whether or not each person would favor laws to make migration easier. Record your decision in the last column.

Activity 1 (continued)

Part 1 (continued):

Migration and My Story: Interview Information Form

Card # and Country	List the person's reasons for migrating OR note how the person was affected by migration	Would the person you interviewed support or oppose more immigration?

Activity 1 (continued)

Part 2: Role Cards

Card #1

You are a computer engineer from India who has migrated to the United States to find a higher paying job.

Card #2

You are a computer engineer in the United States who accepted a job at lower pay than you expected. You discovered that skilled immigrants from India and other countries are competing for skilled jobs in the United States.

Card #3

You are a physician trained in Nigeria. You decide to move to the United States to practice medicine. You anticipate making considerably more income than you would in Nigeria.

Card #4

You are an unskilled migrant worker from Mexico who works in the United States. You work mostly in agriculture, but do other part-time jobs in the winter.

Activity 1 (continued)

Part 2 (continued):

Card #5

You are a babysitter from the Dominican Republic, living in the United States and taking care of two children for a family in which both parents work in highly paid jobs.

Card #6

You are a child who is picked up after school by a babysitter from the Dominican Republic. The babysitter watches you until your parents come home from work.

Card # 7

You are a 30-year-old roofer in Illinois. You just had to take a pay cut because your employer can now hire migrant workers at a lower wage.

Card #8

You have lived in Kenya all your life, and are now ill with tuberculosis. It is difficult to find a doctor to treat your disease. You have heard that many doctors left Kenya to work in other countries.

Activity 1 (continued)

Part 2 (continued):

Card #9

You are a worker in Mexico who receives funds from relatives working in the United States. Because you receive this money you are able to keep your children in school.

Card #10

You own Computechno, a hi-tech company in the United States. Your company has been able to improve its performance and expand by hiring highly qualified computer engineers from India. In earlier years, your company found it difficult to find qualified workers for these jobs.

Card #11

You are the CEO of a firm in India that has just signed its first international contract, supplying services to a firm in the United States. The U.S. firm learned about your company when it hired one of your former employees, who had moved to the United States.

Card #12

You are a teenager in Kenya, and plan to stay in school to get an advanced degree. When you graduate you may decide to work in Kenya or in another country.

Activity 1 (continued)

Part 2 (continued):

Card #13

You are a worker in China, just hired by a new company paying higher wages than most firms in the country. The new company was founded by a Chinese businesswoman who developed her entrepreneurial skills and business contacts working in the United States for the last 10 years.

Card #14

You work in Yerevan for a charity group that supports education programs in Armenia. You have received a large donation from an Armenian businessman who was educated in Armenia but now lives and works in the United States.

Card #15

You are an electrical engineer from Pakistan who moved to the United States. You have not been able to find a job as an electrical engineer, but work as a salesman at a local retail store. While it does not pay nearly what you had expected when you had moved to the United States, it pays more than you made in Pakistan working as an electrical engineer.

Card #16

You are an American farm worker but do not own or farm your own land. Jobs are getting harder to find because migrant workers are willing to work for lower wages than you were paid in recent years.

Activity 1 (continued)

Part 2 (continued):

Card # 17

You are a high school student who applied for a summer job at a local restaurant. You were told those jobs had been filled by migrant workers willing to work all year. You sign up for a summer enrichment course at school instead of working.

Card #18

You buy fruits and vegetables grown in the United States. You read that prices of these products are lower because of the low wages paid to immigrant workers.

Card #19

You are the mayor of Spruceton, a city with a growing population. The city spends more for services such as fire and police protection, education, and maintaining city parks, because of the rising population. The latest census report indicates that much of the recent population growth is made up of people who emigrated from other countries.

Card #20

You are a worker from Brazil with a high school education. You found a job in south Florida installing tile floors, which pays more than you were able to earn in Brazil.

Activity 1 (continued)

Part 2 (continued):

Card #21

You are the owner of a restaurant in the city of Spruceton. You have noticed an increase in your sales and profits as the city has grown. That is due, in part, to more immigrants.

Card #22

You are the owner of a business that sells computer equipment. Sales of your equipment to a local business called Computechno have increased since Computechno expanded its operations by hiring more computer engineers. Many of the engineers hired emigrated from India.

Card #23

You own a large farm in California, and rely heavily on immigrant workers to harvest your crops. You pay these workers minimum wage. If immigrant workers were not available it would be difficult to hire workers at the minimum wage.

Card #24

You are a 56-year-old U.S. citizen who has worked installing tile floors in south Florida for the past 20 years. It is harder for you to find work because immigrant workers are willing to do the same work at lower wages.

LESSON NINE
GLOBALIZATION AND STANDARDS OF LIVING: PREDICTION AND MEASUREMENT

LESSON DESCRIPTION

In this lesson students consider ways to measure and then compare the degree of globalization and the standards of living in different countries. To introduce the idea of tracking complex social issues using different kinds of data, students plot recent changes in per capita technological connectivity–measured by the number of internet users and secure servers–for China, India, and other countries. Then a globalization index that uses the technological connectivity data as one indicator of globalization is presented. This index, developed by A.T. Kearney, Inc. and the Carnegie Endowment for International Peace, is calculated with data that represent four key aspects of globalization: economic, personal, technological, and political.

Students identify which of these dimensions are highest for the five countries at the top of the globalization scale, measured by this index. Then students examine the relationship between levels of globalization and the United Nation's Human Development Index, which is often used to measure the standard of living in different nations.

INTRODUCTION

Economists have long pointed to international trade, technological progress, and economic growth as ways to improve standards of living for people in all nations. Global patterns of economic development have been very uneven in different parts of the world, however, and are likely to remain so well into the future. It is often a difficult process for nations to make the changes in production and consumption patterns that are required to become more integrated with the global economy, and that leads to serious questions about the benefits and costs of higher levels of international trade, economic integration, and globalization.

Using data from an index of globalization and two other indexes of human development and welfare, students see the positive but sometimes uneven relationship between globalization, improvements in the standard of living, and reductions in national poverty levels.

CONCEPTS

Globalization
Globalization index (GI)
International trade
Economic growth
Index numbers
GDP per capita
Human development index (HDI)
Human poverty index (HPI-1)
Standard of living

CONTENT STANDARD

Voluntary exchange occurs only when all participating parties expect to gain. This is true for trade among individuals or organizations within a nation, and among individuals or organizations in different nations.

When individuals, regions, and nations specialize in what they can produce at the lowest cost and then trade with others, both production and consumption increase.

Income for most people is determined by the market value of the productive resources they sell. What workers earn depends, primarily, on the market value of what they produce and how productive they are.

BENCHMARKS

Free trade increases worldwide material standards of living.

Like trade among individuals within one country, international trade promotes specialization and division of labor and increases output and consumption.

The introduction of new products and production methods by entrepreneurs is an important form of competition, and is a source of technological progress and economic growth.

People's incomes, in part, reflect choices they have made about education, training, skill development, and careers. People with few skills are more likely to be poor.

Historically, economic growth has been the primary vehicle for alleviating poverty and raising standards of living.

OBJECTIVES

Students will:

- ♦ Understand that voluntary trade and economic growth increase worldwide levels of production and consumption, promoting higher standards of living.
- ♦ Identify key components used in constructing one of the leading indexes of the level of globalization in different nations.
- ♦ Understand how the United Nation's Human Development Index (HDI) is calculated and used to measure and compare gains in standards of living in different nations.
- ♦ Construct scatter diagrams to illustrate relationships between the degree of globalization and measures of human development or poverty in different nations.
- ♦ Use scatter diagrams to draw inferences about globalization and living standards in different nations.

TIME REQUIRED

Two class periods. In class periods of about one hour, the suggested coverage is: Period 1: Procedures 1 - 17; Period 2: Procedures 18 - 42, Closure, and Assessment.

MATERIALS

- Visual 1: Globalization
- Visual 2: Mutual Gains from Trade
- Visual 3: Economic Growth
- Visual 4: Components of the A.T. Kearney/Carnegie Globalization Index (GI)
- Visual 5: Constructing the Globalization Index (GI)
- Visual 6: Components of the U.N. Human Development Index (HDI)
- Visual 7: Scatter Diagram: GI Rank vs. HDI Rank
- Visual 8: Globalization and Poverty (one copy per student)
- Activity 1: Global Interconnectivity (one copy per student). Copy the Answer Key pages of this activity separately, to hand out later in the activity (one copy per student).
- Activity 2: 2005 Globalization Index: Ranks for Top Five Countries (one copy per student)
- Activity 3: GI Rank vs. HDI Rank (one copy per student). Graph paper for each student (or, optionally, student access to computers with spreadsheet and graphing software. Internet connections may also be used, if available.)

PROCEDURES

1. Ask students to define globalization, and to identify some of the most important effects that globalization has had on the United States and other nations in recent decades. *(Answers will vary–write some of the key points students make on the board or an overhead projector.)*

2. Display Visual 1 and discuss the definition of **globalization** provided by Wikipedia. Compare the key terms used in this definition to the student responses from procedure 1.

3. Ask students whether they believe globalization has improved material standards of living in the United States and other nations over the past few decades. Encourage them to suggest both positive and negative effects globalization has had on how people live. (*Answers will vary. Let students brainstorm on these questions for several minutes, recording major points on the board or an overhead transparency.*)

4. When student responses wind down or you decide the discussion has gone on long enough, point out that these are complex and controversial issues. Announce that this lesson will deal with these questions, first by considering two key reasons why economists typically believe that globalization increases worldwide standards of living over time (though not without creating problems, too), and then by working with some data on these questions. Warn students at the outset that these issues are controversial partly because they are difficult to measure and understand, and partly because the positive effects of globalization are not spread equally across different countries or to all groups in individual nations. In particular, globalization leads to changes in production patterns that displace some firms and workers, at least until they adjust to new production and employment opportunities. (That topic is developed in greater depth in Lessons 8 and 10 of this volume.)

5. Explain that economists point to several key factors that suggest the long-run effects of globalization will be positive for all nations. In particular, they stress the importance of mutual gains from international trade and the benefits of economic growth that results from trade and several other factors associated with globalization–especially technological advances and investments in physical capital and in the education and training of workers (often called human capital).

6. Display Visual 2 (Standard 5 from the *Voluntary National Content Standards in Economics*, published by the National Council on Economic Education in 1997). Emphasize the point that voluntary trade–whether it involves trade between people or firms in the same nation or trade between people and firms in different nations–only takes place when both parties to the trade expect to gain. In other words, people trade when they can get something at a lower cost than they have to pay if they make it themselves, so in that way trade lowers costs and increases levels of production and consumption. This is a basic tenet of economics (covered at greater length in Lesson 2 in this volume), and explains why most economists and all U.S. Presidents since World War II have supported treaties and U.S. participation in international institutions established to make international trade easier and less expensive, to improve social welfare for all nations.

7. Display Visual 3. Define **economic growth** as a sustained increase in a nation's production of goods and services, or real (inflation-adjusted) gross domestic product (GDP). If the production of goods and services increases faster than a nation's population, **GDP per capita** increases and, on average, the people of that nation have

more to consume, increasing their material **standard of living**. Economists have identified several factors that contribute to economic growth in the United States and other nations, including: technological advances, increasing skills of workers through education and training, and investments in capital resources such as factories and machinery. (See lesson 21, "Economic Growth and Development," in the National Council on Economic Education's *Focus: High School Economics*, 2nd edition, published in 2001, for more information and activities on these topics.)

8. Display Visual 1 again, and note that the Wikipedia description of globalization encompasses expanded international trade, economic growth and change, and several of the factors that promote higher levels of trade and growth, as key elements in the process of globalization.

9. Distribute Activity 1 and graph paper. (If students have computer access and appropriate software skills, the computations and graphs can be generated electronically.) Note once again that the description of globalization in Visual 1 suggests the use of new technologies, such as the Internet and secure servers, is part of the process of globalization. Tell students they will use the data in Activity 1 to compare internet users as a percentage of the population for various countries in recent years. If time allows, also have students make similar comparisons using the number of secure servers. Note: for data on internet usage in other countries, and other measures used to construct the globalization index described in later procedures, access www.atkearney.com. Use the site links for "Publications and Online Articles" and "Globalization Index."

10. Tell students to begin the assignment by computing the ratios of internet users to national populations and entering the results in the boxed spaces on Activity 1. Demonstrate the set-up for the first calculation (for China in 1998: 2,100 divided by 1,253,880). Allow time for students to complete their computations and graph the results. Then distribute the Answer Key for Activity 1 and have students check their answers.

11. Ask the following questions: "What common patterns do you see by graphing internet users as a percentage of the population for these four countries in recent years?" *(In all four countries, the percentage rises each year.)* "Are the percentages identical for all countries?" *(No. China, India, and Saudi Arabia are similar in having relatively low–under 2%–but rising percentages. The United States has a much higher level of connectivity, with a 30% internet user ratio in 1998 and close to 60% by 2003.)* "Will internet use continue to be an important form of interconnectivity as globalization continues to increase and spread in the 21st century?" *(Answers may vary, but most students understand the power of the internet in terms of sharing information and facilitating different kinds of interactions, including economic, political, and cultural.)*

12. Point out that technology use is only one of many factors included in the Visual 1 description of globalization. To consider more than one of those factors at the same time, economists and other social scientists often construct indexes. An **index number** or ranking is computed by selecting variables that can be measured statistically and that are considered important and relevant to the overall issue that is being measured (in this case globalization). Formulas are then estimated to assign different weights (importance) to each of the variables selected. Data for each of the selected variables are collected and the formula is then used to compute the value of

the index for a set time period, often one year.

13. Ask students to provide examples of index numbers they are familiar with. *(Answers may vary).* Remind students that business news reported daily on internet sites and in print and electronic media often include the latest figures for the Dow Jones Industrial Average (DJIA) and the Standard and Poor's 500 (S&P 500).

The S&P index is constructed by choosing 500 large, publicly held firms to measure changes in stock market prices, which are often considered a bellwether for the overall health or direction of the economy. The Dow Jones Industrial Average is even more widely reported, and is constructed in basically the same way as the S&P index, but using share prices for only 30 very large, "blue chip" firms.

Price movements for the individual stocks in these indexes are market-value weighted, which means that stock price changes for companies with bigger market valuation have a stronger effect than the same stock price change for a smaller company. Both indexes are used to indicate the overall direction and magnitude of stock price changes for the stock market as a whole, but using only a subset of 500 or 30 firms.

Although these indexes are tracked and widely used by large numbers of individual and institutional investors, they are not perfect measures of all stock market activity, or certainly not the performance of any one company. Nor do they predict with perfect accuracy the near-term or longer-range performance of the economy, though they are often used as one component in broader indexes of leading economic indicators. See http://encyclopedia.thefreedictionary.com for more information on these indexes.

14. Tell students that one leading index of globalization was developed by A.T. Kearney, Inc. and the Carnegie Endowment for International Peace. In 2000, they began gathering data from a variety of sources for 62 countries. As a group, these 62 nations account for 96 percent of global gross domestic product (GDP), and 85 percent of the world's population. Ask students if they agree that calculating an index value to measure the extent of globalization in different countries is probably even more difficult that calculating an index number to indicate changes in prices for the stock exchange, such as the Dow Jones or S&P indexes. *(Students are likely to agree that globalization is a more complex issue than the stock prices, as suggested in the description of globalization in Visual 1, which you may want to display again here.)*

15. Explain that the Carnegie globalization index is calculated using 12 variables, divided into four dimensions (sometimes called "baskets") of globalization: economic integration, technological connectivity, personal contact, and political engagement. For example, the internet users data from Activity 1, combined with data on internet hosts and secure servers, are used to measure the technological connectivity component of the Index. (See "Measuring Globalization" in *Foreign Policy*, May-June 2005. The article can be accessed at www.atkearney.com.)

16. Display Visual 4, which lists the components of the Kearney/Carnegie Globalization Index (GI). Briefly discuss each of the 12 components and prepare students for their upcoming work with the four baskets or categories in Activity 2. Foreign direct investment (FDI) refers to the movement of capital across borders when a foreign investor maintains control of the assets (for example, Toyota builds a new Camry production plant in Indiana). Remittances are personal transfers and other

non-governmental transfers of money sent from one country to another (for example, money sent by U.S. immigrants to family members in their native countries). Government transfers (foreign aid, for example) are included in the political engagement category.

Tell students they will be working with the general globalization index, based on all 12 components, and with the four broad groupings or dimensions that make up the overall index. Rank values for each country will be used, ranging from 1 (representing the nation with highest level of globalization) to 62 (the lowest level of globalization).

17. Display Visual 5. Tell students that for most components of the globalization index, a country's exchanges with other countries are added together, and then the sum is divided by the country's overall level of economic output (GDP) or, for measures involving the number of people engaged in some activity, by the nation's population. For example, the "trade" component of the index is calculated by adding the value of a country's exports and imports together, then dividing by GDP.

The United States is an interesting case with regard to several of the index components. One might assume the U.S. would rank high in economic integration, based upon the volume of its exports and imports and its reputation as a global economic superpower. But even though the United States is the largest trading nation in the world, because its domestic economy is so much larger than most nations, and accounts for the great majority of its total GDP, exports and imports are a comparatively small (but growing) part of the overall U.S. economy. In Ireland, the Netherlands, etc., trade is a much larger part of the national economy, so those nations rank higher on the economic measure of globalization than the United States. In other words, the effect of globalization on those economies is even larger than the effects of globalization on the U.S. economy. Remember, however, that the economic dimension is only one of four dimensions of globalization in the Carnegie index.

18. If this is the start of a new class period, as suggested in the Time Required section, remind students that in order to understand why countries are ranked high or low in certain globalization categories, they need to remember that the ranks are based upon measures that are adjusted for the size of the country's economy (GDP) or its population. Thus a large country with considerable activity in any given category may NOT necessarily receive the lowest numerical ranks (indicating highest globalization).

19. Distribute a copy of Activity 2 to each student. Explain that the five countries shown are the five nations that ranked highest on the overall Carnegie globalization index (GI) in 2005. The lower section of the table shows the rankings for these countries on the four broad components of the overall GI index. Remind students that low numbers indicate nations ranked as having higher levels of globalization, while larger numbers indicate countries that were ranked lower among the 62 nations for which the GI was calculated.

20. Ask students to compare the overall GI rankings for these countries from 2004 and 2005. Were there any changes in the top three nations? *(Yes. Ireland and Singapore switched positions.)* Was the United States in the top five in 2004? *(No, it ranked 7th.)*

21. Display Visual 4 again, and make sure students understand that there are four different dimensions underlying the overall

GI rating: economic, personal, technological, and political. For each country, a rank is established for each globalization dimension. Point out these ranks in Activity 2. For example, the U.S. dimensional ranks are: 60 (economic), 40 (personal), 1 (technological), and 43 (political).

22. Ask students what features of globalization these five countries seem have in common. *(Answers may vary. Point out that Singapore, Switzerland, and the United States each rank 1st in one of the dimensions. Ireland is ranked 2nd in two of the dimensions, and the Netherlands is ranked 4th and 5th in two of the dimensions. Thus, a high overall GI ranking is achieved by ranking high in one or more of the four dimensions.)*

23. Ask students to discuss whether adding together the four dimension ranks could have been how the 62 nations were ranked on the overall GI index, with the lowest total of the four dimensions ranked highest? *(No. If that were true, the Netherlands would rank as more globalized than the United States, because the sum of its four rankings (5 + 11 + 8 + 4 = 28) would be much lower than the sum of the four rankings for the United States (60 +40 + 1 + 43 = 144). Clearly, the numerical rankings in the four categories are not weighted equally to determine the overall globalization index. In fact, a considerably more complex formula is used to combine the four subcategories to derive the overall index. But the rankings in each dimension, and the overall GI rankings, make it possible to compare how different aspects of globalization have larger or smaller effects in different countries, and show that globalization is sometimes achieved in different ways.)*

24. Ask students what rank the U.S. holds in terms of the economic dimension of the index. *(60 of 62 countries)* Are they surprised by this low level of globalization? *(Not if they remember the discussion from procedure 17, above. Answers may vary, but remind students that the GI ranks for a country are based on its global activities relative to the size of its economy or population. If necessary, display Visual 5 again and review the construction of the index. Because the U.S. domestic economy is so large, U.S. exports and imports are a relatively smaller share of national income than in many smaller countries.)*

25. Ask students to discuss the relatively high ranking for the United States in terms of political engagement, indicating a lower degree of globalization. What factors might explain that ranking? *(In recent years, the United States has not participated in several international agreements dealing with such issues as environmental regulations and international trade.)*

26. Discuss the limits of using this globalization index, or any similar technique, to measure the globalization of any country at any given point in time. Consider each of the following issues: choosing which components to include or exclude in the index, assigning weights for the different components, and data measurement and collection problems, especially for variables that are designed to measure how people are affected by changes in economic or political factors.

27. If teachers and students are interested in expanding comparisons of GI rankings beyond the top five countries included in Activity 2, data are available for all 62 countries analyzed by A.T. Kearney at www.atkearney.com, using the site links to "Publications and Online Articles" and "Globalization Index."

28. Tell students they are now going to use another index, called the Human Development Index (HDI). This index was developed by a Pakistani economist, Mahbub ul Haq, and since 1993 has been used as an indicator of the overall quality of life in different countries by the United Nations Development Programme.

29. Display Visual 6, and explain that the HDI index is based on three basic dimensions of human development:

A. a long and healthy life, measured by life expectancy at birth

B. basic knowledge and skills, measured by the adult literacy rate (2/3 weight) and the combined primary, secondary, and tertiary education gross enrollment ratio (1/3 weight)

C. the average financial standard of living, measured by GDP per capita in U.S. dollars, at purchasing power parity (PPP)

(You may want to explain here that international comparisons of GDP using currency exchange rates are usually not good measures of differences in purchasing power, consumption, and living standards in different countries. The basic problem is that currency exchange rates are affected only by things that are internationally traded. Many large items in most peoples' budgets, including housing and many services–including government services–are not traded internationally. The PPP adjustment equalizes the purchasing power of different currencies including items that are not traded internationally.)

30. Discuss the limits of these three dimensions in measuring overall economic and social well being, both in terms of other factors that are not considered and measurement problems associated with the variables that are used to reflect levels of education, income, health care, and the quality of life. Point out that before the introduction of HDI, it was common practice for international institutions like the United Nations, and for economists and other social scientists, to use only real GDP per capita as a proxy for standard of living or economic well being. Some economists still argue that real GDP is a better indicator, because it is simpler to measure, at least in some ways, without having to assign weights to other categories–knowing that the weights themselves will be a matter of some debate or even dispute. Note that HDI still includes real GDP per capita, and weights it as 1/3 of the HDI. But proponents of the HDI and similar indexes argue that measures of average income alone do not adequately reflect the quality of life for all people in a nation, especially those in low-income or disadvantaged groups. A United Nations website devoted to the HDI, http://hdr.undp.org, notes that:

"The HDI was created to re-emphasize that people and their capabilities should be the ultimate criteria for assessing the development of a country, not economic growth."

31. Distribute copies of Activity 3 to each student. Ask them to consider first which countries were chosen for the activity. Explain that 30 countries are included: 10 with the highest ranks for globalization using the 2005 Carnegie GI index, (1-10); 10 with the lowest ranks for globalization (53-62); and 10 spread across the middle range of countries (from 11 to 52).

32. Demonstrate how the data can be used to plot 30 separate points on a scatter diagram. Each country is plotted as a single point, using the GI rank for the horizontal coordinate and HDI rank for the vertical coordinate. Japan and Singapore are already

plotted, so work through those two examples with the students. Although these two demonstration points are labeled to show the country identity, tell students not to label the other 28 points they will plot, because of insufficient space.

33. Remind students that low HDI and GI ranks indicate high levels of human development and globalization, respectively. Point out that the axes for the scatter plot in Activity 3 are labeled with coordinate values in descending order, so that countries with high levels of development will be plotted higher on the vertical axis, and countries with higher rankings for globalization will be shown further right on the horizontal axis. When students fully understand their assignment, tell them to proceed in plotting the remaining 28 points, using the country data provided.

34. After allowing enough time for students to complete their graphs display Visual 7 and let students check their scatter plots. Expect some variation in non-electronic results due to hand plotting without small-grid graph paper. Visual 7 was created using Microsoft Excel and Chart Wizard, and if students know how to use spreadsheets and graphics software they might also do Activity 3 this way. Explain that on Visual 7, although the axes values are shown on the top and right sides of the chart, the values are identical (still in descending order) to those on the version of the chart in Activity 3.

35. Ask students to interpret the scatter diagram shown in Visual 7 and in their version of the chart on Activity 3, after making any necessary corrections. Specifically, ask students what the relationship appears to be between globalization and the standard of living, as measured by the HDI: Are countries ranked higher on the HDI index usually ranked higher or lower on the globalization index? (*Although there is certainly variation, most countries with lower globalization levels–on the left side of the chart–also have lower levels of human development, and so appear in the lower half of the chart. Countries with higher globalization (lower GI ranks) are even more likely to have higher levels of human development (lower ranks on the HDI index), too, appearing in the upper-right quadrant of the chart.*)

36. Caution students that this kind of statistical pattern shows a correlation between two variables–in this case between the HDI and GI indexes–but does not establish the direction of causation between the variables. For example, based only on these data, some people might argue that more globalization in a nation leads to higher levels of human development and standards of living, but others might argue the opposite direction of causation, claiming that higher standards of living lead nations to be more open to globalization. Or both effects might be at work, simultaneously. Explain that, while plotting data points cannot establish causality, there are sometimes other ways to do that.

37. Remind students that, as discussed at the start of this lesson, most economists argue that voluntary trade (including international trade) and economic growth lead to higher standards of living. Display Visuals 2 and 3 again for review, if necessary. Because international trade and, more broadly, economic integration, are components of the globalization index, most economists also argue that countries with policies that promote free trade and other factors that promote integration with the global economy are likely to experience larger gains in standards of living. In other words, the economic ideas and theories concerning the mutual advantages from international trade and the overall (net) benefits of economic growth provide the basis for arguing that there is a causal

relationship, with nations that become more integrated with the global economy improving their standards of living.

38. Explain that some economists and organizations argue that there is a different, or at least another, cause and effect sequence underlying this relationship. The United Nations website on Human Development Reports, http://hdr.undp.org, makes the argument that:

"Economic growth requires investment in human development first."

That statement is broadly consistent with economic models of economic growth, and not necessarily inconsistent with the idea that greater globalization will also promote improvements in standards of living and the HDI. But it does suggest a different kind of causation, and perhaps a different set of priorities in policies designed to promote economic growth and development.

39. Tell students that your investigation of globalization will now incorporate one measure of poverty published by the United Nations. The Human Poverty Index (HPI-1) attempts to capture the lack of choices or opportunities faced by individuals in developing countries. It measures human deprivations in the same three areas covered by the HDI (health, education, and standard of living). In the case of HDI, positive human development in those three areas is measured by life expectancy, adult literacy rates plus school enrollment ratios, and real GDP per capita, respectively. In the case of HPI-1, human deprivations in health are measured by the probability at birth of not surviving to age 40. Education deprivations are measured by the percentage of adults who are illiterate. Deprivations in the standard of living are captured by two measures: the percentage of people not having sustainable access to improved water sources, and the percentage of children below the age of five who are underweight. HPI-1 is used only for developing countries. A separate U.N. index, HPI-2, based on somewhat different variables, is used to measure human deprivation in selected high-income countries.

40. Display Visual 8, which compares globalization index ranks and human poverty index ranks (HPI-1) for 20 developing countries. Distribute one copy to each student.

41. Show students how the index values are measured along each axis of the graph. A low HPI-1 index indicates lower levels of deprivation, while a higher HPI-1 index indicates relatively higher levels of deprivation and poverty. In Visual 8, countries with high levels of globalization and low levels of poverty are found in the upper right corner of the graph. (GI ranks decrease moving from left to right, and HDP-1 ranks decrease moving up the vertical axis.)

42. Assign students to small groups. Using the data from Visual 8, ask them to determine if there is a positive or negative relationship between national levels of globalization and poverty levels, for these 20 less developed nations. Is it a strong relationship? *(Answers may vary. The relationship between poverty and globalization in these developing nations is clearly not as strong as the relationship between globalization and human development seen earlier in Activity 3 and Visual 7. Understanding less developed nations, and how they might become more developed, has been a notoriously difficult problem in economics and other social sciences. Education, health, population growth, institutional and policy reforms, low levels of private and social investment, and other factors are often problems that have to be faced at the same time, but in different mixes in different countries. Therefore,*

expect a variety of responses. But point out that considering the points for only the lower HDI nations in Activity 3 and Visual 7, on the lower ranges of the chart, the patterns are perhaps not really so different. And in general, the scatter diagram in Visual 8 does suggest a positive relationship between globalization and lower levels of poverty. Once again, explain that the correlation does not prove that globalization reduces poverty levels in developing countries; but economic arguments on the mutual benefits from international trade and the overall benefits of economic growth lend more support to that argument, especially over time, as people and firms have more time to make the changes brought about by international trade and globalization.)

CLOSURE

Ask students the following questions:

1. Based on the Kearney/Carnegie Globalization Index (GI), what are the key dimensions to consider in measuring the degree of globalization in different nations? *(economic, personal, technological, and political)*

2. What kinds of patterns or trends in a nation indicate a growing level of globalization? *(increased economic integration through trade and foreign direct investment; increased international personal contacts via telephone, travel, and personal money transfers; rising technological connectivity, especially through internet connections; and increased political engagement, through increased international governmental transfers, membership in international organizations, and participation in multinational peacekeeping activities and treaty agreements.)*

3. Does a nation's increased globalization guarantee an increase in the human development of its people, as measured by the United Nation's HDI and HPI-1? *(There are no ironclad guarantees, especially in terms of the relationship between globalization and reducing poverty levels in developing countries. However, comparisons of globalization ranks and HDI ranks offer clear evidence of a positive correlation between globalization and human welfare.)*

ASSESSMENT

Assign small groups of students to gather additional data related to globalization, economic growth, well-being, and poverty. "Measuring Globalization," *Foreign Policy*, May/June 2005 is a good print source. For HDI-related data, see the website: http://hdr.undp.org.

Tell students to use two or more data series to make simple graphs or scatter plots that support a particular theory about the relationship between globalization and economic growth, well being, or poverty. To accompany the graphs, have students write a short statement that describes the relationships between the variables in their graphs. If class time allows, conduct a classroom debate on globalization issues, with teams presenting their evidence and defending their claims about the relationship between globalization and different measures of human development and welfare.

EXTENSION ACTIVITY

If time permits and internet resources are accessible in the classroom, visit http://hdr.undp.org/statistics with your students. Several links are particularly useful. In the "Highlights" section, click on the Animation–Growth and HD link to view a short presentation with attractive graphics that tracks and compares the relationships of health and education indexes to per capita GDP indexes over time for various groups of countries. There is also a link in the "Highlights" section to an interactive HDI calculator, which shows how the index is calculated for a nation from the data series included in the index. Students can insert their own fictitious or real world figures to see how the formulas work and how sensitive the indexes are to changes in values for different components.

Visual 1
Globalization

"Globalization refers to the worldwide phenomenon of technological, economic, and cultural change, as brought about by expanding facilities for intercommunication and interdependency between traditionally isolated cultures.

The term refers to the overall integration, and resulting increase in interdependence, among global actors, be they political, economic, or otherwise."

Source: http://en.wikipedia.org

Visual 2
Mutual Gains from Trade

Voluntary exchange occurs only when all participating parties expect to gain. This is true for trade among individuals or organizations within a nation, and among individuals or organizations in different nations.[2]

Because all the parties to a voluntary exchange expect to gain from trade, institutions that make trading easier usually improve social welfare.

[2] *Voluntary National Content Standards in Economics, Standard 5*. National Council on Economic Education, New York, NY, 1997, p. 9.

Visual 3
Economic Growth

Economic growth is a sustained increase in a nation's production of goods and services.

If the production of goods and services increases faster than a nation's population GDP per capita increases and, on average, the people of that nation have more to consume, increasing their material standard of living.[3]

[3] *Voluntary National Content Standards in Economics.* National Council on Economic Education, New York, NY, 1997, pp. 29, 35-36.

Visual 4
Components of A.T. Kearney/Carnegie Globalization Index (GI)

1. **ECONOMIC INTEGRATION**
   - TRADE
   - FOREIGN DIRECT INVESTMENT
2. **PERSONAL**
   - TELEPHONE
   - TRAVEL
   - REMITTANCES/PERSONAL TRANSFERS
3. **TECHNOLOGICAL CONNECTIVITY**
   - INTERNET USERS
   - INTERNET HOSTS
   - SECURE SERVERS
4. **POLITICAL ENGAGEMENT**
   - INTERNATIONAL ORGANIZATIONS
   - U. N. PEACEKEEPING
   - TREATIES
   - GOVERNMENT TRANSFERS

Visual 5
Constructing the Globalization Index

1. A complex formula is used, with different weights assigned to the 12 components of the 4 categories (economic, personal, technological connectivity, and political engagement).

2. For most variables used in the GI index, each year's inward and outward flows are added together. The sum of these flows is divided by the country's nominal economic output (GDP) or, where appropriate, its population.

3. Two of the political engagement indicators are absolute numbers (not divided by GDP or population):

- memberships in international organizations
- number of selected treaties ratified

Source: "Measuring Globalization," *Foreign Policy,* March/April 2004

Visual 6
Components of the U.N. Human Development Index (HDI)

HEALTH (LIFE EXPECTANCY)

a long and healthy life, measured by life expectancy at birth

EDUCATION

knowledge, measured by the adult literacy rate (2/3 weight) and the combined primary, secondary, and tertiary education gross enrollment ratio (1/3 weight)

STANDARD OF LIVING (REAL GDP PER CAPITA: GDP/N)

a decent standard of living, measured by gross domestic product (GDP) per capita at purchasing power parity (PPP) in U.S. dollars

Visual 7
Scatter Diagram: GI Rank vs. HDI Rank

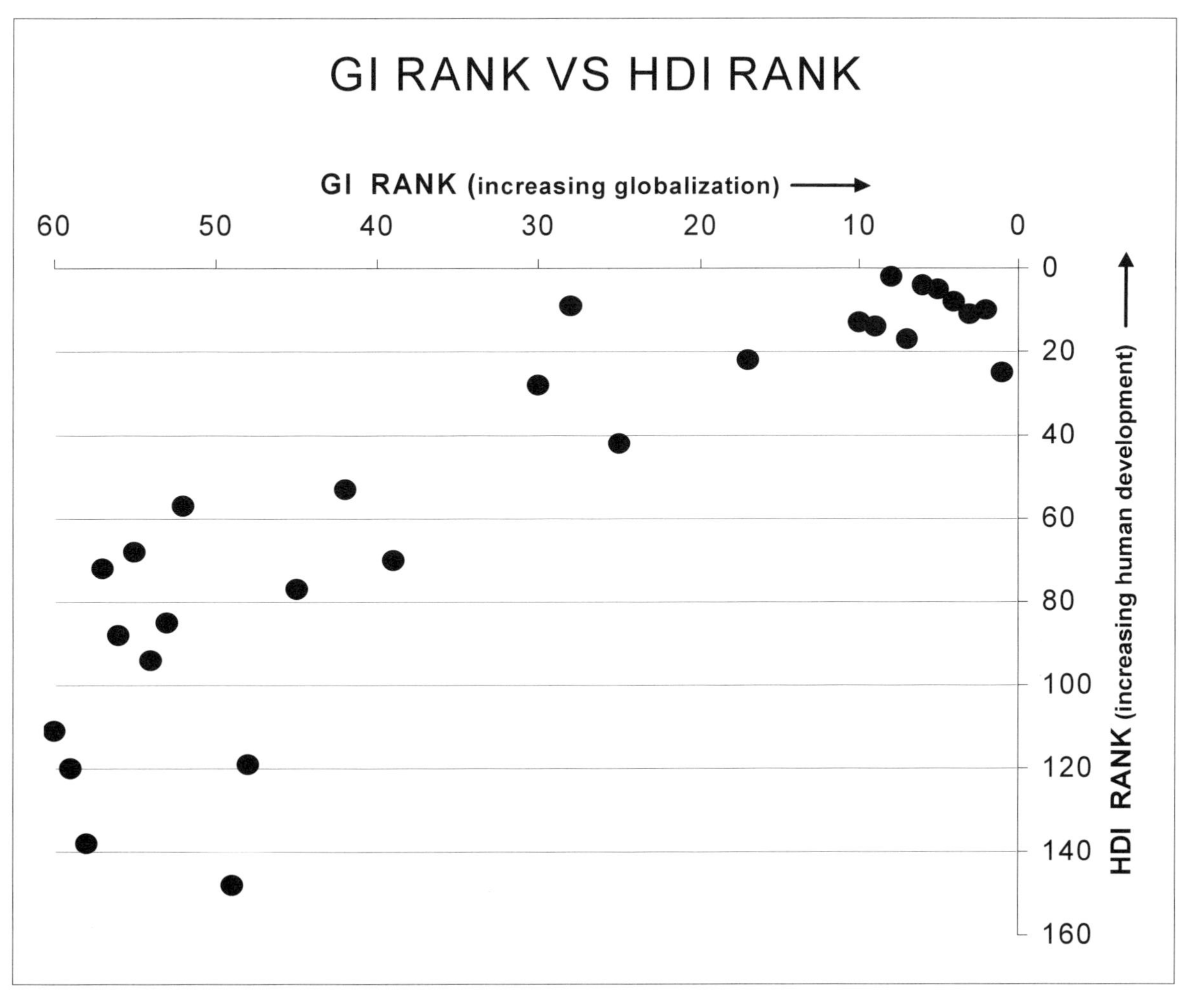

Visual 8
Globalization and Poverty

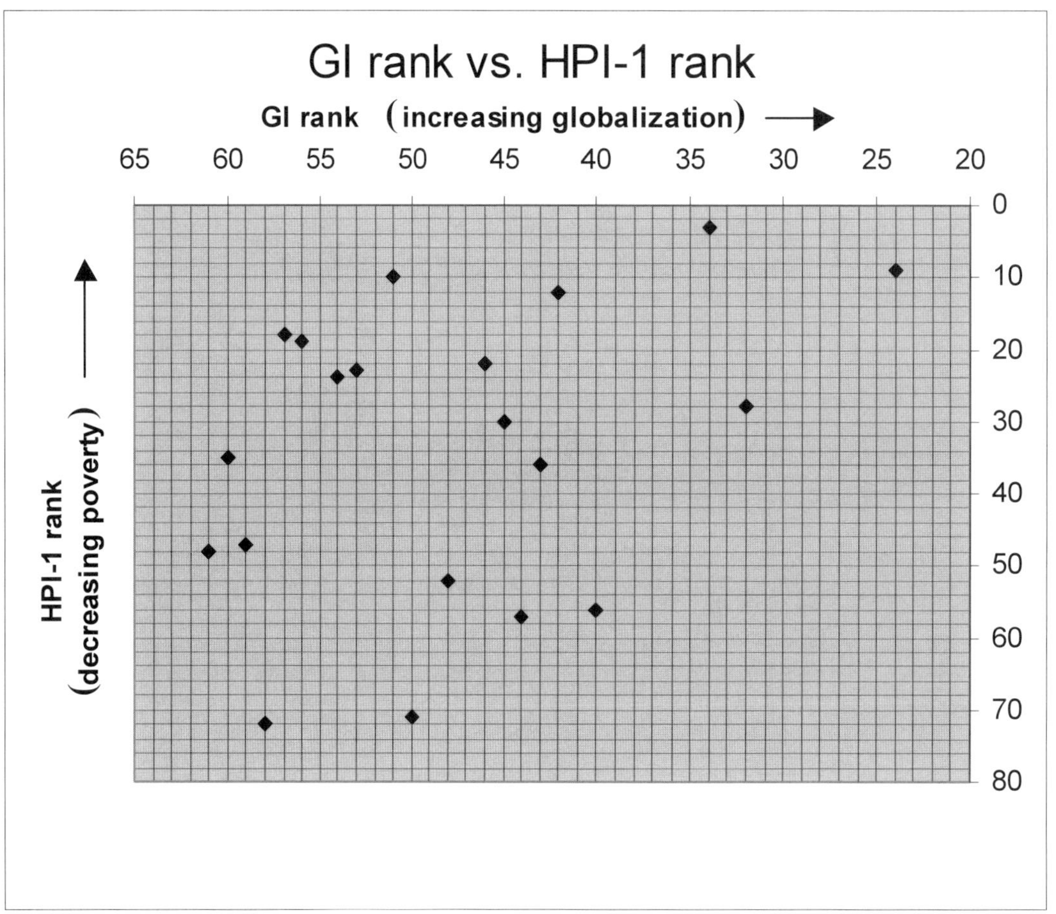

Country	GI rank	HPI-1 rank	Country	GI rank	HPI-1 rank
Morocco	40	56	China	54	24
Chile	34	3	South Africa	48	52
Mexico	42	12	Egypt	59	47
Panama	24	9	India	61	48
Brazil	57	18	Bangladesh	58	72
Colombia	51	10	Peru	53	23
Thailand	46	22	Indonesia	60	35
Saudi Arabia	45	30	Pakistan	50	71
Philippines	32	28	Nigeria	44	57
Turkey	56	19	Sri Lanka	43	36

Activity 1
Global Interconnectivity

Year	1998	1999	2000	2001	2002	2003
China						
Internet users (000)	2,100	8,900	22,500	33,700	59,100	79,500
Population (000)	1,253,880	1,264,760	1,275,220	1,285,230	1,294,870	1,304,200
Users/Population						
Secure servers	28	71	187	206	173	243
India						
Internet users (000)	1,400	2,800	5,500	7,000	16,580	18,481
Population (000)	983,110	1,000,160	1,016,940	1,033,390	1,049,550	1,065,460
Users/Population						
Secure servers	7	22	114	173	230	386
Saudi Arabia						
Internet users (000)	20	100	460	1,016	1,419	1,500
Population (000)	20,796	21,469	22,147	22,829	23,520	24,217
Users/Population						
Secure servers	2	5	10	25	17	41
United States						
Internet users (000)	84,587	102,000	124,000	142,823	159,000	172,250
Population (000)	278,948	281,975	285,003	288,025	291,038	294,043
Users/Population						
Secure servers	23,447	39,460	77,308	93,194	112,359	175,123

All data above were obtained at www.atkearney.com. Original sources for the data series are: International Telecommunications Union Database 2004; International Monetary Fund, *International Financial Statistics*, November 2004; and Netcraft Secure Server Surveys 2004.

Activity 1 (continued)

Answer Key

Year	1998	1999	2000	2001	2002	2003
China						
Internet users (000)	2,100	8,900	22,500	33,700	59,100	79,500
Population (000)	1,253,880	1,264,760	1,275,220	1,285,230	1,294,870	1,304,200
Users/Population	**0.00167**	**0.00704**	**0.01764**	**0.02622**	**0.04564**	**0.06096**
Secure servers	28	71	187	206	173	243
India						
Internet users (000)	1,400	2,800	5,500	7,000	16,580	18,481
Population (000)	983,110	1,000,160	1,016,940	1,033,390	1,049,550	1,065,460
Users/Population	**0.00142**	**0.00280**	**0.00541**	**0.00677**	**0.01580**	**0.01735**
Secure servers	7	22	114	173	230	386
Saudi Arabia						
Internet users (000)	20	100	460	1,016	1,419	1,500
Population (000)	20,796	21,469	22,147	22,829	23,520	24,217
Users/Population	**0.00096**	**0.00466**	**0.02077**	**0.04450**	**0.06033**	**0.06194**
Secure servers	2	5	10	25	17	41
United States						
Internet users (000)	84,587	102,000	124,000	142,823	159,000	172,250
Population (000)	278,948	281,975	285,003	288,025	291,038	294,043
Users/Population	**0.30324**	**0.36173**	**0.43508**	**0.49587**	**0.54632**	**0.58580**
Secure servers	23,447	39,460	77,308	93,194	112,359	175,123

Activity 1 (continued)

Answer Key (continued)

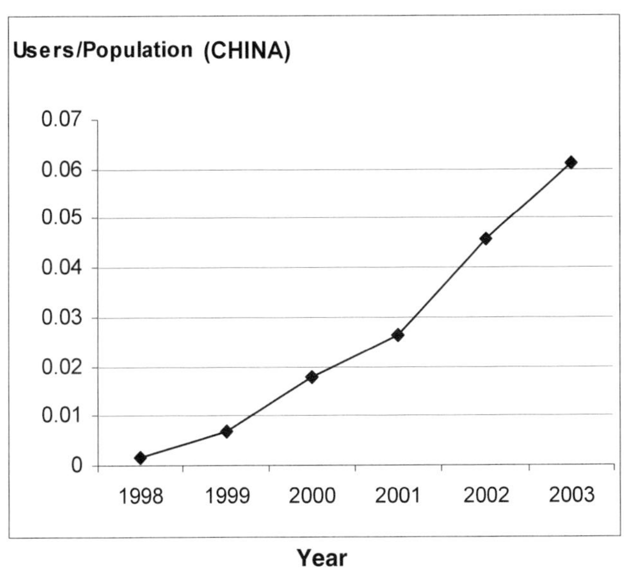

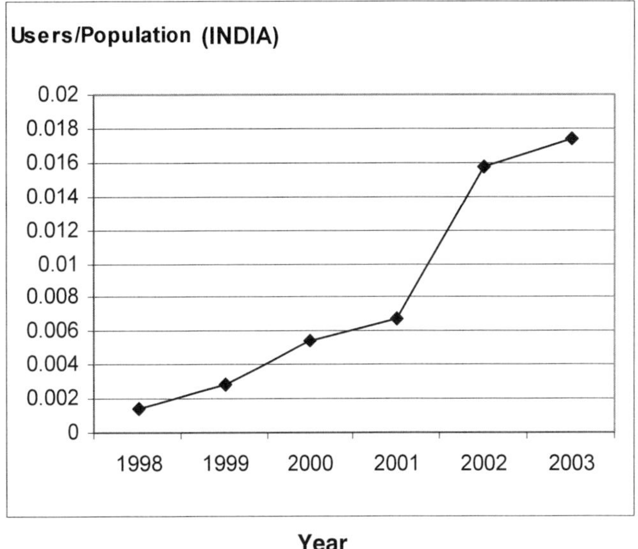

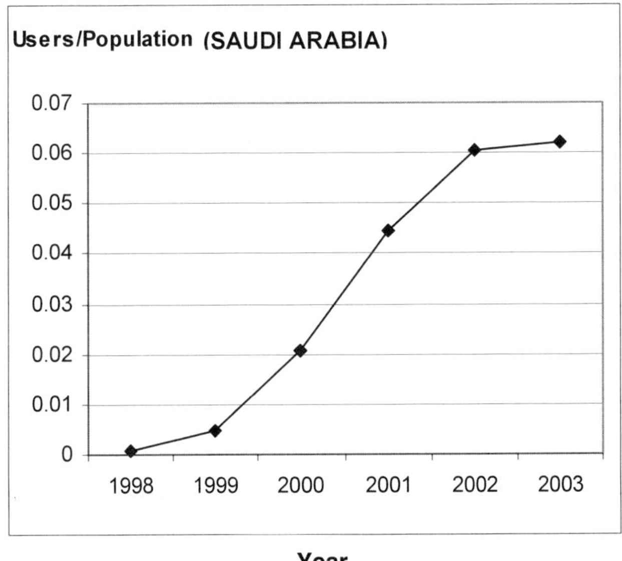

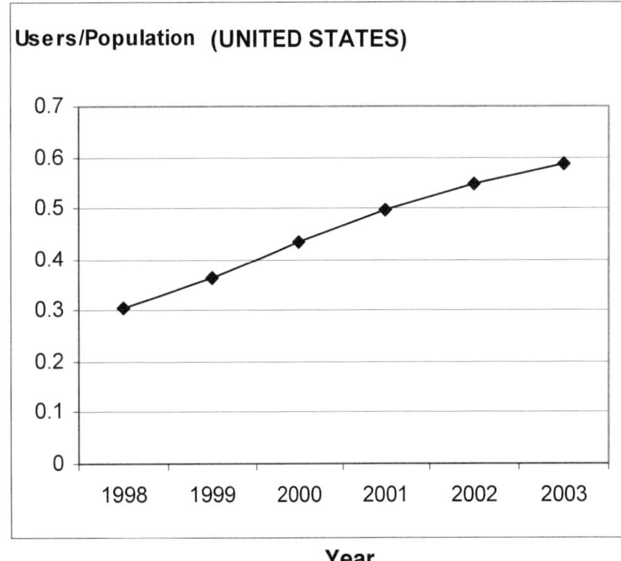

Activity 2

2005 Globalization Index Ranks for Top Five Countries

	5 Most Globalized Countries				
	Singapore	Ireland	Switzerland	United States	Netherlands
2005 GI ranking	1	2	3	4	5
2004 GI ranking	2	1	3	7	4
Change from 2004	1	–1	0	3	–1
Economic dimension rank	1	2	9	60	5
Personal dimension rank	3	2	1	40	11
Technological dimension rank	11	13	7	1	8
Political dimension rank	32	19	29	43	4

Details of Dimensional Ranks					
	Singapore	Ireland	Switzerland	United States	Netherlands
Economic Integration	1	2	9	60	5
Trade	1	4	18	61	8
Foreign direct investment	1	2	5	42	4
Personal Contact	3	2	1	40	11
Telephone	1	3	2	19	6
Travel	5	3	4	34	13
Remittances/personal transfers	47	6	1	58	45
Technological Connectivity	11	13	7	1	8
Internet users	10	24	11	4	9
Internet hosts	9	18	14	1	4
Secure servers	11	7	5	1	13
Political Engagement	32	19	29	43	4
International organizations	29	12	29	1	5
U.N. peacekeeping	3	11	13	28	17
Treaties	41	28	41	57	6
Government transfers	47	22	10	38	6

Note: For all rankings, 1 = most globalized, 62 = least globalized of 62 ranked countries

Activity 3
GI Rank vs. HDI Rank

Plot the country data. For illustration, Japan and Singapore are marked

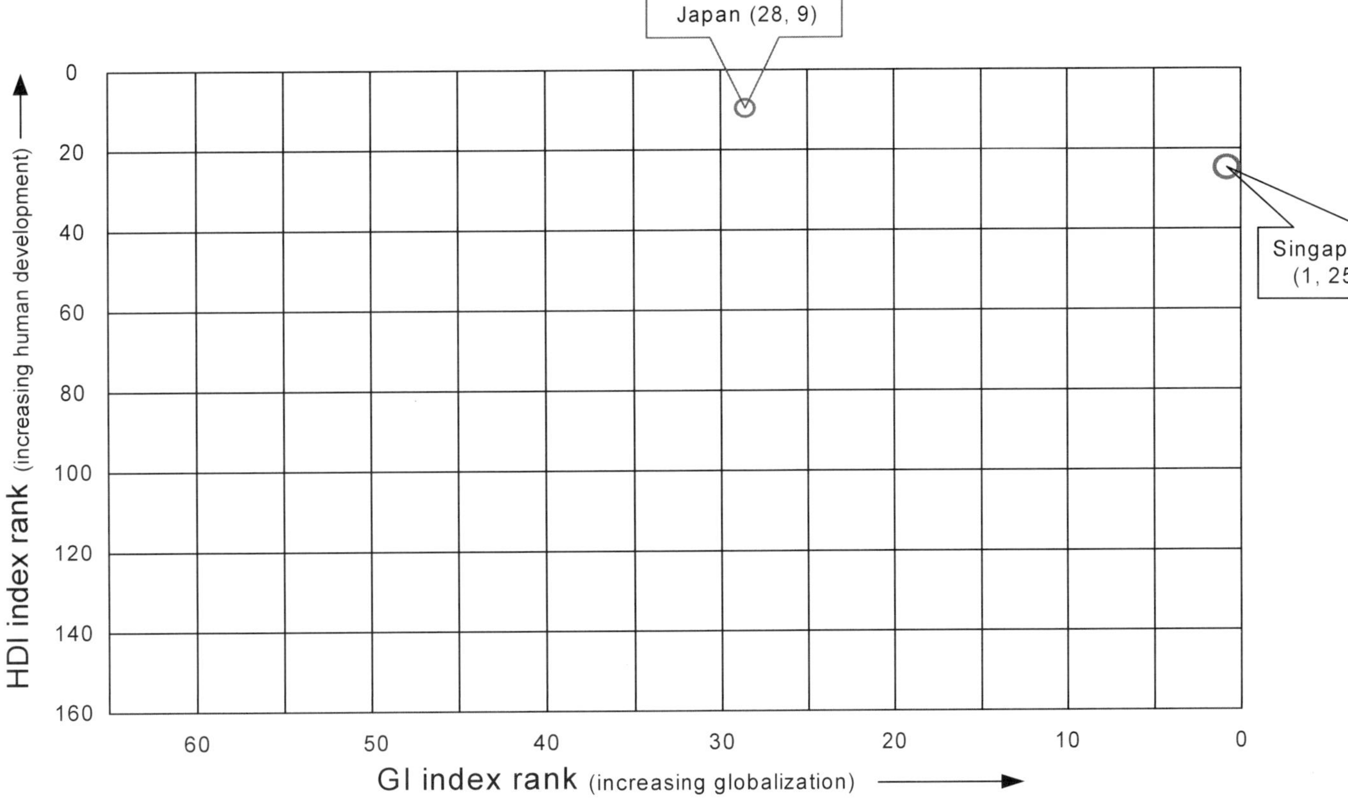

Country	GI rank 2005	HDI rank 2002
Singapore	1	25
Ireland	2	10
Switzerland	3	11
United States	4	8
Netherlands	5	5
Canada	6	4
Denmark	7	17
Sweden	8	2
Austria	9	14
Finland	10	13
Israel	17	22
Slovak Republic	25	42
Japan	28	9
South Korea	30	28
Ukraine	39	70

Country	GI rank 2005	HDI rank 2002
Mexico	42	53
Saudi Arabia	45	77
South Africa	48	119
Kenya	49	148
Russian Federation	52	57
Peru	53	85
China	54	94
Venezuela	55	68
Turkey	56	88
Brazil	57	72
Bangladesh	58	138
Egypt	59	120
Indonesia	60	111
India	61	127
Iran	62	101

LESSON TEN
PROTECTING THE U.S. SUGAR INDUSTRY FROM FOREIGN OUTSOURCING: A BITTERSWEET IDEA

LESSON DESCRIPTION

Students participate in a small group activity–taking roles as consumers, producers, taxpayers, or workers–to review the costs and benefits of programs that keep U.S. prices for sugar two or three times higher than the world price. A class debate on the overall effectiveness of these programs is held, followed by a discussion of U.S. laws and policies that assist workers who are hurt by imports of foreign products or outsourcing of jobs to other countries. A brief activity then provides a summary measure of the high costs of protecting selected U.S. jobs from foreign competition.

INTRODUCTION

In the early 19th century one of the leading practitioners of the new field of economics, David Ricardo, led the call for repeal of the Corn Laws in England. (At that time corn and the Corn Laws referred to wheat. What we call corn today in the United States was then called maize in Europe.) These laws imposed high tariffs on imported grain, which protected the interests of wealthy landowners because land rents were higher when the domestic price of grain was high. English farmers also supported the Corn Laws, which let them sell grain at a higher price.

British consumers were, of course, hurt by the higher grain prices–at that time bread and flour were a much larger part of household budgets than they are today. Ricardo pointed out that countries with more land, lower wages, and drier climates could grow wheat at a lower cost than England, which would find better ways to use its land, labor, and other resources once the artificially high price of grain fell to the lower price that prevailed in the rest of the world.

The same kinds of debates go on today, for agricultural and many other products. There are overall gains from specialization and trade along the lines of low-cost production (also known as comparative advantage, as developed in other lessons in this volume); but groups that benefit from laws protecting them from foreign competition understandably do not want those policies to change.

When protectionist policies for an industry are eliminated or curtailed, it can be very costly for domestic producers to move resources into other uses, and workers in industries that lose the special protection often have to be retrained to do new kinds of jobs, or perhaps even move to a different community where jobs are available. Fortunately, the overall gains from such policy reforms are typically high enough to compensate workers for a substantial part of these costs, and in recent decades laws and policies have been adopted to do that for U.S. workers who lose jobs because of international trade.

But there are still controversies about these policies and the costs and benefits of protective policies versus free trade. The debate Ricardo and other early economists helped to start centuries ago still goes on.

CONCEPTS

Barriers to trade (tariffs, quotas, and subsidies)
Competition
Special interest issues
Trade adjustment assistance
Imports
Exports
Domestic price
World price
Outsourcing
Offshoring

CONTENT STANDARDS

Competition among sellers lowers costs and prices, and encourages producers to produce more of what consumers are willing and able to buy.

Costs of government policies sometimes exceed benefits. This may occur because of incentives facing voters, government officials, and government employees, because of actions of special interest groups that can impose costs on the general public, or because social goals other than economic efficiency are being pursued.

BENCHMARKS

Free trade increases worldwide material standards of living.

Despite the mutual benefits from trade among people in different countries, many nations employ trade barriers to restrict free trade for national defense reasons or because some companies and workers are hurt by free trade.

When imports are restricted by public policies, consumers pay higher prices and job opportunities and profits in exporting firms decrease.

Although barriers to international trade usually impose more costs than benefits, they are often advocated by people and groups who expect to gain substantially from them. Because the costs of these barriers are typically spread over a large number of people who each pay only a little and may not recognize the cost, policies supporting trade barriers are often adopted through the political process.

Governments often redistribute income directly when individuals or interest groups are not satisfied with the income distribution resulting from markets; governments also redistribute income indirectly as side-effects of other government actions that affect prices or output levels for various goods and services.

OBJECTIVES

Students will:

- Identify the gains to themselves and others, and compare the overall benefits and costs, of policies that alter trade barriers between nations (such as tariffs and quotas).
- Explain why the benefits of trade barriers are highly concentrated, providing higher income and employment for producers of the protected products, while costs are spread widely across millions of consumers and firms that purchase the protected product.
- Review provisions in several U.S. laws passed in recent decades that provide special assistance to workers who lose their jobs because of international trade, and relate the rationale for providing this public assistance to workers to the distribution of costs and benefits of policies that promote or restrict free trade, as well as the overall gains from trade.

TIME REQUIRED

Two class periods. In class periods of about one hour, the suggested coverage is: Period 1: Procedures 1-15; Period 2: Procedures 16-31, Closure, and Assessment.

NOTE: You may want to hold the debate on U.S. sugar policies a day or two after completing Procedures 1-15, to allow students time to consult additional information sources, including those listed with Activity 1.

MATERIALS

- Visual 1: A Brief History of U.S. Policies Protecting Sugar
- Visual 2: Outsourcing
- Visual 3: Offshoring
- Visual 4: Summary of Benefits and Costs of Protecting U.S. Sugar Producers
- Activity 1: Talking Points on U.S. Sugar Policies
  - Part 1: U.S. Producers of Sugar (one copy for every fifth student)
  - Part 2: U.S. Consumers of Sugar (one copy for every fifth student)
  - Part 3: U.S. Taxpayers Alliance (one copy for every fifth student)
  - Part 4: Workers Helped by U.S. Sugar Policies (one copy for every fifth student)
  - Part 5: Workers Hurt by U.S. Sugar Policies (one copy for every fifth student)
- Activity 2: U.S. Trade Adjustment Assistance: Fact Sheet (one copy per student)
- Activity 3: The High Cost of Protecting U.S. Jobs (one copy per student), with the second page–the Answer Key–copied separately and distributed later in the activity
- Activity 4: (for optional extension activity or general reference), Readings on Foreign Outsourcing/Offshoring
- A candy bar or other kind of candy, and/or a regular (not diet) soft drink

PROCEDURES

1. Hold up a popular candy bar, roll of hard candy, or a regular soft drink (not sugar free) and ask students if they like this type of food or drink. (*Answers will vary, but many will say yes.*) Point out that millions of people must like the product(s), based on annual sales.

2. Ask students what makes the product sweet. *(sugar, corn syrup, or other "natural" sweeteners)* Ask, "What would happen to the prices of this product, and of other products sweetened with sugar, if the price of sugar increased?" *(Answers may vary initially. Guide students to responses that connect higher input or ingredient costs with higher prices for products made with the inputs.)*

3. Tell students that today they will examine the effects on different groups in the economy resulting from high sugar prices caused by government policies that protect U.S. sugar producers from foreign competition.

4. Define the **domestic price** of a product as the price that results when goods are traded within a country, with only domestic sources for both demand and supply. This situation is sometimes referred to as a closed economy, because the market is closed to trade from other countries.

5. Define the **world price** as the price of a product that results when goods are freely traded in nations all around the world, reflecting global sources of both demand and supply.

6. Ask students what would happen to the domestic price for a good if imports of the products are reduced or eliminated by laws passed in a country that had been

importing the product? *(the domestic price will rise above the world price)*

7. Ask students if they can name several kinds of policies that restrict imports. (*Answers will vary based on how much material on international trade students have seen in earlier lessons or other courses.*) Briefly explain that tariffs, quotas, and subsidies to domestic producers all reduce imports of the affected products. **Tariffs** are taxes on imports and **quotas** are limits on quantities of products that can be imported. Both increase the domestic price of protected products, as suggested above. **Subsidies,** paid by the government to producers of a product, lower the domestic price of the product, but are paid for by taxpayers, so in that sense they also raise the cost of the product to domestic consumers. Lesson 11 in this volume covers these trade barriers in more detail, if you want to do more.

8. Display Visual 1, revealing one bullet point at a time:

- In the early 19th century, the U.S. imposed high tariffs on sugar to help sugar producers in the newly acquired Louisiana territory.
- Southern plantation owners demanded continued protection before the Civil War, fearing the collapse of both land and slave values if cheaper sugar imports were allowed to come into the country.
- In the 1930s, as part of a futile effort to use trade barriers to protect U.S. jobs in many industries, sugar import quotas were added to existing high tariffs on sugar and production subsidies paid to U.S. sugar producers.
- By 1945, to promote recovery efforts after WWII and avoid another depression, many international agreements and institutions (including GATT, which later became the WTO) were adopted that encouraged international trade and discouraged trade barriers. Worldwide, trade barriers for most products began to fall sharply, but not for sugar.
- Since 1981, the U.S. sugar industry has successfully lobbied to protect itself from international competition and is now one of the most protected industries in the world.

9. Explain to students that the special protection enjoyed by the U.S. sugar industry today is related to broader concerns about workers losing their jobs because other workers, and especially workers in other countries, are willing to work for lower wages. Display Visual 2 and define **outsourcing**. Ask students if they have heard about outsourcing, and if they can offer examples. *(Answers may vary, but most likely students will have heard stories about outsourcing in the context of jobs leaving the U.S. for Mexico, China, or other developing nations.)*

10. Discuss the following example: the hospital in your area hires a local company called Sanitizers-R-Us to perform all of its housekeeping services, from mopping floors to cleaning beds, surgical areas, and linens. The workers who perform these duties are employees of Sanitizers-R-Us, not the hospital. Ask students if they believe this is an example of outsourcing. *(Answers may vary, but some students might argue no, since both companies are local.)* Many students think outsourcing always involves jobs "lost" to other countries. Review the definition again and confirm that this example involving two local companies does represent outsourcing, because the housekeeping duties and employment are moved from the firm that runs the hospital to a third-party provider.

11. Display Visual 3. Define **offshoring**. Note that some kinds of outsourcing can also be considered

offshoring, if production tasks and employment are transferred to a different company in another country. This kind of outsourcing, as well as cases of offshoring in which a firm moves production to facilities in other countries that it owns and operates itself, have become very controversial in recent years, and regularly featured in the print and electronic media. Point out that media reports often use the term outsourcing, not offshoring, to refer only to cases of foreign outsourcing, or offshoring. But in fact many U.S. firms hire other U.S. firms and workers domestically. For example, hospitals, airports, schools, and professional sports teams often negotiate contracts with other firms to make and sell food or other products in their facilities, rather than trying to make and sell these products themselves.

12. Tell students they will participate in a group activity that explores the costs and benefits of sugar trade restrictions from the standpoint of five different groups: U.S. sugar producers, U.S. sugar consumers, U.S. taxpayers, and two different groups of workers.

13. Divide students into five groups of approximately equal size. Identify Group 1 as U.S. Sugar Farmers, and give each student in the group a copy of Activity 1, Part 1. Identify Group 2 as U.S. Consumers of Sugar and give one copy of Activity 1, Part 2 to each member of that group. Identify Groups 3, 4, and 5 as the U.S. Taxpayers Alliance and Workers Helped or Hurt by the Sugar Policies, respectively, and give each student in those groups one copy of Activity 1, Parts 3, 4, or 5, as appropriate.

14. Tell students that the handout they received provides information relevant to their assigned roles. They will be given 15-20 minutes to discuss the points in their groups and develop a brief summary statement representing their position on whether U.S. policies that protect the domestic sugar industry from imports of sugar grown and processed in other nations should be continued. Each group should select a spokesperson to present their summary statement. Tell all of the groups to create a summary statement in their own words that reflects their group discussion, and not to just read one or more points from their handout. Announce that each spokesperson will have one minute to explain their team's summary position, and then the class as a whole will debate the policies.

15. You may want to hold the debate a day or two later, and have students do additional research on the topic, but still in the framework of their assigned roles as sugar producers, consumers, taxpayers, or workers. Sources of the talking points on Activity 1, Parts 1-5, available on the Internet, include:

- www.fff.org/freedom/0498d.asp "The Great Sugar Shaft" by James Bovard, April 1998;
- www.knowledgeproblem.com/archives/000726.html Walter Williams on Sweets, February 2004;
- www.townhall.com/opinion/columns/dougbandow/2005/02/07/14460.html "Sugar Subsidy: How Sweet It Is" by Doug Bandow, February 2005;
- www.ppionline.org/ppi_ci.cfm?knlgAreaID=108&subsecID=900003&contentID=253294 "U.S. Subsidies: $1.2 Billion a Year," Progressive Policy Institute, April 2005;
- www.ers.usda.gov/Briefing/Sugar Sugar Briefing Room: Sugar and Sweeteners, Economic Research Service, United States Department of Agriculture;
- www.ciponline.org/SugarIPR.pdf Sugar Program, Citizens Against Government Waste; "A Time for

Change: The Outrageous Federal Sugar Subsidy Program," by Wayne S. Smith, Center for International Policy;

- www.taxpayer.net/TCS/wastebasket/environment/8-3-00.htm "Taxpayers Sour on Sugar Subsidies," *Taxpayers for Common Sense,* Vol. 5, No. 26, August 3, 2000;
- www.aworldconnected.org/article.php/561.html "Trade & Protectionism" by Daniel T. Griswold, A World Connected;
- www.ers.usda.gov/Briefing/Sugar Sugar Briefing Room: Sugar and Sweeteners: Background, Economic Research Service, U.S. Department of Agriculture;
- www.cagw.org/site/PageServer?/pagename=issues_agriculture "Sugar Program";
- www.ers.usda.gov/Publications/SSS/aug05/sss24301/ "Sweetener Consumption in the United States: Distribution by Demographic and Product Characteristics";
- www.free-eco.org/articleDisplay.php?id=459 "Big Sugar's Sugar Daddy," by David G. Sands;
- http://www.taxpayer.net/agriculture/learnmore/factsheets/TCSSugarCommodityFactSheet_2003.pdf "Federal Sugar Subsidies: A Sweet Deal for Sugar Processors";
- www.heritage.org/Research/TradeandForeignAid/bg1868.cfm "DR-CAFTA Yes, Sugar No," by Daniella Markheim, July 13, 2005;
- www.reason.com/0602/fe.dg.six.shtml "Six Reasons to Kill Farm Subsidies and Trade Barriers," by Daniel Griswold and others, 1 Feb 2006;
- www.marketaccesscoalition.com/Sugar.htm "Truth and Consequences: Sifting through Sugar Exclusions";
- www.house.gov/georgemiller/rel6900.html "GAO: Government Protection of Sugar Growers Costs Consumers $2 Billion," July 9, 2000

16. Assemble students in one large group for the debate. Allow members of each small group to sit in close proximity. Remind students that they should remain in their assigned roles as consumers, producers, etc., until the debate is over, even if their personal opinions differ from the talking points associated with the roles they are playing. After the debate, an additional discussion will take place (see procedures 20-23), during which students are encouraged to express opinions they hold or have formed as a result of the debate on protecting the sugar industry.

17. Begin the activity with brief opening statements from each of the five spokespersons that summarize the position of their group. Remind spokespersons to identify the group they represent (consumers, producers, etc), and tell other students to listen carefully and make notes to use in supporting or opposing arguments when the class debate begins.

18. Announce that all students should participate in the class debate of these issues, not just the spokespersons. Encourage challenges of claims made by other students, but make it clear that challenges are to be made in a civil manner, and that you will enforce that policy. Conduct the debate.

19. After the debate, instruct students to consult with the members of their small group (consumers, producers, etc). Tell each group to prepare a closing statement, summarizing where the group stands on

sugar subsidies in light of the public debate over this issue. Explain that this statement may or may not be similar to their opening statement, but it should reflect additional information and insights gathered during the debate. Each group will be allowed one minute to present their closing statement to the class. You may want to have each group designate a new spokesperson. Allow 5-10 minutes to prepare the closing arguments, and have the groups present them to the class.

20. Announce that the debate is over and their assigned role-playing duties are completed. Ask students to think broadly and to consider the overall benefits and costs of the U.S. sugar policies, for all groups in society–even workers who produce sugar in other countries.

21. Display Visual 4, which summarizes points that were probably made by the different groups. Explain any points that the students did not address adequately in their presentations.

22. To review, end the display of Visual 4 and ask the following questions, reviewing the correct answers as you go:

A. Has sugar production in the United States increased or decreased in recent decades? *(increased)*

B. Why? *(Price supports and protection from international competition allow U.S. producers to sell sugar at prices much higher than the world price, so much more sugar is produced than would be if the world price prevailed in the U.S. market for sugar.)*

C. Why can some other countries produce sugar at a lower cost than U.S. producers? (*The other countries may have more arable farmland in tropical climates, and lower wages.)*

D. Who in the United States benefits from the government policies that support the domestic production of sugar? *(A small number of sugar producers benefit most. The Government Accounting Office estimates that more than 40% of the benefits from policies that support U.S. sugar production–including government backed loans, price supports, and import quotas–go to the largest 1% of farms, which are usually owned by large corporations. Also, more U.S. jobs are available in sugar production, and in corn and corn syrup production.)*

E. Who in the United States is hurt by the government policies that support the domestic production of sugar? *(consumers of sugar and sugar-based products pay higher product prices; firms and workers in industries that use sugar or sweeteners as inputs, such as soft drink, candy, and bakery firms; export industries subject to retaliation by trading partners; and taxpayers who cover the cost of government backed loans, price supports, and import quotas that benefit sugar producers; in addition, taxpayers bear the cost of storing surplus sugar that the government purchases to maintain high U.S. prices)*

F. From the point of view of society as a whole, are the benefits of sugar subsidies greater than their costs? *(Answers may vary at this point, although most of the evidence from Activity 1 suggests that benefits are fairly small relative to the costs.)* Provide additional evidence by citing the following statistic: the U.S. International Trade Commission estimates that the cost of each job "saved" in the sugar industries is more than $1.5 million–far more than workers in those jobs are paid, of course. Those costs take into account the higher prices paid by consumers and job losses in export industries and industries that use sugar or other sweeteners as a major input.

G. If U.S. sugar policies result in more costs than benefits, why are they allowed to continue? *(Benefits are concentrated among a small number of sugar producers who have been effective in lobbying Congress to maintain protection, and the relatively small number of workers in the industry. Sugar producers contribute 17% of total farm campaign donations in the United States, even though sugar farms represent only 1% of total U.S. agricultural production. Several sugar-producing states are considered "swing" states that are especially important in tightly contested national elections. Much larger numbers of consumers and taxpayers are adversely affected by the policies, so the costs to individual consumers and taxpayers are relatively small, and many of them do not even know that these policies are in place and increasing prices and taxes. As many jobs are lost as are saved by the sugar policies, but the jobs lost are widely dispersed among many different industries, while the jobs saved are concentrated in sugar production and processing, so those firms and workers are more likely to know about and support the programs than the firms and workers who are hurt by the policies. This pattern of highly concentrated benefits and widely dispersed costs is a classic example of a special interest issue.)*

H. How do sugar subsidies affect relationships with U.S. trading partners? *(You may want to refer to Activity 1 in Lesson 11 of this volume, or give students a copy of that reading here, if you do not plan to cover that lesson separately. In short, trade barriers for sugar and other agricultural products in the United States, the European Union, Japan, and other wealthy nations in the world have clearly slowed progress toward general tariff reductions and the trade liberalization movement. This was especially clear at the World Trade Organization's Doha Round of trade negotiations. The extremely high sugar trade barriers have been especially devastating to developing nations that can produce sugar at much lower costs than the United States, including nations in Central and South America and Africa. Displaced sugar farmers and agricultural workers in those countries have sometimes turned to other cash crops, including marijuana and cocaine. Some countries have also retaliated with their own trade barriers to protest the U.S. sugar policies. For example, Australia imposed restrictions on imports of U.S. wheat and pharmaceuticals, which reduces U.S. employment in these industries.)*

23. Tell students to consider, one last time, all the issues and perspectives raised during the debate about the U.S. sugar policies. Ask them to indicate with a show of hands whether they support the continuation of the programs to protect U.S.

production of sugar. *(responses will vary)* Ask students if their response would be the same if they lived in a different region of the United States. Point out that students who live in states that depend heavily on sugar production might well respond differently from those who live in other states.

24. Tell students to imagine themselves in the following situation: they live in a family where their parents' income and employment is tied to sugar production, and it has just been announced that the government will soon eliminate all trade restrictions on imported sugar. (Note: at the time this was written, there has been no such indication, and students are only being asked to consider a hypothetical situation here.) Government representatives say this is best for the nation as a whole, because the overall benefits of ending the sugar programs are much greater than the costs. But they recognize that those who bear the costs will be significantly hurt.

25. Ask students the following questions: Do you believe the government should help workers who lose their jobs? For how long? Should workers who lose their jobs because of international trade issues receive more assistance than workers who lose their jobs for other reasons (such as plants relocating to another location in the United States, or closing because consumers stop buying the products they make to buy goods made by other U.S. companies)? *(Answers will vary. Ask students to discuss the costs and benefits of the support, including costs to taxpayers.)*

26. Tell students that, in fact, the United States and some other countries have adopted **Trade Adjustment Assistance** programs, which are special programs to assist workers who are hurt by international trade, and in particular by the reduction or termination of government policies that protected workers in some industries from foreign competition and imports. Distribute Activity 2, which reviews the major U.S. Trade Adjustment Assistance programs adopted over the past 50 years, and give students time to read it.

27. Explain that, although being unemployed and without income is a serious problem for anyone, not just workers who were hurt by international trade, there are some special reasons for the trade assistance programs, too. First, by reducing opposition to agreements that promote more international trade, trade assistance policies make it politically easier to negotiate those agreements and gain the advantages from trade (including lower prices for consumers, more jobs in U.S. export industries, etc.). Second, unemployment caused by changes in trading patterns and policies is likely to be concentrated in certain industries and regions of the nation, and perhaps more likely to entail relocation and retraining expenses for workers who lose their jobs. Third, the overall gains from allowing more trade are in some sense available to help pay for the trade assistance programs, which is not always the case with other kinds of unemployment. In the final analysis, of course, the Trade Assistance programs were adopted because there was enough political support to have the legislation passed.

28. Conclude the discussion of trade adjustment assistance by asking students why it is important that the help offered to affected workers be limited and temporary. *(Answers will vary. Guide students toward responses that suggest society's welfare is highest when workers quickly find new permanent employment that best matches their skills and training. Full compensation for losses with no time limit on benefits severely reduces workers' incentives to find and move into new jobs.)*

29. Distribute the first page of Activity 3, showing the number of jobs saved by trade restrictions and the total annual costs for those restrictions in 20 protected industries in the United States. Briefly review again the types of costs associated with protecting jobs, including higher prices for the good and other goods that use the product as an input. For example, students saw that U.S. sugar policies increased sugar prices, and prices for candy bars, soft drinks, bakery goods, etc. Costs also include "secondary" job losses in those industries. Another example could be U.S. autoworkers losing jobs when U.S. steel production was protected and trading partners retaliated with limits on their imports of U.S. automobiles. Or, once again with sugar policies, production of Life Savers candy was moved from the United States to Canada to avoid the higher U.S. price of sugar after imports were restricted, even though the wage rates for workers were similar in both countries.

30. Have students calculate the average cost of saving one job in each of the protected industries shown in Activity 3. When they have finished, distribute the second page of Activity 3–the Answer Key–to check their calculations.

31. Ask students to decide whether the annual cost per job saved in any of these industries is low enough to support such policies, from a purely economic point of view. *(Most students are likely to answer no, because the annual costs of saving a job are far higher than the typical wages of the jobs that are saved.)* Point out that it would be less expensive to spend part of that amount supporting workers with temporary unemployment insurance, or with assistance for retraining or relocation costs.

CLOSURE

Review the key points of the lesson using the following questions:

1. Who wins and who loses when U.S. sugar producers are protected from foreign competition? *(Winners: sugar and corn producers and some sugar and corn farm workers, who would otherwise not be employed in those industries if U.S. sugar prices were as low as the world price. Losers: consumers of sugar and sugar-sweetened products, who pay higher prices for those goods; firms and workers in industries that use sugar as an input, such as candy, bakery, and soft drinks; workers in countries that can produce sugar at a lower cost but who are unable to compete when U.S. sugar is protected; and U.S. taxpayers, who pay higher taxes to provide the revenues necessary to fund the additional government expenditures.)*

2. If the overall costs of protecting U.S. sugar production are higher than the benefits, why does this program have enough political support to continue? *(The costs are spread widely across many affected parties while the benefits are concentrated among a smaller number of firms and individuals–classic conditions for a special interest issue. The large group of losers is typically not organized or motivated enough to block the actions of the small, highly motivated group of gainers.)*

3. If sugar protection is removed, what types of assistance would be available to workers who are hurt by this policy change? *(extended unemployment compensation, and financial support for retraining or relocation, for periods of one to two years)*

EXTENSION ACTIVITY

Conduct a classroom debate on foreign outsourcing issues, assigning readings to students from the list in Activity 4, or letting students choose their own sources from this list and their own research.

ASSESSMENT

Have students write a letter to the editor or a short "op ed" piece for the local newspaper editorial page, supporting or opposing trade liberalization (freer trade rules) by the United States. A discussion of the benefits and costs of those policies, and which groups benefit and lose from policies promoting or restricting trade, should be prominently featured in their letter or article.

Visual 1
A Brief History of U.S. Policies Protecting Sugar

- Early 19th century–High tariffs imposed on imported sugar to favor growers in newly acquired Louisiana territory
- Mid-19th century–Southern plantation owners demand continued protection to prevent collapse of land and slave values
- 1930s–tariffs, quotas, and subsidies are adopted in an attempt to save American jobs in many industries, including sugar
- Post WWII–efforts to promote economic recovery from the war and avoid another Great Depression, often led by the United States, propel a move toward free trade and the establishment of international organizations and agreements such as the UN, IMF, and GATT (which later becomes the WTO)
- Since 1981–sugar industry successfully lobbies for protection against international competition. For example, in 1981 President Reagan reimposed import quotas. Throughout the 1980s, quotas were reduced (tightened), allowing smaller amounts of imported foreign sugar. The 1981 Farm Bill created a commodity loan program that sets a support price for sugar. Legislation passed in 2002 continued similar forms of protection and subsidies.

Sources:

- www.fff.org/freedom/0498d.asp "The Great Sugar Shaft," by James Bovard, April 1998;
- www.reason.com/0602/fe.dg.sixshtml "Six Reasons to Kill Farm Subsidies and Trade Barriers," by Daniel Griswold et al. February 2006;
- www.taxpayer.net/agriculture/learnmore/factsheets/ TCSSugarCommodityFactSheet_2003.pdf "Federal Sugar Subsidies: A Sweet Deal for Sugar Processors"

Visual 2
Outsourcing

Outsourcing (or contracting out) is often defined as the delegation of non-core operations or jobs from internal production within a business to an external entity (such as a subcontractor) that specializes in that operation.

[It is]… the management and/or day-to-day execution of an entire business function by a third party service provider.

Source: Wikipedia
http://www.en.wikipedia.org/wiki/outsourcing

Visual 3
Offshoring

Offshoring is the movement of a business process done at a local company to a foreign country, regardless of whether the work done in the foreign country is still performed by the local company or a third party. Typically, work is moved due to a lower cost of operations in the foreign location.

Source: Wikipedia
http://www.en.wikipedia.org/wiki/offshoring

Visual 4
Summary of Benefits and Costs of Protecting U.S. Sugar Producers

U.S. sugar producers–Producing sugar and other sweeteners (such as corn syrup) in the United States costs substantially more than the world price of sugar. To produce these products profitably, U.S. producers must receive government subsidies, or have imports of sugar restricted so that the U.S. price of sugar increases substantially, or both.

U.S. sugar consumers–The U.S. is the largest consumer of sweeteners in the world. Higher U.S. sugar prices affect the prices of many products consumers buy every day.

Workers (positive effects)–Some U.S. jobs (growing sugar cane, sugar beets, or processing sugar) are saved as a result of the policies. There is also more U.S. employment in growing corn and processing corn syrup sweeteners, as some manufacturers replace sugar with corn syrup.

Workers (negative effects)–High sugar prices reduce jobs in U.S. industries that use sweeteners, and create incentives to produce sugar-sweetened goods outside the United States. If U.S. consumers spend more on sweetened food products but less on other goods and services, employment in producing other goods and services also falls. In sugar exporting nations, including many very poor nations in Africa, Latin America, and the Caribbean, when sugar producers are unable to export

Visual 4 (continued)

products to the United States employment and income fall. U.S. sugar policies may lead to retaliation by trading partners, which reduces U.S. exports to those nations and U.S. jobs in export industries.

U.S. taxpayers–The costs of government policies protecting sugar are high relative to their benefits, and concentrated among large farmers and companies that produce sugar or other sweeteners. The costs of production subsidies and higher prices for sugar and sweeteners are spread widely across millions of consumers and taxpayers.

Sources:

- www.fff.org/freedom/0498d.asp "The Great Sugar Shaft," by James Bovard, April 1998;
- www.knowledgeproblem.com/archives/000726.html Walter Williams on Sweets, February 2004;
- www.ers.usda.gov/Briefing/Sugar Sugar Briefing Room: Sugar and Sweeteners, Economic Research Service, United States Department of Agriculture;
- www.ciponline.org/SugarIPR.pdf Sugar Program, Citizens Against Government Waste; "A Time for Change: The Outrageous Federal Sugar Subsidy Program," by Wayne S. Smith, Center for International Policy;
- www.taxpayer.net/TCS/wastebasket/environment/8-3-00.htm "Taxpayers Sour on Sugar Subsidies," *Taxpayers for Common Sense*, Vol. 5, No. 26, August 3, 2000;
- www.cagw.org/site/PageServer?/pagename=issues_agriculture "Sugar Program"

Activity 1
Talking Points on U.S. Sugar Policies

Part 1, U.S. Producers of Sugar

- Sugar is produced from sugar cane or sugar beets. Cane grows in tropical/semi-tropic climes, including four states (FL, LA, HI, TX). Beets grow in temperate climes, including 12 states (CA, WA, OR, ID, WY, MT, CO, NE, ND, MN, MI, OH).

- The number of U.S. farms devoted to sugar production fell from 1997 to 2002, from 1,079 to 953, but average acreage per cane farm rose from 825 to 1,027. The number of sugar beet farms decreased from 7,059 to 5,057, but average acreage per beet farm rose from 202 to 272.

- From the 1980s to the early 2000s, average U.S. production of sugar increased from 6 million short tons, raw value (STRV) to approximately 8.4 million STRV of sugar.

- U.S. sugar farmers produce only 1% of total U.S. agricultural production, but contribute 17% of all political donations from U.S. farmers.

- The American Sugar Alliance estimates that trade restrictions on imported sugar help protect 372,000 jobs in the U.S. sugar industry.

Sources:

- www.ciponline.org/SugarIPR.pdf Sugar Program, Citizens Against Government Waste; "A Time for Change: The Outrageous Federal Sugar Subsidy Program," by Wayne S. Smith, Center for International Policy;
- www.ers.usda.gov/Briefing/Sugar Sugar Briefing Room: Sugar and Sweeteners: Background, Economic Research Service, U.S. Department of Agriculture

Activity 1 (continued)

Part 2, U. S. Consumers of Sugar

- American consumers pay 2 to 3 times the world price of sugar because of limits on sugar imported from other countries.

- The United States consumes more sweeteners than any nation in the world. Higher sugar prices lead to only small decreases in the consumption of products that use sugar or other sweeteners.

- The U.S. General Accounting Office (GAO) estimates that consumers pay about $2 billion more each year in higher prices for goods such as soft drinks, bakery goods, candy, and processed foods, because of the higher U.S. price of sugar.

- The U.S. per capita consumption of sugar has increased in recent decades. Therefore, the cost to consumers of policies that raise the price of sugar has also increased, and is relatively greater for low-income households.

- Low-income households spend a larger percentage of their income on food and beverages than high-income households, but nearly all consumers buy and use goods that contain sugar. Therefore, the impact of higher sugar prices is very widespread.

- Higher sugar prices distort supply and prices of other goods. For example, Coca Cola and Pepsi Cola switched from sugar to corn syrup as a sweetener in 1984, reducing the amount of sugar demanded by 500,000 tons. The additional demand for corn syrup increases corn prices and production, so corn and corn syrup producers also support policies that raise sugar prices.

- Sugar price supports are often impediments in trade negotiations with other nations. Retaliation by trading partners usually takes the form of trade barriers on goods they import from the United States, which reduces U.S. exports of those products.

Activity 1 (continued)

Part 2, (continued)

- The Organization for Economic Co-operation and Development (OECD) estimates that higher domestic food prices caused by U.S. farm programs (all agricultural products, not just sugar) transferred $16.2 billion from American consumers to domestic agricultural producers in 2004

Sources:

- www.fff.org/freedom/0498d.asp "The Great Sugar Shaft" by James Bovard, April 1998;
- www.ciponline.org/SugarIPR.pdf Sugar Program, Citizens Against Government Waste; "A Time for Change: The Outrageous Federal Sugar Subsidy Program," by Wayne S. Smith, Center for International Policy;
- www.cagw.org/site/PageServer?/pagename=issues_agriculture "Sugar Program";
- www.ers.usda.gov/Publications/SSS/aug05/sss24301 "Sweetener Consumption in the United States: Distribution by Demographic and Product Characteristics";
- www.free-eco.org/articleDisplay.php?id=459 "Big Sugar's Sugar Daddy," by David G. Sands;
- www.reason.com/0602/fe.dg.six.shtml "Six Reasons to Kill Farm Subsidies and Trade Barriers," by Daniel Griswold and others, 1 Feb 2006;
- www.house.gov/georgemiller/rel6900.html "GAO: Government Protection of Sugar Growers Costs Consumers $2 Billion," July 9, 2000

Activity 1 (continued)

Part 3, U. S. Taxpayers Alliance

- Government subsidies paid directly to sugar producers transfer much of the cost of producing sugar and sweeteners in the United States to U.S. taxpayers. Taxpayers also pay for U.S. trade policies that restrict imports of sugar, through higher prices for sugar and products made with sugar or sweeteners.

- Subsidies and higher prices for sugar lead to increased output of sugar, and even to surpluses. In 2003, to keep U.S. sugar prices from falling, the U.S. government purchased $400 million worth of surplus sugar production and paid $1 million a month to store it.

- Higher sugar prices mean higher costs for other government programs, including school lunch programs and food stamp programs for low-income families. The Government Accounting Office (GAO) estimates taxpayers pay $90 million more annually for food programs because of higher prices for sugar and sugar-sweetened products used in those programs.

- Because of the adverse effects U.S. restrictions on imported sugar have on sugar producers in other countries, including many very poor countries, the U.S. government has agreed to compensate governments of these countries, through foreign aid. In other words, U.S. taxpayers are paying to subsidize sugar producers in the United States **AND** in other countries, too.

- Although government programs that protect U.S. agricultural producers are sometimes defended as a way to protect small "family farms," more than 40% of the benefits of the sugar protection program are received by the largest 1% of sugar producers, which turned out to be 17 individuals or firms in 2000.

- Lobbyists for the U.S. sugar industry claim that 372,000 U.S. jobs are affected by the sugar price supports, but the U.S. International Trade Commission estimates the figure to be much lower, around 61,000 jobs.

Activity 1 (continued)

Part 3, (continued)

- Sugar growers make political campaign contributions of about $18 million a year, far more than growers and producers of most other agricultural products.

Sources:

- www.fff.org/freedom/0498d.asp "The Great Sugar Shaft," by James Bovard, April 1998;
- www.townhall.com/opinion/columns/dougbandow/2005/02/07/14460.html "Sugar Subsidy: How Sweet It Is," by Doug Bandow, February 2005;
- www.ciponline.org/SugarIPR.pdf Sugar Program, Citizens Against Government Waste; "A Time for Change: The Outrageous Federal Sugar Subsidy Program," by Wayne S. Smith, Center for International Policy;
- "Sugar Lobby's Clout Threatens Economic Decay," *USA Today*, August 19, 2002;
- www.taxpayer.net/TCS/wastebasket/environment/8-3-00.htm "Taxpayers Sour on Sugar Subsidies," Taxpayers for Common Sense, Vol. 5, No. 26, August 3, 2000;
- www.cagw.org/site/PageServer?/pagename=issues_agriculture "Sugar Program"

Activity 1 (continued)

Part 4, Workers Helped by U.S. Sugar Policies

- Sugar farmers. Although the number of farms is decreasing, the number would be lower without subsidies, because many farms would not be profitable without the higher U.S. prices of sugar that result from government protection policies.

- Corn farmers. As a result of higher sugar prices, more acres of U.S. farmland are planted in corn for the production of high-fructose corn syrup (HFCS). From 1980 to 2000, domestic corn production devoted to HFCS rose from 2.2 million tons to 9.2 million tons, which represents about 5 percent of the total U.S. corn crop.

- In regions of the country where employment and income in sugar or corn farming and processing increase as a result of government policies that protect domestic producers from foreign competition, other businesses also benefit. For example, in certain parishes of Louisiana or counties in Florida, when the sugar industry expands the demand for farm equipment, clothing, restaurants, housing, and other goods and services also increases.

Sources:

- www.ers.usda.gov/Briefing/Sugar Sugar Briefing Room: Sugar and Sweeteners: Background, Economic Research Service, U.S. Department of Agriculture;
- www.heritage.org/Research/TradeandForeignAid/bg1868.cfm "DR-CAFTA Yes, Sugar No," by Daniella Markheim, July 13, 2005

Activity 1 (continued)

Part 5, Workers Hurt by U.S. Sugar Policies

- U.S. manufacturers of goods containing sugar. Higher costs of production result in higher product prices and lower quantities demanded, and therefore lower production and employment levels, compared to free trade prices.

- U.S. bakers, candy makers, and other producers that use sugar to make their products. Some U.S. companies that use sugar as a major input and can ship their final products into the United States at a low cost moved their production to other countries, where sugar prices were lower. Wage rates were also lower in some cases, but not always. For example, Kraft moved the production of Life Savers to Canada, where wages were comparable but the price of sugar was half the U.S. price. That alone saved Kraft $10 million a year in production costs. In 1970, employment in candy manufacturing around Chicago was about 15,000 workers–by 2004 it had fallen to 8,000. Fannie May and Brach's have shut down; Ferrara Candy is expanding in Mexico, Canada, and other countries.

- Workers in U.S. export industries. When a country limits imports of products, in this case sugar, other countries often retaliate by limiting their imports of other products from the same country. For example, in response to U.S. policies limiting sugar imports, Australia limited its imports of U.S. wheat and pharmaceuticals. That reduces employment in U.S. export industries. Employment in U.S. export industries also falls if countries that were selling sugar to the United States before the U.S. import restrictions were adopted have fewer dollars to buy U.S. exports.

- Foreign sugar producers and workers. Although sugar can be produced at a lower cost in other countries, with U.S. sugar policies it is impossible for firms in those countries to sell their product in the United States. In some of these countries where income levels were very low, workers who lost jobs producing sugar turned to the production of illegal drugs, or came to the United States to look for work, sometimes as illegal immigrants.

Sources:

- www.knowledgeproblem.com/archives/000726.html Walter Williams on Sweets, February 2004;
- http://www.reason.com/0602/fe.dg.six.shtml "Six Reasons to Kill Farm Subsidies and Trade Barriers," by Daniel Griswold and others, Feb.1 2006;
- www.marketaccesscoalition.com/Sugar.htm "Truth and Consequences: Sifting through Sugar Exclusions," April 2006

Activity 2
U.S. Trade Adjustment Assistance: Fact Sheet

Rationale for Trade Adjustment Assistance: Even though the nation as a whole benefits from free trade policies, workers and firms in some industries are hurt by removing trade barriers or production subsidies. The benefits are very widely dispersed to millions of consumers and taxpayers, but the costs are much more concentrated, and fall mainly on relatively small numbers of workers and firms. In light of that, several U.S. laws have authorized special assistance programs for workers hurt by international trade, including:

A. Trade Expansion Act of 1962

1. Authorized President Kennedy to engage in GATT negotiations with other world leaders for trade liberalization (Kennedy Round); and

2. Established Trade Adjustment Assistance (TAA) to compensate workers if employment is negatively affected by increased imports.

   Until 1974, very few people qualified due to rigid eligibility rules.

   In 1974 Congress eased eligibility criteria, and the relaxed rules provided 52 weeks of income maintenance for eligible workers (beyond the usual 26 weeks of unemployment insurance payments) including training, job search, and relocation assistance. In 1981, enrollment in training programs was required for workers to qualify for income maintenance, and weekly payments were reduced to match each state's unemployment insurance payments instead of being set at the national average manufacturing wage.

B. North American Free Trade Agreement of 1993

Authorized North American Free Trade Agreement Transitional Adjustment Assistance (NAFTA-TAA), a separate program for workers who lost jobs in industries facing increased imports from Mexico or Canada, or from U.S. firms relocating production to Canada and Mexico.

Activity 2 (continued)

C. Trade Adjustment Assistance Reform Act of 2002

1. Extends assistance eligibility to workers at firms that are negatively affected by "secondary" effects of imports and other trade policy adjustments, including suppliers of firms that cut back or relocate their production (for example, a worker in a spark plug factory that supplies a U.S. auto manufacturer);
2. Strengthens the quality of the on-the-job training program, and customizes training to meet employers' needs;
3. Provides an additional 26 weeks of income support for workers participating in training, meaning that TAA payments can be paid for up to 104 weeks, instead of the 26 weeks that is usually allowed for unemployment benefits);
4. Provides limited health care benefits to eligible workers;
5. Creates a TAA program for farmers, administered by the Department of Agriculture;
6. Provides alternative TAA programs for eligible workers who are 50 years old or older.

Sources:

- www.doleta.gov/tradeact/2002act_summary.cfm "Trade Adjustment Assistance Reform Act of 2002: Summary";
- www.heritage.org/Research/Labor/HL714.cfm "Trade Adjustment Assistance: A Flawed Program," by Denise H. Froning, July 31, 2001;
- www.iie.com/publications/papers/paper.cfm?ResearchID=450 "Reforming Trade Adjustment Assistance: Keeping a 40-Year Promise," by Howard F. Rosen, February 26, 2002

Activity 3
The High Cost of Protecting U.S. Jobs

Protected Industry	Jobs saved	Annual total cost (millions)	Annual cost per job saved
Benzenoid chemicals	216	$ 297	
Luggage	226	290	
Softwood lumber	605	632	
Sugar	2,261	1,868	
Polyethylene resins	298	242	
Dairy products	2,378	1,630	
Frozen concentrated orange juice	609	387	
Ball bearings	146	88	
Maritime services	4,411	2,522	
Ceramic tiles	347	191	
Machine tools	1,556	746	
Ceramic articles	418	140	
Women's handbags	773	204	
Canned tuna	390	100	
Glassware	1,477	366	
Apparel and textiles	168,786	33,629	
Peanuts	397	74	
Rubber footwear	1,701	286	
Women's nonathletic footwear	3,702	518	
Costume jewelry	1,067	142	

Source: Federal Reserve Bank of Dallas, *Annual Report 2002.*

Activity 3 (continued)

Answer Key:

Protected Industry	Jobs saved	Annual total cost (millions)	Annual cost per job saved
Benzenoid chemicals	216	$ 297	$ 1,376,435
Luggage	226	290	1,285,078
Softwood lumber	605	632	1,044,271
Sugar	2,261	1,868	826,104
Polyethylene resins	298	242	812,928
Dairy products	2,378	1,630	685,323
Frozen concentrated orange juice	609	387	635,103
Ball bearings	146	88	603,368
Maritime services	4,411	2,522	571,668
Ceramic tiles	347	191	551,367
Machine tools	1,556	746	479,452
Ceramic articles	418	140	335,876
Women's handbags	773	204	263,535
Canned tuna	390	100	257,640
Glassware	1,477	366	247,889
Apparel and textiles	168,786	33,629	199,241
Peanuts	397	74	187,223
Rubber footwear	1,701	286	168,312
Women's nonathletic footwear	3,702	518	139,800
Costume jewelry	1,067	142	132,870
Total	**191,764**	**$ 44,352**	
Average (weighted by number of jobs in each industry)			**$ 231,289**

Source: Federal Reserve Bank of Dallas, *Annual Report 2002.*

Activity 4
Readings on Foreign Outsourcing/Offshoring

"A Survey of Outsourcing," *The Economist*, November 13, 2004.

"Outsourcing Jobs: U.S. Dilemma," Bruce Stokes. www.greatdecisions.org (paper listed under 2005 program)

"Do What You Do Best, Outsource the Rest," Federal Reserve Bank of Dallas, *Southwest Economy*, November/December 2003.

"Globalization: Threat or Opportunity for the U.S. Economy," Federal Reserve Bank of San Francisco, *Economic Letter*, Number 2004-12, May 21, 2004.

"Trade and Jobs," remarks by Ben S. Bernanke.
http://www.federalreserve.gov/boarddocs/speeches/2004

"Demystifying Outsourcing," Mary Amiti and Shang-Jin Wei, *Finance & Development*, December 2004.

"Where Did All the Jobs Go? Nowhere," Daniel W. Drezner, *NY Times*, September 29, 2004. Available at www.-news.uchicago.edu/citations/04/040929.drez

"Why Are We Losing Manufacturing Jobs?" Eric O'N.Fisher, *Economic Commentary*, Federal Reserve Bank of Cleveland, July 2004.

"Job Losses and Trade: A Reality Check," Brink Lindsey. Cato Institute, Trade Briefing Paper, March 17, 2004.

"The Outsourcing Bogeyman," Daniel W. Drezner, *Foreign Affairs*, May/June 2004.

"Is Your Job Going Abroad?" *Time* magazine, March 1, 2004.

"Outsource, Outsource, and Outsource Some More," Daniel T. Griswold.
http://www.freetrade.org/pubs/articles/dg-05-03-04.html

"The Facts about Insourcing: Top 20 States with Greatest Number of "Insourced" Jobs,"
http://www.ofii.org/insourcing/top_twenty.cfm

"Offshoring Service Jobs: Bane or Boon and What to Do?"
http://www.brookings.edu/printme.wbs?page=/comm/policybriefs/

"Outsourcing" and "Offshoring" at Wikipedia:
http://www.en.wikipedia.org/wiki

LESSON ELEVEN
LIMITING TRADE–WHO GAINS, WHO LOSES?

LESSON DESCRIPTION

This lesson introduces three types of trade barriers: tariffs, quotas, and subsidies. In a small group activity, students determine who wins and who loses when each type of trade barrier is imposed. A reading on agricultural subsidies provides students with a real-world glimpse of the complexity of international trade issues in the 21st century. An optional exercise is included for instructors who choose to develop these ideas in simple graphical models.

INTRODUCTION

Over the past decade the volume of global trade has doubled to more than $9 trillion per year. Greater economic interdependence and global integration have led to higher levels of production and consumption, but some groups are hurt by increased competition from foreign producers. Similarly, trade barriers help some groups but hurt others, which explains why they are often adopted even in nations that generally support expanding international trade.

This lesson examines how trade barriers affect patterns of international trade, and gains and losses by different groups in the economy. Subsidies are reviewed in greater detail, to illustrate the political as well as economic complexities in debates over these policies.

CONCEPTS

Closed economy
Open economy
Tariff
Quota
Subsidy
Opportunity cost
Comparative advantage

CONTENT STANDARDS

Voluntary exchange occurs only when all participating parties expect to gain. This is true for trade among individuals or organizations within a nation, and among individuals or organizations in different nations.

When individuals, regions, and nations specialize in what they can produce at the lowest cost and then trade with others, both production and consumption increase.

Costs of government policies sometimes exceed benefits. This may occur because of incentives facing voters, government officials, and government employees, because of actions by special interest groups that can impose costs on the general public, or because social goals other than economic efficiency are being pursued.

BENCHMARKS

Despite the mutual benefits from trade among people in different countries, many nations employ trade barriers to restrict free trade for national defense reasons or because some companies and workers are hurt by free trade.

When imports are restricted by public policies, consumers pay higher prices and job opportunities and profits in exporting firms decrease.

As a result of growing international economic interdependence, economic conditions and policies in one nation increasingly affect economic conditions and policies in other nations.

Although barriers to international trade usually impose more costs than benefits, they are often advocated by people and groups who expect to gain substantially from them. Because the costs of these barriers are typically spread over a large number of people who each pay only a little and may not recognize the cost, policies supporting trade barriers are often adopted through the political process.

OBJECTIVES

Students will:

- ♦ Compare the benefits and costs of policies that alter trade barriers between nations, such as tariffs and quotas.
- ♦ Explain why political leaders may support policies that help only a few while harming many, such as a tariff on imported luggage or an import quota on sugar.
- ♦ Analyze international trade scenarios to identify the benefits and costs of free trade policies and policies that restrict international trade.

TIME REQUIRED

50–60 minutes if the optional graphical material is not covered; an additional 50–60 minutes if it is. Note that Activity 2 may either be done as an overnight assignment or in class.

MATERIALS

- Visual 1: In the Words of Adam Smith…
- Visual 2: Common Barriers to International Trade
- Visual 3: Trade Barriers: Winners and Losers (one copy per student)
- Visual 4: Answer Key to Trade Barriers: Winners and Losers

Note: Visuals 5–10 are optional, only used to present the graphical analysis of trade barriers

- Visual 5: Domestic Supply and Demand
- Visual 6: Opening the Domestic Economy to International Trade
- Visual 7: Trade Barrier: Tariff = $10 Per Unit
- Visual 8: Trade Barrier: Quota = 15 Units
- Visual 9: Trade Barrier: Subsidy = $6 Per Unit
- Visual 10: Larger Subsidies May Lead Domestic Producers to Export Some Goods

- Activity 1: Some International Effects of Agricultural Subsidies (one copy per student)

PROCEDURES

1. Display Visual 1. Allow students a few minutes to read the statement. Discuss the following questions:

   A. What is Adam Smith's main point in this passage? (*Answers will vary. The key point to make is that people are better off when they specialize and do not try to produce for themselves everything they consume. People usually accept that when local or domestic specialization and trade are involved–few people really want to try to be self-sufficient, like the pioneers who had few opportunities to trade. Smith argued that the same thing is true when it comes to international trade, which is harder to see and becomes more controversial, as shown in the rest of this lesson.*)

B. How does a family or a nation decide what to produce themselves and what to let others produce for them? (*Answers will vary. Have students consider Smith's claim that people produce things they can make at a lower cost than what they would have to pay to buy it from someone else. Therefore, the tailor makes clothing for himself and others, but buys meat from the butcher, medical care from a doctor, etc. Specialization increases the amount of clothing, meat, and medical care produced, and lowers the cost of producing the goods and services.*)

C. Do things we make ourselves cost anything? *(Yes. The resources needed to produce it are not free, and even your own labor is not free. There is an* ***opportunity cost*** *because the time spent producing a good for your own use could have been used making something else, or to earn income working at a paid job, or for leisure activities–including sleeping or playing video games.)*

2. Tell students that Adam Smith, the founding father of modern economics, was a strong advocate of free trade. The passage they read *from Wealth of Nations* is just one of many in that book that support his position on this issue. Another famous classical economist, David Ricardo, agreed with Smith and used the concept of opportunity cost to make the case for free trade. Ricardo argued that people and countries should specialize in producing goods for which they have a **comparative advantage**,[*] which means they can produce the product at a lower cost, as Smith suggested.

[*] The topics of comparative advantage and gains from specialization and trade are developed at greater length in Lesson 2 of this volume.

3. Explain that when people specialize and voluntarily agree to trade with each other, they both expect to gain. For example, if the tailor trades a shirt to the butcher for a steak year after year, they are both better off. Smith and Ricardo argued that international trade works the same way, and only takes place when the traders in both countries expect to be better off by trading. There is typically not a winner and a loser in an exchange when two friends trade comic books or other goods, or when two people or firms in different countries buy and sell goods and services to each other. Instead, both gain.

4. Ask students, "If it is true that international trade benefits buyers and sellers in both countries, and we have known about these ideas for more than 200 years, there should be free trade in the world economy today. Is that what we see?" (*Not really. Although there is a lot of international trade, and more today than ever before, there are also persistent policies in most nations that limit international trade, and many groups oppose at least some kinds of international trade, or international agreements that would encourage more trade between nations.*)

5. Ask students to suggest examples in which free trade is violated. (*Answers will vary, but may include export or import limits on certain farm products, such as sugar or cotton; trade embargoes on all goods from certain countries, such as Cuba or North Korea; and tariffs on imported textiles or electronics.*)

6. Display Visual 2, and use it to explain the basic features of three common trade barriers (tariffs, quotas, and subsidies), as described in the next few procedures.

7. Define a **tariff** as a tax on imported goods. The tax may be levied on each

measured unit of the good (liter bottles, meters of cloth, dozen of hats, metric tons, etc.), which is called a specific or unit tariff. Or instead, tariffs may be based on the value of the good (usually as a percent of the selling price), which is known as an *ad valorem* tariff.

8. Explain that tariffs are collected from the exporter by government agencies. Tariffs increase tax revenues for governments that adopt them, but exporters view tariffs as an additional cost of selling goods, so as with other producer costs tariffs increase the prices producers charge consumers.

9. Tell students to consider an economy with no tariffs on imported shoes. At the current price for the imported shoes, consumers demand a certain quantity. If a tariff is then imposed on imported shoes, the price of these shoes will increase. That will lead some consumers to buy shoes made by domestic producers instead–if there are any domestic producers of shoes–but when that happens the price of domestic shoes will also increase, because of the increase in demand for domestic shoes. The end result is that consumers will pay higher prices for shoes whether they buy imported or domestic shoes. Fewer imported shoes will be purchased, which may lead to more domestic shoes being purchased, and to higher production, profits, and employment in the domestic shoe industry.

10. Define a **quota** as a limit on the quantity of imports allowed into a country. Explain that a decrease in the supply of the imported products–for example, beef–will lead to an increase in the price for the smaller number of imported goods that may still be brought into the country. When the price of the imported goods increases, consumers will buy more goods from domestic producers (if there are domestic producers of the products, or of products that are close substitutes for the imported products). That means, just as with tariffs, as consumers buy more of the domestic products, prices of those goods will also rise. A quota will result in a reduction in the amount of the imported products that are sold, an increase in the price of both domestic and imported goods that are affected by the quota, and an increase in prices, profits, production, and employment in the affected domestic industries. Unlike a tariff, however, quotas do not directly increase tax revenues for the government.

11. Define a **subsidy** as a government payment to domestic consumers or producers of a good or service. If domestic firms receive a subsidy from the government for each unit of product they produce, they will increase the amount they produce. In other words, the subsidy shifts the domestic producer supply curves to the right. Without subsidies, domestic producers of beef must be at least as efficient as their global competitors to sell their goods. With the government subsidies, they can supply more beef and sell it at lower prices, even if they are not as efficient as international producers. The subsidies therefore increase domestic production, employment, and profits, lower prices for consumers and lead them to buy more of the product, but reduce the amount of foreign production and imports. The subsidies also increase government spending, which means that taxpayers will ultimately have to cover the costs of the subsidies.

12. Assign students to small groups (3 or 4 students per group). Distribute one copy of Visual 3 to each student. Tell them to begin with the case of a tariff on imported shoes, and in their groups discuss which groups win or lose when the tariff is imposed. In the first column, labeled "Tariff," they should mark the winners and losers with Xs in the appropriate rows, and then indicate whether the direct effect of the

tariff on the government budget balance (revenues minus expenditures) will be positive (+), negative (−), or no change (0). Tell students not to consider the other two trade barriers until the class discussion of the tariff is completed.

13. Allow several minutes for students to analyze the tariff questions in their small groups. Review student answers and correct any misconceptions by displaying Visual 3 and filling in the tariff items in the first column, or by displaying only the Tariff column in the Answer Key provided on Visual 4.

Tariff Effects
winners: domestic producers
foreign consumers
losers: domestic consumers
foreign producers
effect on government budget: positive (+) *because tax revenues increase*

A. Are domestic consumers winners or losers? (*Domestic consumers lose because fewer imported goods are available and both domestic and imported goods sell at a higher price.)*

B. Are domestic producers winners or losers? (*Domestic producers of the product win because they face less competition from imports, allowing them to increase prices, sales, output, employment levels, and profits.)*

C. Are foreign consumers winners or losers? (*Foreign consumers win because fewer goods are sent to the country that has imposed the tariff. That means more goods will be available to sell in other countries, decreasing prices there.)*

D. Are foreign producers winners or losers? (*Foreign producers of the product lose because they sell fewer units in the country that imposed the tariff, and must sell at lower prices in other countries.)*

E. What is the effect of tariffs on the government budget? (*positive, +, although tariff revenues are very small relative to the size of the U.S. government's budget, and for governments in most other developed nations)*

14. When the discussion of the tariff is completed, tell students to continue working in small groups on the remaining two trade barriers, recording their answers on Activity 1.

15. Review student answers for the quota, writing the answers in the second column of Visual 3 or displaying the appropriate column in Visual 4.

Quota Effects
winners: domestic producers
foreign consumers
losers: domestic consumers
foreign producers
effect on government budget: neutral (0), typically, although some governments adopt hybrid "tariff-based quotas," which trigger tariffs on imported products after the number of imports exceeds a certain quantity/quota. That kind of hybrid policy could increase tax revenues, but the other effects, including "winners and losers," are not changed.)

A. Are domestic consumers winners or losers? (*Domestic consumers lose because fewer imported goods are available, and both domestic and imported goods sell at a higher price.)*

B. Are domestic producers winners or losers? (*Domestic producers of the product win because they face less competition from imports, allowing them to increase prices, sales, output, employment levels, and profits.)*

C. Are foreign consumers winners or losers? (*Foreign consumers win because fewer goods are sent to the country that has imposed the quota. That means more goods will be available to sell in other countries, decreasing prices there.)*

D. Are foreign producers winners or losers? *(Foreign producers of the product lose because they sell fewer units in the country that imposed the tariff, and must sell at lower prices in other countries.)*

E. What is the effect of quota on the government budget? (*typically neutral, 0, as explained above)*

16. Review student answers for the case of a subsidy, writing the answers in the third column of Visual 3 or displaying that column in Visual 4:

Subsidy Effects
winners: domestic consumers
domestic producers
foreign consumers
losers: foreign producers
effect on government budget:
negative (–) because government expenditures increase

A. Are domestic consumers winners or losers? (*Domestic consumers win because the subsidy increases the supply of the good and lowers its price.)*

B. Are domestic producers winners or losers? (*Domestic producers of the product win because the subsidy provides additional revenues to offset some production costs and increases their profits.)*

C. Are foreign consumers winners or losers? (*Foreign consumers win because the supply of the good increases, lowering its price.)*

D. Are foreign producers winners or losers? *(Foreign producers of the product lose because the price of the product decreases. It is especially difficult for them to export this product into the country adopting the subsidies, but the price decrease will affect prices in the rest of the world, too.)*

E. What is the effect of subsidies on the government budget? *(negative, –, because the subsidies represent additional government expenditures that must be financed with increased taxes or borrowed funds)*

17. (Optional material featuring graphical analysis in Visuals 5–10. If this material is not to be covered, skip ahead to procedure 28.) Tell students they will now use supply and demand graphs to see more clearly who wins and who loses when trade barriers are imposed.

18. Display Visual 5 and explain that it represents a domestic market for some product, before there is any international trade. Point out that, as usual, consumer demand is downward sloping: at higher prices consumers buy fewer units, and at lower prices they buy more. The supply curve is upward sloping: at higher prices producers are willing and able to sell more units of the product than at lower prices. The equilibrium (or market clearing) price

and quantity occur where the two curves intersect, and where quantity demanded (30) equals the quantity supplied (30). If this is a **closed economy**, meaning there are no imports from or exports to other countries, the market clears at the price of $40.

19. Display Visual 6. Define an **open economy** as one in which trade with other countries is allowed. A country may export or import goods, depending on whether the world price for the product is higher or lower than the price would be in the domestic economy, without any imports or exports.

20. Ask students: "If the domestic economy price for this good is $40 and the world price is $50, what will domestic producers of this product want to do?" (*Export to other countries if transportation costs are relatively low, to receive the higher price. The amount exported is shown as the difference between domestic quantity supplied and domestic quantity demanded at the world price of $50.)*

21. Ask students: "If the domestic economy price for this good is $40 and the world price is $20, what will domestic consumers want to do? (*purchase the good at the world price, by importing some units made by foreign producers*) "How much will be imported?" (*30–at the price of $20 imports will equal the difference between the total quantity demanded, 40, and the domestic quantity supplied, which is 10. 40 – 10 = 30*) Show this carefully, and more than once if necessary, to make sure students understand what is happening.

22. Ask students what will happen if domestic producers are able to convince the government to limit the number of imports? After some general comments, announce that it is easy to show this using the supply and demand model. Display Visual 7 and explain that this graph still has the world price of $20, but now shows the domestic government imposing a tariff of $10 on each unit of the product that is imported. The $10 tariff raises the price above the world price of $20 by the amount of the tariff, to $30 ($20 + $10). Ask students, "What quantity will be imported after the $10 tariff is imposed?" (*15–the difference between quantity demanded at a price of $30, which is 35, and the quantity that will be supplied by domestic producers at this price, which is 20.*) Ask, "Who gains and who loses from this change?" (*Answers are the same as shown in Column 1 of Visuals 3 and 4 above. Point out the higher price to consumers after the tariff, the lower import sales by foreign producers, and the higher level of production by domestic producers.*)

23. Display Visual 8, illustrating a quota. The quota raises price above the world price of $20 because it limits the amount of imports allowed. Imports are again shown as the difference between the quantity supplied by domestic producers and the total quantity demanded. Therefore, the quota raises the price until the gap between D and S equals the quota limit, which in this example is assumed to be 15 units. Show this on the graph and make sure students understand how the quota is illustrated. Then ask students:

A. "What price will domestic consumers pay if the quota is imposed?" (*$30*)

B. "Who gains and who loses from the quota?" (*Answers are the same as shown in Column 2 of Visuals 3 and 4. Once again, make sure students see that consumers pay a higher price, imports decrease so foreign producers sell less, and domestic producers sell more after the quota is imposed.)*

24. Point out that although tariffs and quotas both raise the price of the good to domestic consumers, with tariffs the government collects tax revenues, but with a traditional quota it does not. With quotas, the higher price paid for the imports all goes to foreign producers, but with tariffs some of the higher price is captured by the domestic government.

25. Display Visual 9, which shows the effects of a government subsidy paid to the domestic producers of a good, such as subsidies paid for agricultural products grown in many developed nations in the world, including the United States. The subsidy shifts the domestic supply curve down (and to the right) by the amount of the subsidy, because in effect the government now pays that much of the cost of producing each unit of the product. Point out that with a $6 subsidy, all points of the new supply curve are $6 lower than the original supply curve.

26. Remind students that in an open economy without subsidies or other trade barriers, the world price for this product is $20 and the quantity sold is 40 (10 from domestic sources and 30 from imports). Ask students:

A. "After the subsidy, will domestic consumers buy more or fewer imports?" (*fewer*)

B. "Who gains and who loses from the subsidy?" (*Answers are the same as shown in Column 3 of Visuals 3 and 4. Make sure students see that imports or sales by foreign producers of the product decrease, and output and sales by domestic producers of the product increase.*)

27. Display Visual 10. This shows the case of a highly subsidized domestic industry. The subsidy is now so large that it shifts the domestic supply curve so far down that the domestic price is lower than the world price. That would entirely eliminate imports of the product, and lead domestic producers to start exporting some units of the product to other countries. That is exactly what happens with many U.S. agricultural products, as discussed in a later reading. That means U.S. taxpayers pay to subsidize the production of goods that will be consumed by people in other countries. It also makes it difficult, if not impossible, for agricultural producers in very poor nations to sell their crops in world markets.

28. Distribute one copy of Activity 1 to each student, either as an overnight assignment or to complete in class. Use the answers provided below to review the correct responses.

A. Why does agriculture play such an important role in international trade discussions? (*The 2005* Human Development Report *of the United Nations estimates that developing countries lose about $24 billion a year in agricultural income from this kind of protectionism and subsidies in developed nations. Although agriculture is shrinking as a percentage of world trade, many poorer countries are heavily reliant upon earnings from agricultural exports. More than 50 developing countries depend on agriculture for at least one-fourth of their export earnings.*)

B. When wealthy countries protect domestic producers with subsidies, who gains and who loses? (*Domestic producers of the subsidized product gain because subsidies allow them to compete against foreign producers that would otherwise be more efficient, sometimes even to the point of exporting the product to other nations that can produce it at a lower cost. Both domestic and foreign consumers benefit from lower product prices for subsidized goods. Competing foreign producers are hurt because, without subsidies in their own countries, many are unable to produce at the artificially low world prices resulting from the subsidies.*)

C. What happens when U.S. cotton farmers receive subsidies of $4.7 billion/year? (*The subsidy is shared by 20,000 U.S. farmers, although most of the funds go to a small number of corporate mega-farms. The subsidy induces greater production, which lowers the world price of cotton by an estimated 9-13%. As a result of the subsidy, the United States dominates production in this market even though it does not have a comparative advantage. Some of the poorest countries in Africa are among the nations most negatively affected by the cotton subsidies to U.S. farmers.*)

D. What happens when EU farmers are paid $51 billion/year in agricultural subsidies? (*Agricultural producers represent just 2% of EU employment, but receive payments that absorb more than 40% of the EU budget. Subsidies to sugar producers and processors are so large–four times the world market price–that a surplus of 4 million tons of sugar is sent to world markets, depressing prices by about one-third. The countries most harmed by EU sugar subsidies are Brazil [$494 million], South Africa [$151 million]), and Thailand [$60 million].)*

CLOSURE

Ask students to compare and contrast the effects of tariffs, quotas, and subsidies in terms of their impacts on prices, government budgets, and world trade (imports and exports, or in other words production by domestic and foreign producers.) Use Visuals 2 - 4 to review the main points of comparison:

SIMILARITIES of Tariffs, Quotas, and Subsidies:

- *all three are trade barriers that reduce international trade, compared to a policy of free trade, and move production from more efficient producers to less efficient producers*
- *all three benefit domestic producers and foreign consumers*

DIFFERENCES of Tariffs, Quotas, and Subsidies:

- *tariffs and quotas raise prices, hurting domestic consumers; subsidies lower prices, helping domestic and foreign consumers*
- *tariffs increase government revenue, subsidies increase government expenditures, quotas have no direct effect on government revenues*
- *tariffs and quotas reduce imports; subsidies sometimes increase exports, usually if the subsidies are very large*

ASSESSMENT

Divide the class into four groups: 1) domestic consumers, 2) domestic producers, 3) foreign consumers, and 4) foreign producers.

Explain that in this assignment each group should consider ONLY its own self-interest, not the overall effects of barriers to trade. That is, they should assume the identity of the group assigned to them and make decisions that benefit their particular interests.

Announce that the task for each group is to determine which of the trade barriers covered in this lesson–tariffs, quotas, and subsidies–they will support, based on their own self-interest. Then they will prepare a rationale for their position on each type of trade barrier and present the rationales to the entire class

Allow sufficient time for discussion among group members, then ask a spokesperson from each group to make a brief presentation summarizing their choices and rationales.

When the presentations have been made display Visual 4, Answer Key for Trade Barrier Winners and Losers, and review whether each of the groups took the positions on each type of trade barrier that were in line with their self-interest.

Visual 1

In the Words of Adam Smith...

"It is the maxim of every prudent ... family, never to attempt to make at home what it will cost ... more to make than to buy. The tailor does not attempt to make his own shoes, but buys them of the shoemaker. The shoemaker does not attempt to make his own clothes, but employs a tailor.

What is prudent in the conduct of every private family, can scarce be folly in that of a great kingdom. If a foreign country can supply us with a commodity cheaper than we ourselves can make it, better buy it of them with some part of the produce of our own industry, employed in a way in which we have some advantage."

Source: *An Inquiry into the Nature and Causes of the Wealth of Nations*, 1776. (IV.2.11-12). London: Methuen and Company, Ltd., ed. Edwin Cannan, 1904. Fifth edition. Spelling has been modernized.

Visual 2
Common Barriers to International Trade

Tariff–a tax on imported goods. Creates revenue for domestic government.

Quota–a limit on the quantity of imports allowed. Restricts the amount supplied by foreign producers.

Subsidy–a government payment to domestic producers or consumers of a product. Producers who receive government subsidies may sell part of their output to foreign consumers.

Visual 3
Trade Barriers: Winners and Losers

Tariff–government imposes $5 tax on each pair of imported shoes

Quota–government limits auto imports to 4 million vehicles per year

Subsidy–the government pays rice farmers $3 for each bushel of rice they produce

	Tariff	Quota	Subsidy
WINNERS			
Domestic consumers			
Domestic producers			
Foreign consumers			
Foreign producers			
LOSERS			
Domestic consumers			
Domestic producers			
Foreign consumers			
Foreign producers			
Effect on Government			
Budget (+, −, 0)			

Visual 4
Answer Key for Trade Barriers: Winners and Losers

Tariff–government imposes $5 tax on each pair of imported shoes

Quota–government limits auto imports to 4 million vehicles per year

Subsidy–the government pays rice farmers $3 for each bushel of rice they produce

	Tariff	Quota	Subsidy
WINNERS			
Domestic consumers			X
Domestic producers	X	X	X
Foreign consumers	X	X	X
Foreign producers			
LOSERS			
Domestic consumers	X	X	
Domestic producers			
Foreign consumers			
Foreign producers	X	X	X
Effect on Government			
Budget (+, −, 0)	+	0	−

Visual 5

Domestic Supply and Demand

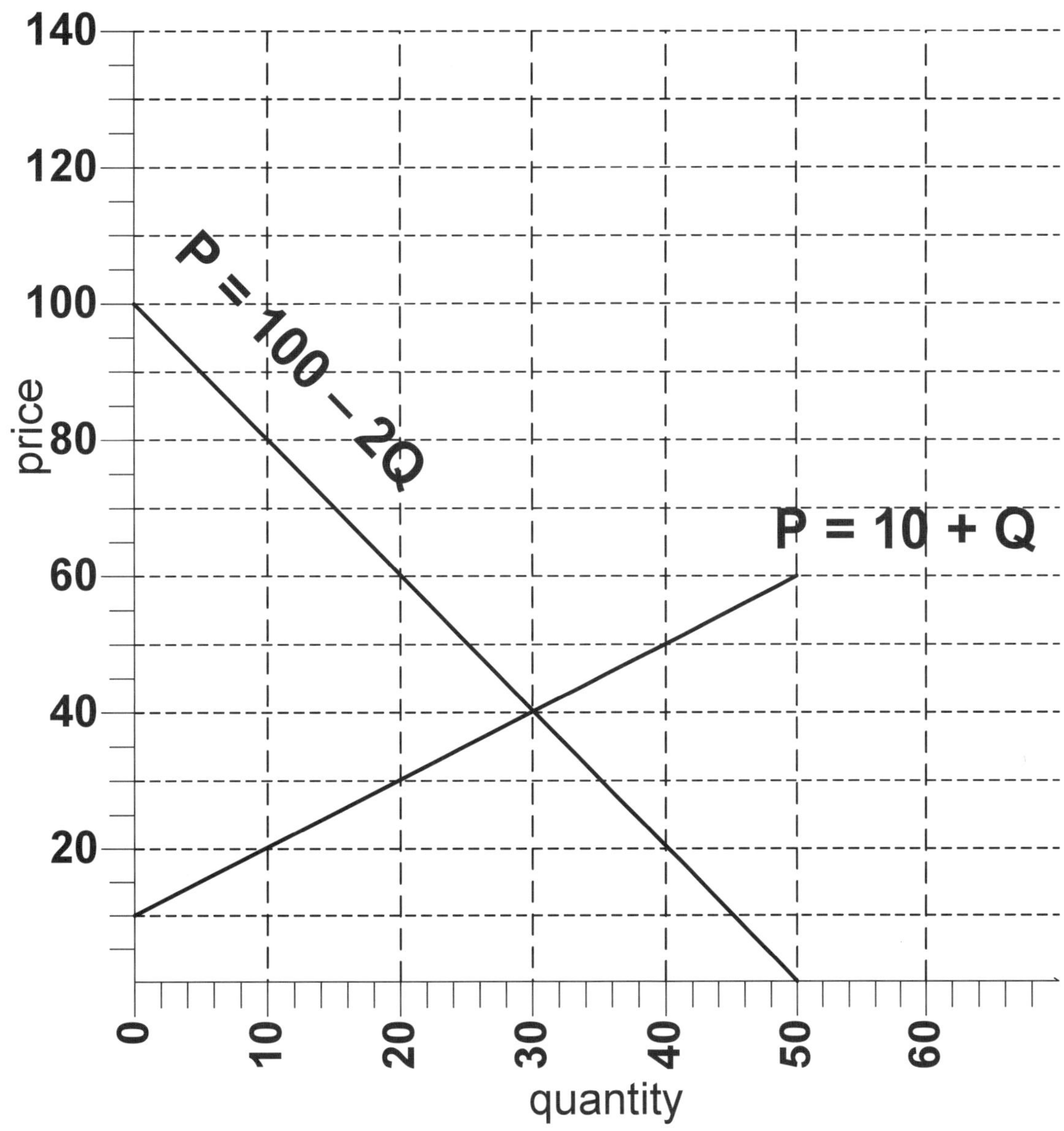

Visual 6

Opening the Domestic Economy to International Trade

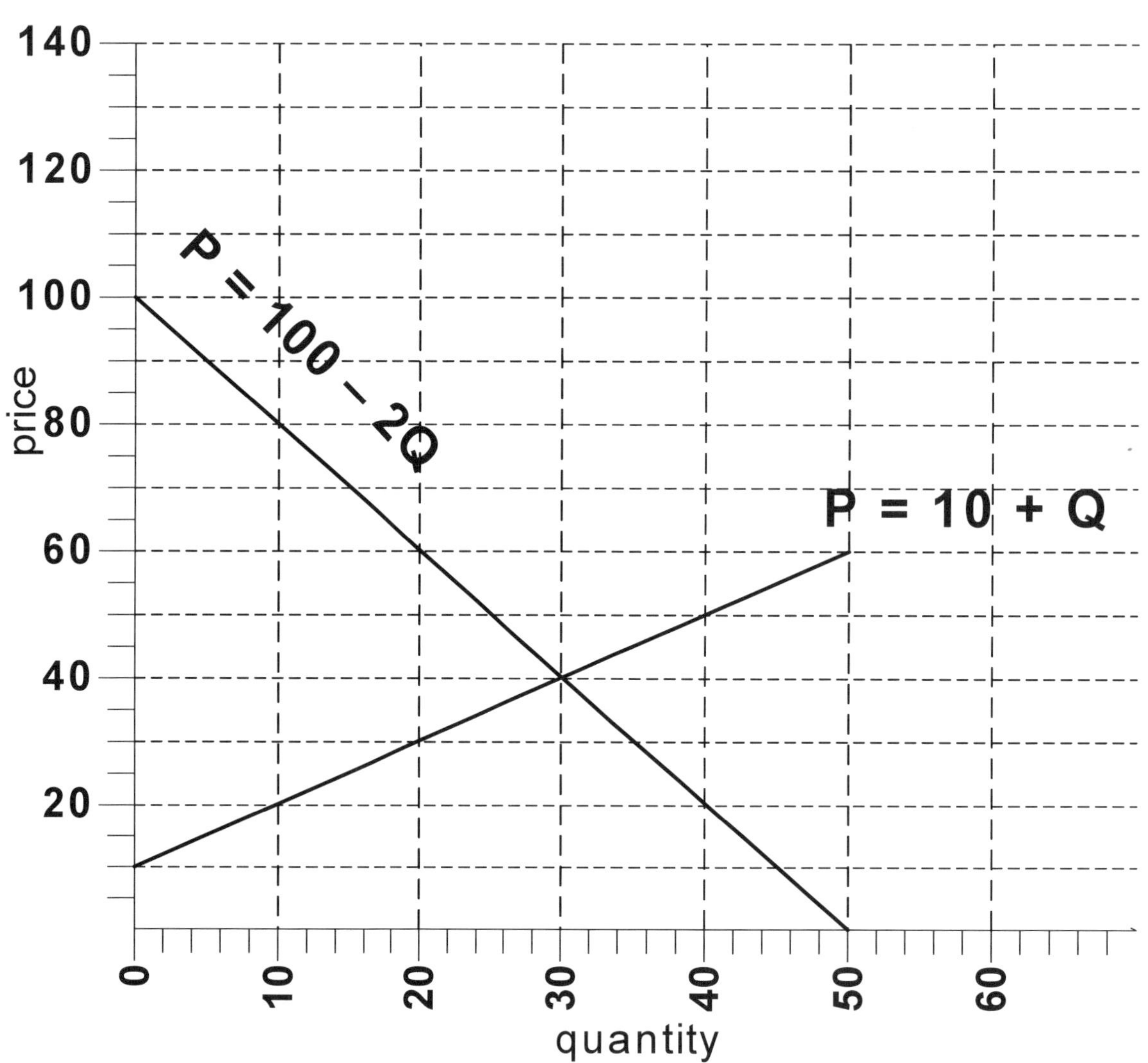

International Trade

If the domestic economy is closed to trade, what price is charged? ____ What quantity is sold? ____

If the economy is open to trade and the world price is $20, will this country export or import? ________

How much? _____ Why?

Visual 7

Trade Barrier: Tariff = $10 Per Unit

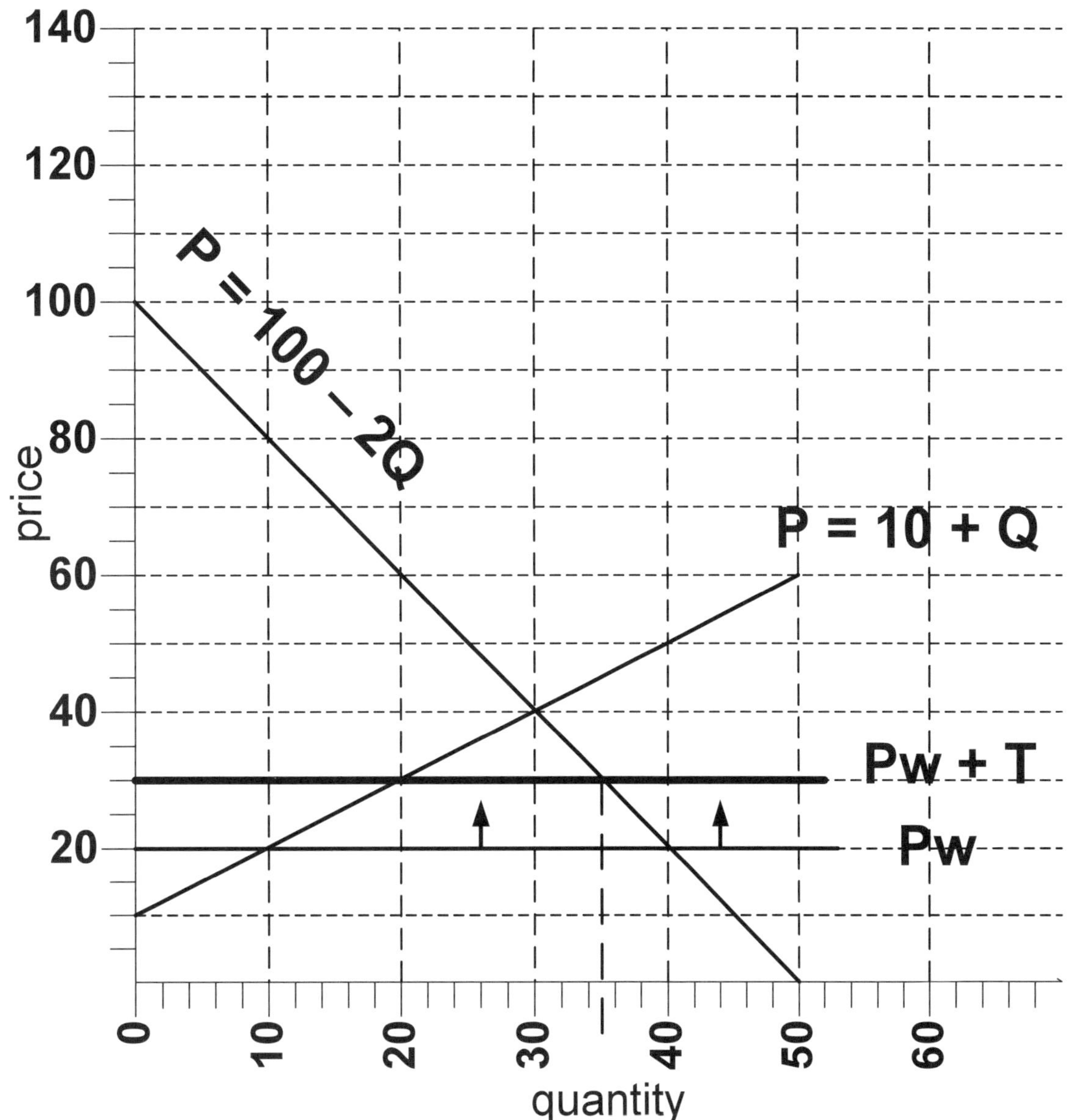

With free trade, the country imports 30 units at the world price of $20. A tariff raises the price to $30, P_w + $10. What quantity is imported now? _____

Who gains and who loses from a tariff?

Visual 8

Trade Barrier: Quota = 15 Units

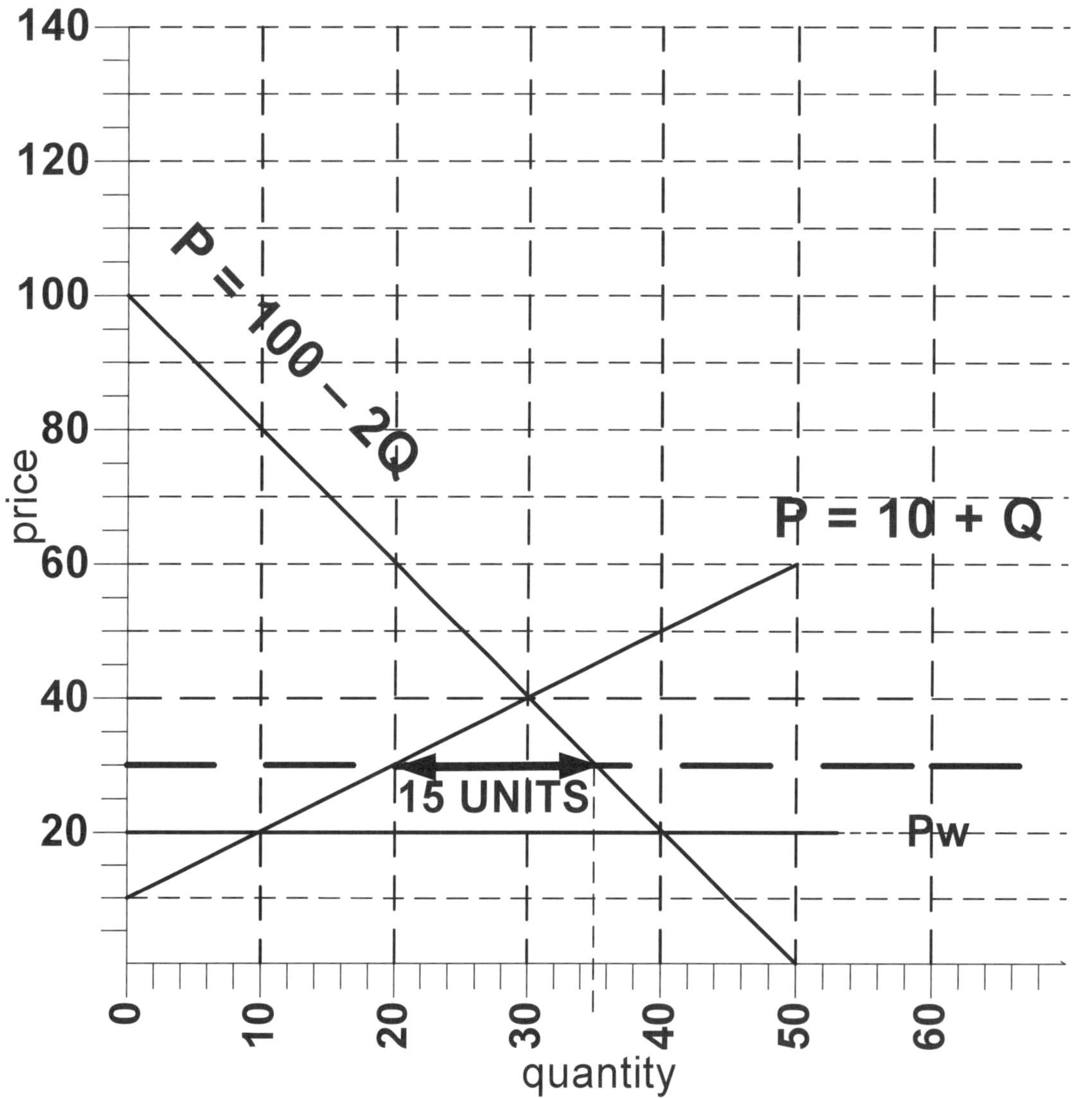

Under free trade, the country imports 30 units at the world price of $20. A quota limits the amount imported to 15 units. What price will domestic consumers now pay?

Who gains and who loses from the quota?

Visual 9

Trade Barrier: Subsidy = $6 Per Unit

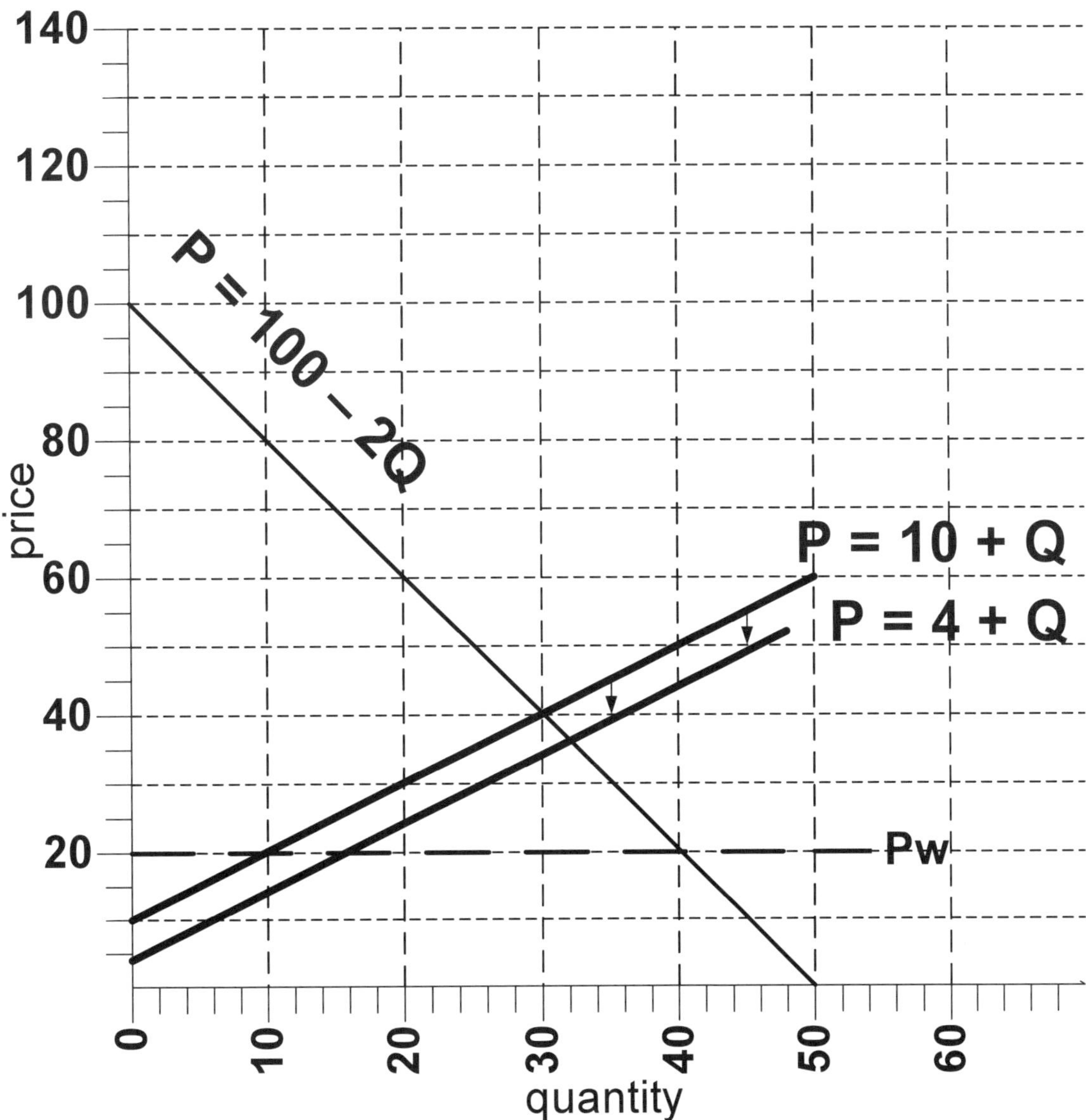

A $6 subsidy to domestic producers shifts the supply curve as shown. Will domestic consumers buy more or fewer imports now? ____

Who gains and who loses from the subsidy?

Visual 10

Larger Subsidies May Lead Domestic Producers to Export Some Goods

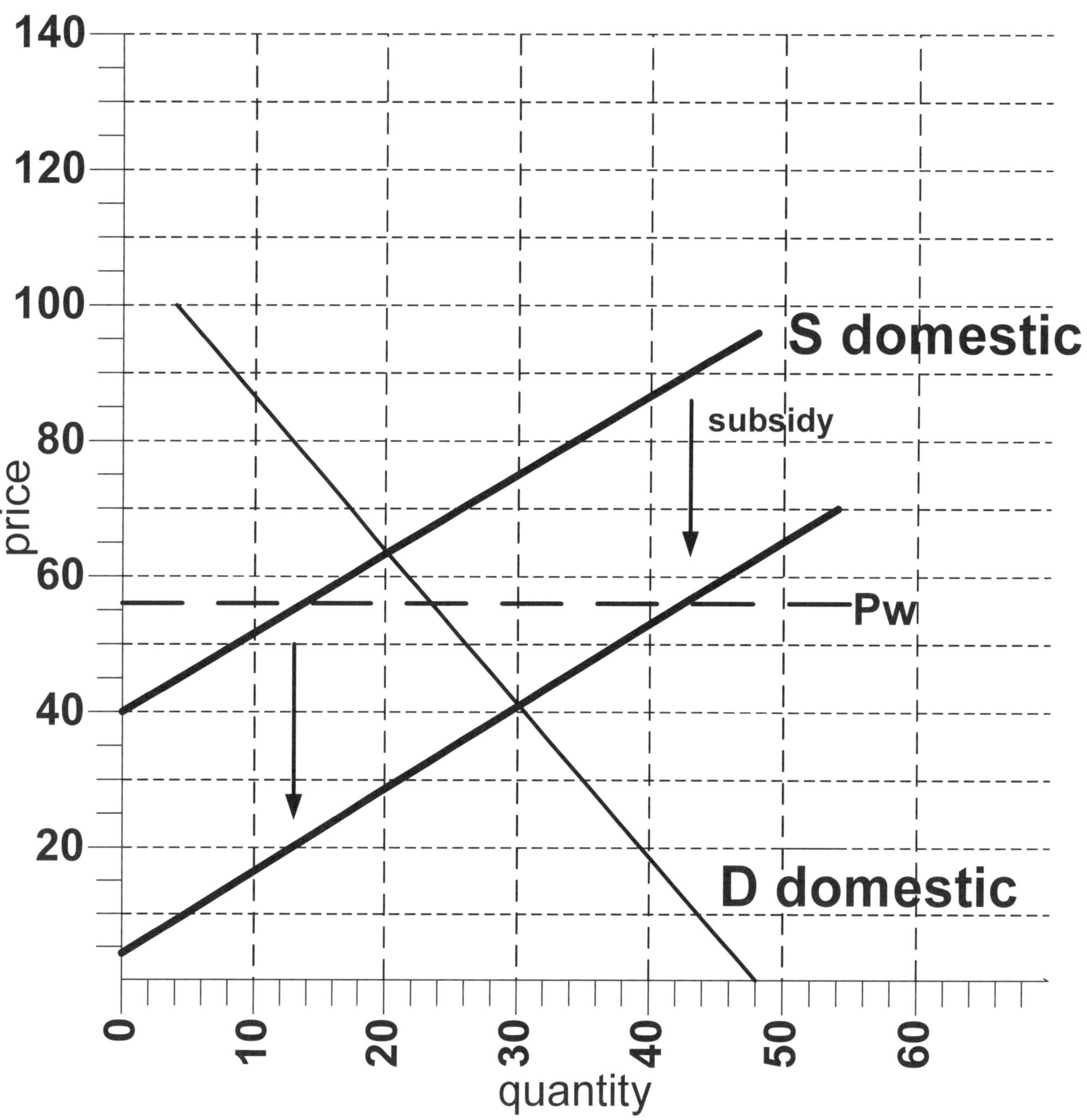

Activity 1

Some International Effects of Agricultural Subsidies

This reading consists of excerpts taken from United Nation's Human Development Report 2005 [HDR 2005]. *The excerpts are reprinted verbatim, with page numbers shown for each passage. Other passages were deleted to keep the reading shorter for more effective classroom use, but there was no attempt or intent to change the tone or meaning of the original document.*

Agriculture may be shrinking as a share of world trade, but many poor countries remain heavily dependent on agricultural exports. More than 50 developing countries depend on agriculture for at least one-quarter of their export earnings. [*HDR 2005*, p. 118]

Rich countries spend just over $1 billion a year on aid to developing country agriculture and just under $1 billion a day supporting their own agricultural systems. When it comes to world agricultural trade, market success is determined not by comparative advantage, but by comparative access to subsidies–an area in which producers in poor countries are unable to compete. [*HDR 2005*, p. 130]

High levels of agricultural support translate into higher output, fewer imports and more exports than would otherwise be the case. That support helps to explain why industrial countries continue to dominate world agricultural trade. Recent estimates suggest that developing countries lose about $24 billion a year in agricultural income from protectionism and subsidies in developed countries.... [*HDR 2005*, p. 130]

Nothing better demonstrates the perverse logic of agricultural subsidies than the European Union's Common Agricultural Policy (CAP)–an arrangement that lavishes $51 billion (€43 billion) in support on producers. The CAP supports a sector that accounts for less than 2% of employment but absorbs more than 40% of the total EU budget. Farmers and processors are paid four times the world market price for sugar, generating a 4 million ton surplus. That surplus is then dumped on world markets with the help of more than $1 billion in export subsidies paid to a small group of sugar processors. [*HDR 2005*, p. 130]

Subsidized EU sugar exports lower world prices by about one-third. As a result, far more efficient sugar exporters in developing countries suffer foreign exchange losses estimated at $494 million for Brazil, $151 million for South Africa and $60 million for Thailand–countries with more than 60 million people living on less than $2 a day. [*HDR 2005*, p. 131]

Activity 1 (continued)

Cotton policy in the United States provides another example of subsidized market distortions that harm human development. As with EU sugar policies, the scale of the subsidies stretches credulity. The U.S. Department of Agriculture estimates that the country's 20,000 cotton farmers will receive government payments of $4.7 billion in 2005–an amount equivalent to the market value of the crop and more than U.S. aid to Sub-Saharan Africa. Of more direct relevance is the effect of the subsidies on cotton producers in poor countries. [HDR, 2005, p. 131]

Price distortions caused by U.S. subsidies have a direct impact on these smallholder producers. These subsidies lower world prices by 9%–13% and enable U.S. producers to dominate world markets, accounting for about one-third of total world exports. These exports would not be possible without subsidies. High levels of government support effectively insulate U.S. producers from world price signals, enabling them to expand production regardless of market conditions. [*HDR 2005*, p. 131]

Not all of the problems in international cotton markets can be traced to U.S. agricultural policy. Rising production elsewhere, especially in China, and heavy subsidies in the European Union, also contribute. However, because the United States is the world's largest exporter, its policies have particularly strong global market effects. [*HDR 2005*, p. 132]

Activity 1 (continued)

Based on the reading, answer the following questions:

1. Why does agriculture play such an important role in international trade discussions?

2. When wealthy countries protect their domestic agricultural producers, who gains and who loses?

3. What happens when U.S. cotton farmers receive subsidies of $4.7 billion/year?

4. What happens when EU farmers are paid $51 billion/year in subsidies for sugar?

LESSON TWELVE
TRADE, INVESTMENT, AND THE BALANCE OF PAYMENTS

LESSON DESCRIPTION

Students use a balance of payments account between two countries, and a hands-on activity that demonstrates the relationship between the current account and the financial account, to understand the relationship between international trade and investment.

INTRODUCTION

The balance of trade for U.S. imports and exports often makes headlines, but does not provide a complete picture of what a balance of trade or current account deficit really is, or the implications of these deficits for other sectors of the economy. This lesson explains the balance of payments and the broader implications of a current account deficit.

CONCEPTS

Balance of payments
Current account
Financial account
Balance of trade
Credits
Debits
Exports
Imports
Investment
Saving

CONTENT STANDARDS

Voluntary exchange occurs only when all participating parties expect to gain. This is true for trade among individuals or organizations within a nation, and among individuals or organizations in different nations.

Money makes it easier to trade, borrow, save, invest, and compare the value of goods and services.

Investment in factories, machinery, new technology, and in the health, education, and training of people, can raise future standards of living.

BENCHMARKS

A nation pays for its imports with its exports.

As a result of growing international economic interdependence, economic conditions and policies in one nation increasingly affect economic conditions and policies in other nations.

As a store of value, money makes it easier for people to save and defer consumption until the future.

Investments in physical and human capital can increase productivity, but such investments entail opportunity costs and economic risks.

OBJECTIVES

Students will:

- Distinguish between the balance of payments, the current account, and the financial account.

- Assign various types of exchanges between countries–including sales of goods and services and assets such as stocks, bonds, and government securities–to the appropriate section of the balance of payments account.

- Explain that a deficit in the current account generally implies a surplus in the financial account, and vice versa.

- Understand that investment in the United States must be funded from savings in the United States or from the rest of the world.

- Identify some of the potential drawbacks of continued international borrowing by the United States or any other nation.

TIME REQUIRED

Two 50-minute class periods. Class 1, procedures 1–17; class 2, procedures 18–31, Closure, and Assessment.

MATERIALS

- Visual 1: Credits and Debits in the U.S. Balance of Payments
- Visual 2: A Simplified U.S. Balance of Payments Account
- Visual 3: Activity 1 Key
- Visual 4: The Relationship Between the Current Account (CA) and the Financial Account (FA)
- Visual 5: U.S. Balance of Payments, 2004: The Current Account, Selected Items
- Visual 6: The U.S. Current Account Balance as a Percent of GDP
- Visual 7: U.S. Balance of Payments, 2004: The Financial Account, Selected Items
- Visual 8: Sources of Funding for U.S. Investment and Government Deficit Spending, 2004
- Visual 9: The International Investment Position of the United States: A Net Debtor Nation
- Visual 10: Activity 2 Key
- Activity 1: The U.S. Balance of Payments Account (one copy of the first four pages in the activity for every three students in the class, and one copy of the cards on pages 292 and 293 of the activity for each group of three students, cut apart)
- Activity 2: The U.S. Balance of Payments Account with Germany (one copy per student)

PROCEDURES

1. Ask students how the United States pays for imported goods. (If students answer exports commend them; but also accept or explain the pragmatic idea that when people or firms import products they must pay for them with money from the nations in which they are purchased, which means trading dollars for those currencies. Exports do ultimately pay for imports, but exporters are usually different people than importers, so currency trading almost always takes place when goods are imported. In the short term imports may be financed by borrowing from the countries that export to the United States, as shown in the rest of this lesson.)

2. Ask students what kind of money people or firms in the United States would have to get to buy goods and services from the United Kingdom? *(Pounds)* Germany? *(Euros)* Mexico? *(Pesos)* Japan? *(Yen)*

3. Ask why foreign citizens and firms would want to acquire U.S. dollars. (*Foreign citizens or businesses often want to buy U.S. goods and services, or to invest in U.S. financial and capital assets–including stocks and bonds, as well as factories, land, and other real assets.*)

4. Explain that the U.S. **balance of payments** is a record of U.S. purchases of foreign goods, services, and financial and capital assets, and sales of U.S. goods, services, and financial and capital assets to people and firms in other countries.

5. Display Visual 1, and use it to show which items represent a **credit** for the United States in its balance of payments

account, and which items represent a **debit**. Credits are shown with a + and debits with a −. Explain that a credit means that people and firms in other nations must acquire U.S. dollars to pay for these items, while debits mean that people and firms in the United States acquire currencies of other nations to pay for those items. Discuss some of the examples to illustrate how that works. For example, if a foreign company buys all or part of a U.S. company, it must use dollars to pay for the purchase, which generates a credit when the foreign firm buys dollars in the currency exchange markets. If a U.S. company buys all or part of a company in another nation, it has to acquire currency from that nation to pay for the purchase, which creates a debit as it sells dollars to buy the foreign currency in the currency exchange markets.

6. Display Visual 2. Explain that the balance of payments is not organized using categories of credits and debits, but rather using accounts that record trades of goods, services, income payments and receipts, and transfers (called the **current account**) and trades of stocks, bonds, and other financial and capital assets (called the **financial account**). (Transfers are funds that are given with nothing received in return. Examples include U.S. government aid programs and money sent to relatives abroad.) (Note: The term financial account recently replaced what was previously called the capital account. See the appendix to this lesson for more information about that change.)

7. Define surplus and deficit as shown in Visual 2: a surplus occurs if the sum of all items in the current account or financial account is positive; a deficit occurs if the sum of all items in the account is negative.

8. Divide the class into groups of three students. Explain that in each trio one student will play the role of firms and consumers in Spain and the other the role of firms and consumers in the United States. The third student will play the role of a bank. Although it really does not matter where the bank is located in terms of conducting the transactions depicted in this activity, to keep the accounting entries for the transactions clear and easier to follow, tell the students the bank is located in the United States. Assign roles to each student in the teams, or let students choose the roles.

9. Give each group one copy of the cards on pages 296 and 297 of Activity 1, cut apart. Tell the student with the role of U.S. firms and consumers to take all the pieces that are denominated in U.S. dollars (the shaded cards) and spread them out on their desk or table. The student acting as Spain takes the pieces denominated in Euros (the cards that are not shaded). Explain that the bank does not receive any cards, but all currency exchanges must be done at the bank.

10. Distribute one copy of the first four pages of Activity 1 to each team. Tell students to complete the actions for Year 1 and then answer the questions for Year 1 working together. They will trade pieces of paper that represent goods, currency, assets, etc. For example, in the first exchange the student representing the United States firm should give the banker $30. In the second exchange, the Spanish player should give the banker €30. The banker then exchanges the dollars for Euros as described in the third exchange. Make sure students use the trading slips as they work through the activity, because moving the slips from "country" to "country" with the trades makes it easier to complete the next part of the Activity. For example, when Spain buys U.S. corn, the paper representing corn should be placed in front of the Spanish role player, showing that corn has become an export credit for the United States.

11. Explain that the dollar and Euro usually do not trade on a one-to-one exchange rate, but that is done here to keep things simple. Also, again for simplicity, no fee is charged by the bank for the foreign exchange conversions here, but point out that banks actually charge a commission on these transactions.

12. At the end of the deals for the first year, have the student representing the U.S. firms and consumers, with the help of their Spanish trading partner and the banker, record the transactions that were made on the U.S. balance of payments account. Explain that students only have to look at the trading slips in front of them to be able to fill out the balance of payments (BOP) account. For example, U.S. corn was sold to Spain, so that is a credit on the U.S. BOP account, while the machinery purchased from Spain will be a debit on the U.S. BOP account. Explain that, once again to keep things simple, you are not also recording the transactions on a balance of payments account for Spain, though of course that is done too when nations really trade. Clarify to the students that the debits and credits are already marked as – and + in the balance of payments worksheet.

13. After the students have completed the questions for Year 1, review the questions and ask students what the balances in the U.S. current and financial accounts were. (*0–both the current account and financial account were balanced, with no surplus or deficit.*) If necessary, review the fact that in this year Spain traded machinery and received corn in return. Because these trades in goods were of equal value, the current account balance is zero. This also means there was no net change in the ownership of financial assets–all of the currency used to trade ended up back in the country where it was initially held, so the financial account balance was also zero.

14. Tell students to return the trading slips for corn, machinery, and currencies back to the starting points for Year 1, with corn and dollars in the United States, and machinery and euros in Spain. Tell students to complete the transactions for Year 2 and then answer the Year 2 and Review questions on the Activity, once again working as a team.

15. When students have completed the questions, display Visual 3 and review the entries for both years. Then review the Year 2 and Review questions: (*In Year 2, the United States had a $20 deficit in its current account, which was offset by a $20 surplus in its financial account. That leaves the overall balance of payments balanced, with an overall total of 0. Foreign investors buy U.S. securities or financial assets if they expect to get a higher rate of return on those investments, or if they feel that the investments are less risky than investments with similar returns that are available in other parts of the world. Foreign investment provides additional funds that may be used to finance private investments or government spending in the United States, but that means foreigners own more U.S. stocks, bonds, and real assets.*)

16. Ask students: "Was there ever a trade in the Activity when something was sent from one country to the other country without ultimately getting something in return?" (*No. Each card representing goods, currency, or other financial assets was always exchanged for something else–in Year 1 corn was ultimately traded for an equivalent value of machinery. In Year 2, only some of the Spanish textiles were paid for by U.S. corn exports to Spain–the rest of the dollars Spain received for the textiles were held as financial assets.*)

17. Ask students to explain why the sum of the current account and the financial accounts was 0 in both Year 1 and Year 2.

(Precisely because something is always received for things that are traded to other nations.) Point out that the balance of payments is set up in such a way that it must balance, so it was no accident that, in this example, the U.S. current account deficit was offset by the financial account surplus.

18. Display Visual 4 and use it to stress the point that the overall balance of payments always "balances," although particular sections of the account may not. For example, if the value of U.S. exports is less than the value of its imports, the dollars that the foreign sellers receive for their goods will be used to invest in U.S. assets such as stocks, treasury securities, or capital assets such as factories and real estate. U.S. imports are "paid for" by U.S. exports or, if the U.S. current account is in deficit, by the sale of U.S. financial assets. Reinforce this idea by noting again that in Year 1 the United States paid for Spanish machinery by exporting corn. In Year 2 the United States paid for Spanish textiles by selling Spain some corn and some U.S. financial assets. (**Notes to teachers:** This example is a simplification of the actual U.S. Balance of Payments in that trade takes place only between the U.S. and Spain. The overall U.S. balance of payments reflects all transactions between the U.S. and the world. The overall balance of payments must equal zero, as shown in Visual 4. However, in real accounts that consider trading between hundreds of countries, the balance of payments between any two countries may not always equal zero, because a deficit with one country could be made up by a surplus with one or more other countries. Using only two countries here to illustrate the overall balance of payments being zero is a simplifying assumption. Also, as explained in the appendix to this lesson, because what is now called the capital accounts section of the balance of payments is a very small part of U.S. accounts it is not included in this activity, once again for simplicity.)

19. Stress that, in the United States or any other country, a current account deficit and financial account surplus are results of choices made by individuals and firms, and by the national government's choices to run a budget deficit by selling treasury bonds or bills. U.S. consumers choose to buy goods and services, including some made in other countries. When they spend more they save less, which leaves fewer domestic funds as savings that can be used to fund investments. By exporting more to the United States than they import from it, foreign citizens and firms choose to invest some of their savings in the United States.

20. Ask students why Spanish investors might purchase U.S. securities. *(U.S. treasury securities may offer a higher interest rate or be seen as less risky than other securities that pay similar rates, and investing in U.S. firms or foreign-owned businesses operating in the United States might offer a higher expected rate of return.)* Note that these choices by consumers and investors are influenced by many factors, including the prices of goods and services in different countries, interest rates paid on savings accounts or bonds, the expected level of profits on investments in different countries, the expected rate of inflation, and political stability and public policies that affect economic conditions.

21. Display Visual 5, which is a simplified version of the U.S. current account for 2004. Explain that indented items are used to show component parts of broader categories. For example, the lines for goods under exports and imports show what part of exports and imports are made up of goods rather than services. Explain that the United States has had a current account deficit since 1991. Over the last decade, its surplus in services has been outweighed by a larger deficit for goods. Note to the students that the news media often reports the **balance of trade**, which is

defined as exports of goods and services minus imports of goods and services. This statistic is based on only part of the current account, because it does not include income payments or net transfers.

22. Display Visual 6 to show historical values for the U.S. current account as a percentage of U.S. GDP. Point out that large deficits in this account have been common for the past 25 years, and especially large in the past 10–15 years.

23. Display Visual 7, which breaks down the Financial Account in the Balance of Payments Account. (Not all subcategories are shown in the table, so the indented items do not equal the totals.) Point out that foreign citizens buy many different types of U.S. assets. Explain that foreign direct investment occurs when foreign individuals or companies buy all or part of a U.S. company, or start or expand their own business in the United States.

24. Ask students if investment is a good thing for the United States and other nations. (*Yes. Investment increases current and future production, creates new jobs, and promotes economic growth.*)

25. Explain that before a nation can invest, someone has to save rather than consume, because if everything produced is consumed there is nothing left to invest. Ask students where they believe funds for investment in the U.S. come from. (*Answers will vary.*)

26. Display Visual 8. Note that in 2004 a large part ($670 billion) of the savings used to finance U.S. private investment and government borrowing came from foreign sources. Stress that, as explained earlier, in order for that to happen the surplus in the U.S. financial account section of its balance of payments account had to be offset by a deficit in its current account, which includes U.S. imports and exports.

27. On Visual 8, also point out that while U.S. private savings are a large source of savings, U.S. savings fell well short of the total amount of borrowing done by U.S. businesses and by the U.S. government, which borrows to cover its budget deficits in many years. In the early years of the 21st century, federal deficits were quite large.

28. Stress again that a current account deficit and a financial account surplus result from choices made by various economic decision makers. Specifically, in 2004:

- U.S. consumers bought more goods and services, including many goods made in other countries, instead of saving to provide more funds for investment.
- The U.S. federal government ran a large budget deficit.
- Foreign investors chose to invest their savings in U.S. government and corporate bonds, or in businesses operating in the United States, rather than buying more U.S. exports of goods and services.

29. Ask students what would have to happen to change a deficit or surplus in the U.S. current or financial section of its balance of payments account. (*Many factors affect the decisions that result in the deficits and surpluses, including household decisions to spend or save; interest rates–which affect both saving and investment decisions; expected profits from investments in the United States and other nations; and political decisions to reduce government borrowing by cutting government spending or increasing taxes.*)

30. Ask students what problems could arise from the continued reliance on foreign savings to fund U.S. investment and government deficits. (*Borrowed funds have*

to be repaid, which will eventually entail a reduction in consumption levels in the United States unless the borrowing funds investments that increase U.S. production by more than enough to repay the borrowed funds.)

31. Display Visual 9. Note that the United States is now a net debtor nation–meaning more assets are owned in the United States by foreign citizens and firms than U.S. citizens and firms own in other countries. Explain that this is directly related to the kinds of trading and borrowing patterns shown in the earlier activity. When the United States runs large current account deficits, more U.S. assets are purchased by foreign investors. If those foreign funds lead to more investments and future growth in the U.S. economy, that can be a good thing for the United States, as it was during the 18th and 19th centuries. But if the foreign borrowing supports more consumption spending by U.S. households and the government, rather than investments in capital projects, the U.S. economy's rate of growth will not increase. In that case the future consumption of goods and services in the United States will have to be reduced when the foreign debt is repaid–perhaps because foreigners become unwilling to hold such a large part of their financial assets in U.S. stocks, bonds, or other assets.

CLOSURE

Review the following points:

- The balance of payments accounts shows that a deficit in the U.S. current account is offset by a surplus in its financial account.
- A current account deficit occurs if a country imports more than it exports.
- A financial account surplus occurs when a country receives more funds for investment from other countries than it sends to other countries.
- The U.S. current account deficit and financial account surplus result from choices made by households, firms, and the federal government. These choices are influenced by interest rates; expected profits; consumer preferences for saving or consuming, and for purchasing domestic or foreign goods and services; and by political decisions about deficit spending.

ASSESSMENT

1. Distribute Activity 2 to each student (or to small groups of students). Ask them to complete the balance of payments table after all the transactions listed have been completed. Remind students to visualize what has happened to the goods, currencies, and financial assets listed, in terms of moving from one country to another.

2. Display Visual 10 and lead a class discussion of the questions on Activity 2: (*The United States receives € 100 for $100, and uses € 70 to buy German stock and € 30 of medical equipment. Both of these transactions are debits on the U.S. balance of payments, the stock in the financial account and the equipment in the current account. Germany uses the $100 to buy $75 worth of wheat and $25 of U.S. Treasury securities. Both of these items are credits in the U.S. balance of payments, the wheat in the current account and the securities in the financial account.*)

3. Ask students whether the current account for the U.S. has a deficit or surplus. *(There is a surplus of $45.)* Ask students whether the financial account for the U.S. has a deficit or surplus. *(There is a deficit of $45.)* Ask students if the United States is sending investment funds to Germany or receiving investment funds from Germany. *(Because there is a deficit in its financial account, the United States is sending funds to Germany, in this case by purchasing German stock.)*

Visual 1
Credits and Debits in the U.S. Balance of Payments

Credits: Dollar values of things the United States sells to citizens or firms in other countries. The citizens or firms in other countries buy dollars to pay for these things. Because the United States receives these payments, they are labeled with a "+" in the U.S. balance of payments account. Examples of things sold include:

- Goods, such as corn, wheat, or machinery
- Services, such as airline travel or insurance
- U.S. securities, such as U.S. Treasury Notes, bonds, or shares of stock in U.S. companies
- Factories or businesses in the United States
- Interest owed to U.S. citizens for their investments abroad

Debits: Values of things U.S. citizens or firms buy from people or firms in other countries. People or firms that make these purchases must buy foreign currency with dollars to make these purchases. Because these payments are made to other countries, they are labeled with a "–" in the U.S. balance of payments account. Examples of things purchased include:

- Goods, such as automobiles, oil, or clothing
- Services, such as U.S. tourists taking a trip to France
- Foreign securities, such as stocks in foreign businesses
- Factories or businesses in other countries
- Interest paid to foreign citizens on their investments in the United States

Visual 2
A Simplified U.S. Balance of Payments Account

Current Account (CA): Summarizes Trade in Goods and Services, Income Payments and Receipts, and Transfers

Exports of goods and services	+ 50
Imports of goods and services	− 100

Financial Account (FA): Summarizes Trade in Assets

U.S. assets owned by foreign citizens	+ 75
Foreign assets owned by U.S. citizens	− 25

The balance of payments is divided into different accounts. An individual account is said to have a surplus if the sum of all the items in the account is positive. It is said to have a deficit if the sum of all the items in the account is negative.

Visual 3
Activity 1 Key

U.S. Balance of Payments

Current Account: Summarizes Trade in Goods and Services, Income Payments and Receipts, and Transfers	**Year 1**	**Year 2**
Exports of U.S.-made goods and services	+ *30*	+ *10*
Imports of foreign goods and services	− *30*	− *30*
Balance of Current Account (Exports − Imports)	*0*	− *20*
Financial Account: Summarizes Trade in Assets		
U.S. assets sold to residents in other nations, including:		
U.S. currency	+	+
U.S. stocks	+	+
U.S. treasury bonds	+	+ *20**
Foreign assets purchased by U.S. residents, including:		
Foreign currency	−	−
Foreign stocks	−	−
Foreign treasury bonds		
Balance of Financial Account (U.S. assets owned by world residents − Foreign assets owned by U.S. residents)	*0*	*20*
Balance of Payments (Current Account + Financial Account) (Should be zero)	*0*	*0*

+ items are credits, − items are debits

* Spain might also have elected to buy U.S. stocks or hold U.S. currency. Note that this does not change the balance of the financial account.

Visual 4
The Relationship between the Current Account (CA) and the Financial Account (FA)

When a country sells something (a good, its currency, or another kind of financial asset), it receives something in return (a good, foreign currency, or another kind of financial asset). On its Balance of Payments account, that means a country's credits must equal its debits. While it may have a balance in one part of the account–for example on the current account– the overall account must be balanced, so the sum of all the accounts within the balance of payments must total zero.

For the United States, which has run a large current account deficit over the past decade, those deficits were offset by surpluses in its financial account. Or put differently, for the United States,

$$CA + FA = 0$$

[Note: Another part of the balance of payments account, called the capital account, is a very small item for the United States, and so was ignored here. For some countries, the capital account is much larger.]

Visual 5
U.S. Balance of Payments, 2004: The Current Account, Selected Items (in billions of dollars)

	Current Account: Summarizes Trade in Goods and Services, Income Payments and Receipts, and Transfers	
	Exports of U.S.-made goods and services and income receipts	+ 1530
	Goods	+ 807
	Services	+ 344
	Income receipts	+ 380
	Imports of foreign goods and services and income payments	− 2118
	Goods	− 1473
	Services	− 296
	Income payments	− 349
	Net transfers*	− 81
CA	**Balance of Current Account (Exports – Imports – Net Transfers)**	− 668

+ items are credits, − items are debits

* Net transfers refer to assistance provided to other nations (foreign aid, for example). That is a debit item, because it sends dollars from the United States to other nations.

The balance of trade in goods and services, which is often reported in news reports, is the value of U.S. exports of goods and services minus the value of U.S. imports of goods and services. The balance of trade in goods and services does not include income payments or receipts or net transfers. The U.S. had a balance of trade deficit of $618 billion in 2004.

Source: www.bea.gov, Table 1: U.S. International Transactions, June 17, 2005.

Visual 6
The U.S. Current Account Balance as a Percentage of GDP

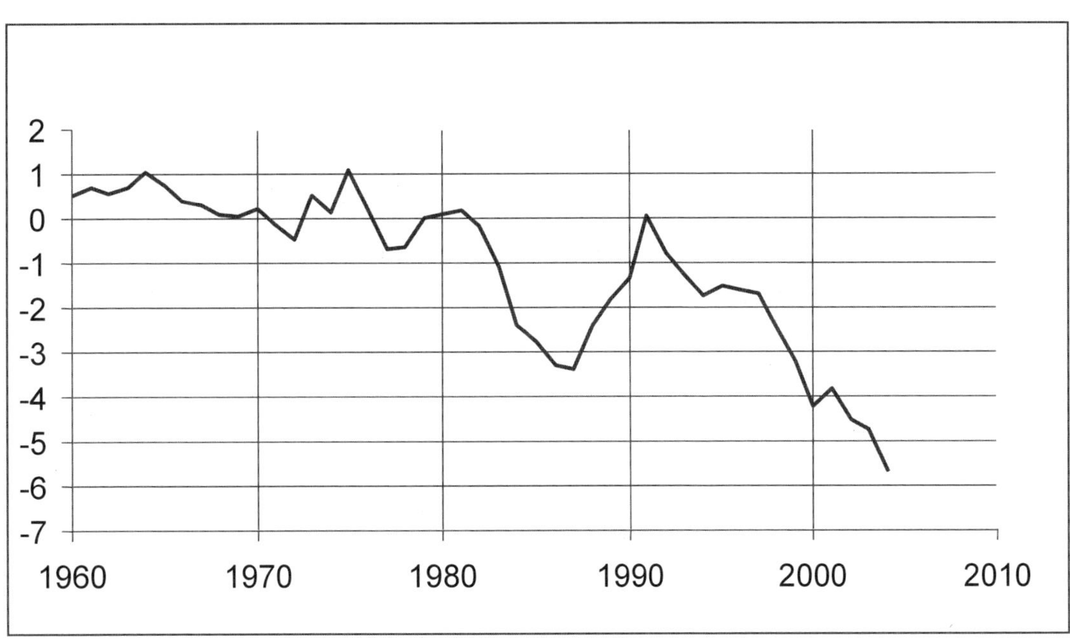

Source: Bureau of Economic Analysis, www.bea.gov, GDP tables, international transactions tables.

Visual 7

U.S. Balance of Payments, 2004: The Financial Account, Selected Items (in billions of dollars)

	Financial Account: Summarizes Trade in Assets*	
	Foreign Assets owned by U.S. residents or government, total:	− 856
	Direct investment	− 252
	Foreign stocks	− 102
	U.S. assets owned by world residents or governments, total:	+ 1440
	U.S. assets held by foreign governments	+ 395
	Direct investment	+ 107
	U.S. currency	+ 15
	U.S. stocks	+ 370
	U.S. treasury bonds	+ 107
FA	**Balance of Financial Account** (U.S. assets owned by world residents – foreign assets own by U.S. residents)	+ 584
SD	**Statistical Differences***	+ 85
CA+ FA+ SD	**Balance of Payments (Current Account + Financial Account)**	0

+ items are credits, − items are debits

* Not all subcategories are shown for Foreign and U.S. Assets, so the total value for those categories is not equal to the sum of the selected items that are shown. Also, because all figures are estimates by the Bureau of Economic Analysis (BEA), and not exact accounting figures, the estimates often do not sum to a zero balance of payments. The "statistical differences" line is used to suggest the overall level of error in the BEA estimates.

Source: www.bea.gov, Table 1: U.S. International Transactions, June 17, 2005.

Visual 8
Sources of Funding for U.S. Investment and Government Deficit Spending, 2004

Investment must be funded by savings, but the saving may be done by people in other countries. Savings are also used to fund government deficits.

In 2004 U.S. private investment spending was $1,930 billion. The sources of those funds were:

	Billions of Dollars
Private savings in U.S.	1760
Government savings in U.S.	– 560
World savings invested in U.S.	670

Note that:

- Savings by U.S. households and firms almost meets private investment.
- Government and businesses are both net borrowers in the United States; households are net savers.
- World savings invested in the United States are taken from the U.S. financial account surplus in its balance of payments account.

Note: Due to statistical discrepancies, rounding, and using an estimate for world savings taken from the international transactions accounts, the value for total savings here is $60 billion less than investment spending and government borrowing.

Source: Bureau of Economic Analysis, www.bea.gov, National Income and Product Accounts, Tables 3.1 and 5.1, and International Transactions Data, Table 1.

Visual 9

The International Investment Position of the United States: A Net Debtor Nation

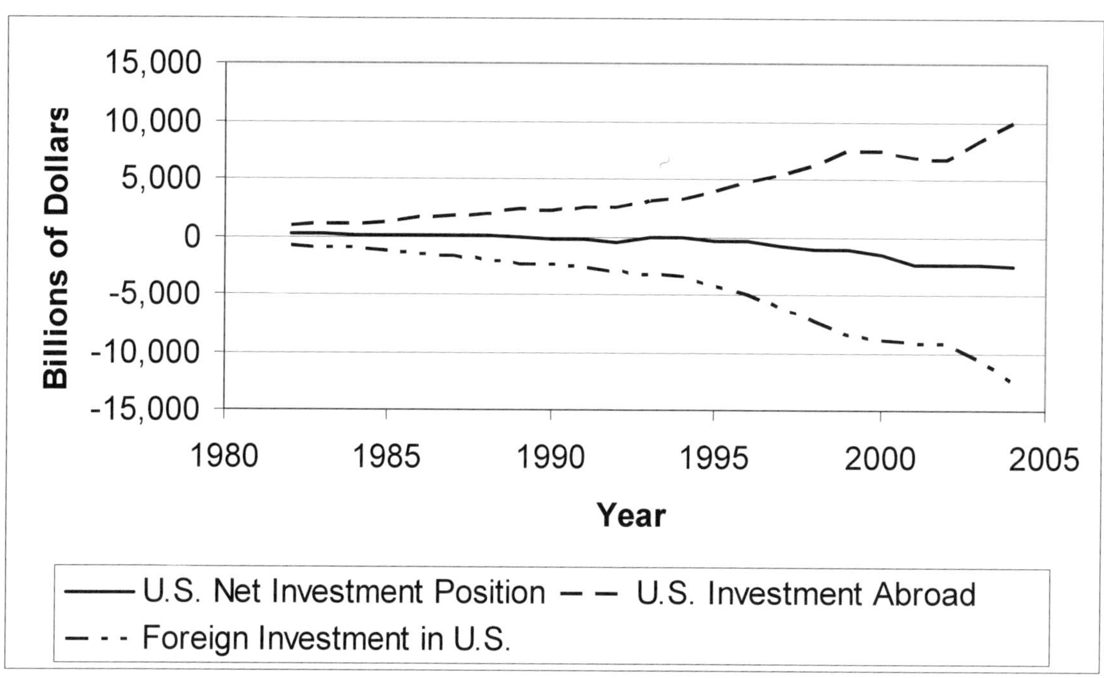

Source: Bureau of Economic Analysis, www.bea.gov, Table 2. International Investment Position of the United States at Year End.

Visual 10

Activity 2 Key: The U.S. Balance of Payments Account with Germany

Current Account: Summarizes Trade in Goods and Services, Income Payments and Receipts, and Transfers	
Exports of U.S. goods and services	+ 75
Imports of foreign goods and services	– 30
Balance of Current Account (Exports – Imports)	+ 45
Financial Account: Summarizes Trade in Assets	
U.S. Assets sold to residents in other nations, including:	
U.S. currency	+
U.S. stocks	+
U.S. treasury bonds	+ 25
Foreign assets purchased by U.S. residents, including:	
Foreign currency	
Foreign stocks	– 70
Foreign treasury bonds	–
Balance of Financial Account (U.S. assets owned by world residents – foreign assets owned by U.S. residents)	– 45
Balance of Payments (Current Account + Financial Account) (Should be zero)	0

Activity 1
The U.S. Balance of Payments Account

Current Account: Summarizes Trade in Goods and Services, Income Payments and Receipts, and Transfers	**Year 1**	**Year 2**
Exports of U.S. goods and services	+	+
Imports of foreign goods and services	–	–
Balance of Current Account (Exports – Imports)		
Financial Account: Summarizes Trade in Assets		
U.S. assets sold to residents in other nations, including:		
U.S. currency	+	+
U.S. stocks	+	+
U.S. treasury bonds	+	+
Foreign assets purchased by U.S. residents, including:		
Foreign currency	–	–
Foreign stocks	–	–
Foreign treasury bonds		
Balance of Financial Account (U.S. assets owned by world residents – foreign assets owned by U.S. residents)		
Balance of Payments (Current Account + Financial Account)		

items marked + are credits; items marked – are debits.

Activity 1 (continued)

Exchanges in Year 1

Assume that the exchange rate is 1 Euro = $1.

Exchange # 1: A U.S. firm wants to buy machinery from a Spanish firm worth 30 Euros. Have the firm send 30 dollars to the bank to be exchanged for Euros.

Exchange # 2: People and companies in Spain decide to buy corn from the Unites States that costs $30. Have the firm in Spain send 30 Euros to the bank to be exchanged for dollars.

Exchange # 3: The bank exchanges Euros for dollars by giving dollars to Spain and Euros to the United States.

Exchange # 4: The United States buys the machinery from Spain with its Euros.

Exchange # 5: Spain buys corn from the United States with its dollars.

Year 1 Summary: Examine the cards held by each country. Any card that came from the other country represents an international transaction that will be recorded someplace on the Balance of Payments account. Fill in the Year 1 column in the Balance of Payments table for the United States, shown above.

Does the U.S. have a current account deficit or surplus? ______ If so, how much? ____________

Does the U.S. have a deficit or a surplus in its financial account? _______ If so, how much?__________

If the current account and the financial account are added together, what is the total? ___________

What did Spain receive in return for its machinery? ____________

RETURN ALL THE CARDS TO THEIR ORIGINAL COUNTRY. A NEW YEAR IS ABOUT TO BEGIN!

Activity 1 (continued)

Exchanges in Year 2

Assume that the exchange rate is still 1 Euro = $1.

Exchange # 1: A U.S. firm wants to buy textiles from a Spanish firm worth 30 Euros. Have the U.S. firm send 30 dollars to the bank to be exchanged for Euros.

Exchange # 2: People and companies in Spain decide to buy corn from the Unites States that costs $10. Have the firm in Spain send 10 Euros to the bank to be exchanged for dollars.

Exchange # 3: People in Spain want to invest some of their savings in the United States. To do so, they will need to acquire dollars. Have Spain send 20 Euros to the bank to be exchanged for dollars.

Exchange # 4: The bank exchanges the Euros for dollars by giving dollars to Spain and Euros to the United States.

Action # 5: The United States buys the textiles from Spain with its Euros.

Action # 6: Spain buys corn from the United States with its dollars.

Action # 7: Spain buys a U.S. asset worth $20 that will pay savers a good rate of return on the investment.

Year 2 Summary: Examine the cards held by each country. Any card that came from the other country represents an international transaction that will be recorded someplace on the Balance of Payments account. Fill in the Year 2 column in the Balance of Payments table for the United States, shown above.

Does the U.S. have a current account deficit or surplus? _____ If so, how much? ____________

Does the U.S. have a deficit or a surplus in its financial account? _____ If so, how much? __________

If the current account and the financial account are added together, what is the total? ___________

What two things did Spain receive in return for its textiles?

____

Activity 1 (continued)

Review Questions:
Why do you suppose foreign investors, in this example investors from Spain, sometimes decide to buy financial assets (invest) in the United States?

How does the United States benefit from foreign investments?

If the United States continues to run a current account for many years, how will that affect the ownership of financial assets in the United States?

Activity 1 (continued)

Cards

Stock in U.S. Company Worth $20	Stock in Spanish Company Worth € 20
United States Treasury Note Worth $20 Paying 5% Interest	Spanish Treasury Note Worth € 20 Paying 3% Interest
$20 Worth of U.S. Grown Corn	€ 30 Worth of Spanish Machinery
$10 Worth of U.S. Grown Corn	€ 30 Worth of Spanish Textiles

Activity 1 (continued)

Cards (continued)

$10	€ 10
$10	€ 10
$10	€ 10
$10	€ 10

Activity 2

The U.S. Balance of Payments Accounts with Germany

Current Account: Summarizes Trade in Goods and Services, Income Payments and Receipts, and Transfers	
Exports of U.S. goods and services	+
Imports of foreign goods and services	–
Balance of Current Account (Exports – Imports)	
Financial Account: Summarizes Trade in Assets	
U.S. assets sold to residents in other nations, including:	
U.S. currency	+
U.S. stocks	+
U.S. treasury bonds	+
Foreign assets purchased by U.S. residents, including:	
Foreign currency	–
Foreign stocks	–
Foreign treasury bonds	
Balance of Financial Account (U.S. assets owned by world residents – foreign assets own by U.S. residents)	
Balance of Payments (Current Account + Financial Account)	

Fill in the figures for the U.S. current account and financial account after the following transactions. Assume the exchange rate is $1 = €1.

A U.S. company exchanges $100 for 100 Euros, which are supplied by someone in Germany.

The U.S. company buys €70 of a German company's stock and €30 worth of German medical equipment.

Someone in Germany buys $75 dollars of U.S. wheat and $25 worth of U.S. Treasury bonds.

Appendix
Recent Changes in Accounting Procedures and Names of Accounts in the Balance of Payments

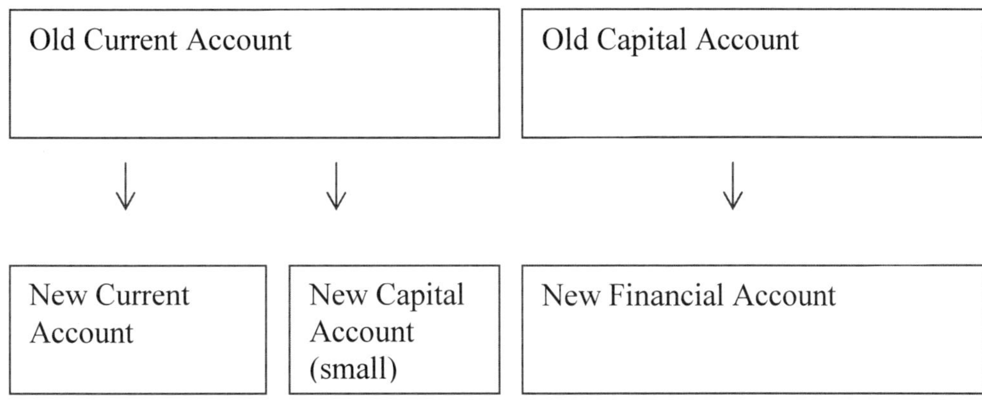

In June 1999, the United States changed its classification system for the balance of payments. The new balance of payments is divided into three groups–the current account, the capital account, and the financial account. Under the new system, the old current account is divided into two parts–the new current account (as presented in the lesson) and the new capital account. The new capital account is a record of capital transfers, one example of which is the assets a migrant brings when he or she enters or exits a country. Another example would be debt forgiveness. Because these items are very small for the United States (although important in the balance of payments in other countries), we ignore this category in the lesson.

The old capital account has now been renamed the financial account (as presented in the lesson). For more information see the February 1999 issue of the *Survey of Current Business*, published by the U.S. Department of Commerce.